Introduction to Video Game Engine Development

Learn to Design, Implement, and Use a Cross-Platform 2D Game Engine

Victor G Brusca

Apress®

Introduction to Video Game Engine Development

Victor G Brusca
Edison, NJ, USA

ISBN-13 (pbk): 978-1-4842-7038-7   ISBN-13 (electronic): 978-1-4842-7039-4
https://doi.org/10.1007/978-1-4842-7039-4

Managing Director, Apress Media LLC: Welmoed Spahr
Acquisitions Editor: Spandana Chatterjee
Development Editor: Matthew Moodie
Coordinating Editor: Divya Modi

Cover designed by eStudioCalamar

Cover image designed by Freepik (www.freepik.com)

Distributed to the book trade worldwide by Springer Science+Business Media New York, 1 New York Plaza, New York, NY 10004. Phone 1-800-SPRINGER, fax (201) 348-4505, e-mail orders-ny@springer-sbm.com, or visit www.springeronline.com. Apress Media, LLC is a California LLC and the sole member (owner) is Springer Science + Business Media Finance Inc (SSBM Finance Inc). SSBM Finance Inc is a Delaware corporation.

For information on translations, please e-mail booktranslations@springernature.com; for reprint, paperback, or audio rights, please e-mail bookpermissions@springernature.com.

Apress titles may be purchased in bulk for academic, corporate, or promotional use. eBook versions and licenses are also available for most titles. For more information, reference our Print and eBook Bulk Sales web page at http://www.apress.com/bulk-sales.

Any source code or other supplementary material referenced by the author in this book is available to readers on GitHub via the book's product page, located at www.apress.com/978-1-4842-7038-7. For more detailed information, please visit http://www.apress.com/source-code.

Printed on acid-free paper

To Mamamama and Papi. I love you both very much.

Table of Contents

About the Author

Victor G Brusca is an experienced software developer specializing in building cross-platform applications and APIs. He regards himself as a self-starter with a keen eye for detail, an obsessive protection of systems/data, and a desire to write well-documented, well-encapsulated code. With over 14 years of software development experience, he has been involved in game and game engine projects on J2ME, T-Mobile Sidekick, WebOS, Windows Phone, Xbox 360, Android, iOS, and web platforms.

About the Technical Reviewer

 **Prasanth Sahoo** is a thought leader, an adjunct professor, a technical speaker, and a full-time practitioner in Blockchain, Cloud, and Scrum working for PDI Software. He was awarded the "Blockchain and Cloud Expert of the Year Award 2019" from TCS Global Community for his knowledge share within academic services to the community. He is passionate about driving digital technology initiatives by handling various community initiatives through coaching, mentoring, and grooming techniques.

Prasanth has a patent under his name, and to date, he has interacted reaching over 50,000 professionals, mostly within the technical domain. He is a working group member in the Blockchain Council, CryptoCurrency Certification Consortium, Scrum Alliance, Scrum Organization, and International Institute of Business Analysis.

Acknowledgments

I'd like to take the time to acknowledge my wife, Katia, for putting up with me writing and coding at my desk for days on end. Love you, bbg:-*.

Introduction

This book is, first and foremost, about the design and development of a 2D game engine. The examples and code presented in this text are from the Java implementation of the game engine, but this book includes functionally equivalent implementations of the engine written in both Java and C#. The API-level code is very similar between the two programming languages, so it should be very easy to follow along in C# if you should desire to do so.

This book will cover, at the class level, each piece of the game engine along with explanations and demonstrations. As you review the code through this text, you'll begin to see the structure of the design patterns that power the engine. These patterns, or interactions of classes, are what give the game engine life. It's what makes the software an engine as opposed to an implementation of a game.

This book is broken down into three parts. Part 1 of the text, Chapters 1–8, reviews all the base classes that support the engine and define its capabilities. In Part 2 of the text, Chapters 9–14, we dive into the application-level code. We review, again class by class, the code responsible for loading resources, game settings, preparing the game's window and drawing surfaces, and mapping user input from different input sources. Finally, in Part 3, we apply what we've learned and build games from the ground up using only the code we've reviewed in this text and an IDE (Integrated Development Environment).

The game development world is a large and complex place. If you're interested in building the next great games, then you need experience working with advanced game development tools. Learning these tools can be a daunting task to say the least. You'll have to learn at least two complex pieces of software, at least one intricate API, and at least one programming language.

This book is designed to give you experience building and working with game engines, at the code level, by providing an example implementation to review in detail. This book will give you experience working with IDEs (Integrated Development Environments), complex cross-platform APIs (Game engine APIs in Java and C#), game engine design patterns, and building games using the game engine introduced in the text. By the end of this book, you'll be able to make your own games directly in code, and you'll be poised to take on the next challenges in your game development career.

PART 1

CHAPTER 1

MmgBase API Introduction

Part 1 of this book contains a comprehensive review of a 2D game engine written in both Java and C#. Both implementations are included with this text along with full code documentation, 137 unit tests for verifying API functionality, an example program that demonstrates key game engine features, and two complete games that you will build on your own, with a little help from me. Like any good TV cooking show however, there is a finished copy of each game also included so you can work with the expected results.

The included game engine contains two APIs: a low-level API that includes many game building tools like sprites, sounds, containers, game screens, UI widgets, event handlers, and much more and a mid-level API that handles launching the game and loading in settings and resources. In this way, the game engine is expressed as a software development kit containing two core APIs and including a number of examples and documentation.

You may be wondering what sort of player this game engine needs and what are the requirements for it, but this game engine does not use a player. Instead, the game is compiled with the engine code built in so each game you make is a full copy of the game engine runtime code and game engine classes. This gives you full control and a full view of the code that powers the engine.

Through the course of this book, you will see how the game engine is built, and you'll have access to both a Java/Swing implementation that requires NetBeans and a C#/MonoGame implementation that requires Visual Studio. The Java version uses Swing with OpenGL acceleration and works on any platform that runs Java – Windows, Mac OSX, Linux, and so on.

© Victor G Brusca 2021
V. G. Brusca, *Introduction to Video Game Engine Development*, https://doi.org/10.1007/978-1-4842-7039-4_1

The C# version runs on SDL, Simple DirectMedia Layer, and uses OpenGL and OpenAL. By having the ability to explore the implementation of one 2D game engine on multiple platforms, you will gain invaluable experience and knowledge building and working with game engines. The intricacies of API abstraction and generalized 2D game engine design will become readily apparent to you as you review this book and compare the cross-platform implementations.

MonoGame is a free, open source, game development technology that is based on the defunct XNA SDK from Microsoft. The community has done a wonderful job of resurrecting this software and utilizing the latest tools and technologies to get MonoGame to run on the following platforms:

- Windows

- Mac

- Linux

- Android

- iOS

- PlayStation 4

- PlayStation Vita

- Xbox One

- Nintendo Switch

- Google Stadia

Source: `https://docs.monogame.net/articles/platforms/0_platforms.html`

Whatever your coding experience or preferred platform, you'll have a choice of which codebase to use, Java or C#. You'll be able to target several different platforms with your new game, and what is more, you'll have every line of code in the game engine under your direct control. Now that is exciting. Let's get started!

Game Engine SDK Overview

Before we get into a detailed review of the classes and example code, let's talk a little bit about the MmgGameApi. In general, when I mention the MmgGameApi, I'm talking about both the Java and C# implementations. In fact, the low-level API implementations are about 95% the same. It's only when you get to the mid-level API that larger differences occur.

That being said, the C#/MonoGame implementation is more efficient than the Java/Swing implementation. It has nothing to do with the game engine code and everything to do with the frameworks the two different implementations use. The C#/MonoGame implementation is built for gaming, so it runs faster overall than the Java/Swing implementation. Both are still viable solutions for implementing your next 2D game.

Let's talk a little bit about the MmgGameApiJava project's packages. These align with the MmgGameApiCs project's namespaces. You're going to see a lot of features, both in the programming languages themselves and in the API implementation, that are completely different from an implementation standpoint but functionally equivalent.

Packages/Namespaces

1. net.middlemind.MmgGameApiJava.MmgBase

    net.middlemind.MmgGameApiCs.MmgBase

    This is the lowest-level API in the game engine SDK. It sits on top of the underlying framework technology. For the Java project, it plugs into the Java Swing and AWT APIs. For the C# project, it plugs into MonoGame APIs that use OpenGL and OpenAL.

2. net.middlemind.MmgGameApiJava.MmgCore

    net.middlemind.MmgGameApiCs.MmgCore

    This is the mid-level API in the game engine SDK. It sits between the low-level API, MmgBase, and the actual game implementation. It handles tasks like setting up the application window and drawing surfaces, loading resources, and processing input. It also handles XML-driven configuration, events, and more robust game screens.

3.   net.middlemind.MmgGameApiJava.MmgTestSpace

net.middlemindMmgGameApiCs.MmgTestSpace

This package represents the application level and really isn't
an SDK API. It is an example of an implementation of the SDK
with runtime code included. This application, when executed,
demonstrates how to use classes from the MmgBase and
MmgCore APIs.

So, with that, let's begin our code review with the lowest-level API, the MmgBase
API. We'll cover key classes in a logical order. This will give you a solid understanding of
how things work, how a general game engine is designed and structured from the point
of view of code, classes and their interactions. Lastly, we'll conclude each class review
with a demonstration of the class in use giving you a solid foundation from which to
build.

The classes we'll cover in this text are loosely organized into the following categories.

Base Classes

- MmgObj

- MmgColor

- MmgRect

- MmgFont

- MmgSound

- MmgPen

- MmgVector2

- MmgBmp

Helper Classes

- MmgApiUtils

- MmgHelper

- MmgScreenData

- MmgFontData

- MmgDebug

- MmgBmpScaler

- MmgMediaTracker

Advanced Classes

- Mmg9Slice

- MmgContainer

- MmgLabelValuePair

- MmgLoadingBar

- MmgSprite

- MmgDrawableBmpSet

Widget Classes

- MmgTextField

- MmgTextBlock

- MmgScrollVert

- MmgScrollHor

- MmgScrollHorVert

- MmgMenuContainer

- MmgMenuItem

Screen Classes

- MmgSplashScreen

- MmgLoadingScreen

- MmgGameScreen

Animation Classes

- MmgPulse

- MmgPosTween

- MmgSizeTween

Other Classes

- MmgCfgFileEntry

- MmgEvent

- MmgEventHandler

There are a lot of powerful tools for creating games out there. Many of them will require you to learn a programming language, a framework API, game creation software, the game engine API, and an IDE to write the code in. This can pose a daunting challenge for a beginner.

This book hopes to make your journey into the universe of video game creation a great one by showing you how a 2D game engine works from the code up. Giving you access to two different implementations of the game engine, you'll gain experience using two IDEs, if you choose to review the code in both languages. With the tools available to you here, you'll build your own games and gain invaluable experience writing games directly in code.

While some of the knowledge you gain here will be specific to one codebase, much of it will be general, broad knowledge you can apply to future projects and game development experiences.

Setting Up Your Environment

The code that accompanies this book comes in two flavors, Java and C#. That being said, this book mainly follows the Java code. All the method breakdowns are done while reviewing the Java code. However, there is a complete C# implementation of the game engine, and the MmgBase API is very similar between both engine versions.

You can follow along with the C# project if you like though you'll have to do a little bit more work due to the line number differences. I recommend following along in Java first and then viewing the C# code once you have finished absorbing the Java code. This should make you notice the differences between the two implementations more than the similarities.

The next sections will show you how to set up your environment for viewing the associated projects in NetBeans for the Java project and Visual Studio for the C# project.

Installing the NetBeans IDE

For this section, you'll need Internet access to download a copy of the IDE and the project that is associated with this book. Once you're online and settled, navigate your favorite browser to the NetBeans IDE main site, `http://netbeans.org`.

Locate the downloads link. This will direct you to a list of recent versions of the IDE. Scroll down until you see the latest LTS, long-term support, entry in the list. At the time of this writing, the latest LTS version is 12.1. Download and install the software. While the NetBeans IDE is installing, go to this URL, `http://www.apress.com/source-code`, and download the zip file for the Java version of the game engine project.

When the project file is done downloading, decompress it, and then move it to the location of your Java projects. If you are new to this and don't have a place, create a new folder in the location where you like to keep your documents. Once the IDE is finished installing and the project file is unzipped and moved to the desired location, launch the NetBeans IDE. Select "File ➤ Open Project..." from the menu. Find the location of the project folder you just downloaded and unzipped.

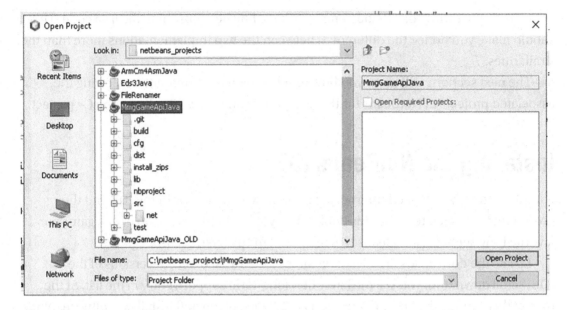

Figure 1-1. *NetBeans IDE Install 1*

When the project is done loading, we need to check a few things. Right-click the MmgGameApiJava project and select the **Properties** entry. The project settings window will pop up. Select the **Packaging** option from the list of sections on the left-hand side of the window. You should make sure your project has the options set as shown in the following screenshot.

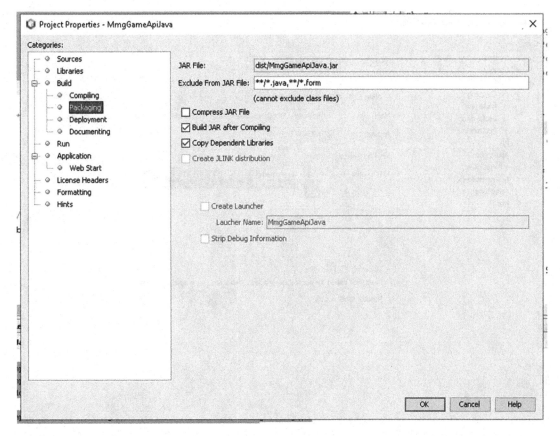

Figure 1-2. *NetBeans IDE Install 2*

Make sure that the **JAR File** field at the top of the screen starts with the **dist** folder. Once that's done, click the **Run** entry on the left-hand list of categories. We're going to make sure that the proper runtime settings are in place.

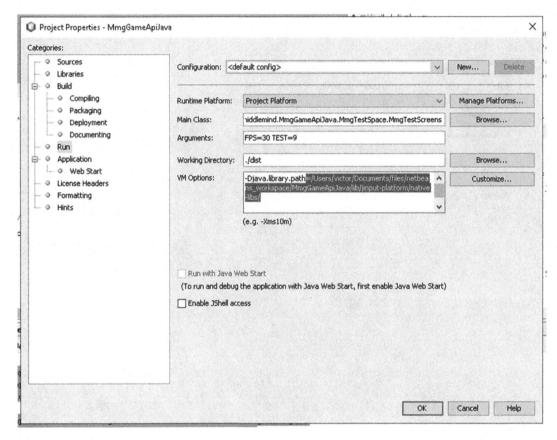

Figure 1-3. *NetBeans IDE Install 3*

With regard to the runtime settings, you're going to want to make sure that the main class is set; choose the MmgTestScreens class of the MmgTestSpace package. The Arguments field can be left blank, or you can experiment with different FPS settings. It's best to work with a frame rate between 15 and 60 FPS. Notice the path that is highlighted in blue in the preceding image. This is the path to the native libraries on my development environment.

You should change that path to the equivalent folder in your environment. That will enable native OS library support for the game engine project. Before you can run anything, we should make sure the project can compile. Right-click the project in the list and select the **Clean and Build** option.

After the project compiles, you should familiarize yourself with how to run the example game screens project. Find the MmgTestSpace package in the MmgGameApiJava project's package list. Locate the MmgTestScreens file, right-click it, and select **Run File**. Give the application a few seconds to load up. After a short wait, you should see something similar to the screenshot shown in the following.

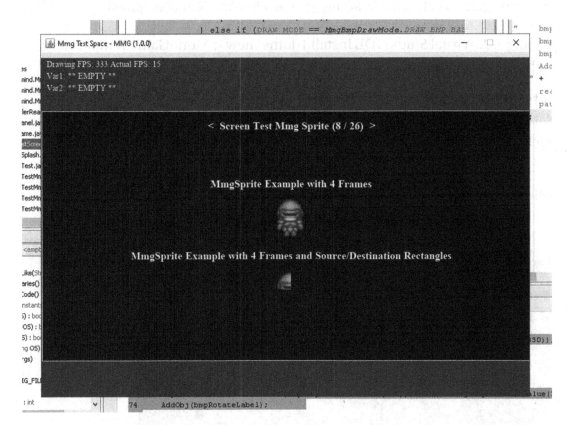

Figure 1-4. *NetBeans IDE Install 4*

This concludes the NetBeans IDE installation and configuration process. If you want to use the C# version of the game engine, check out the next section.

Installing the Visual Studio IDE

For this section, you'll need Internet access to download a copy of the IDE and the C# version of the project that is associated with this book. Because the C# version of the game engine requires the Visual Studio IDE, some Linux users may not have access to Visual Studio. Please follow along by viewing the source code using your favorite text editor. For Mac and Windows users, once you're online and settled, navigate your favorite browser to the Visual Studio IDE main site, `https://visualstudio.microsoft.com/`.

Locate the links for your operating system and then download and install the IDE. Once Visual Studio is done installing, open up a command prompt; type cmd.exe in the Windows search bar. Run the following commands in the command prompt.

Listing 1-1. Visual Studio IDE Install 1dotnet new -i MonoGame.Templates. CSharp::3.8.0.1641

```
dotnet tool install -g dotnet-mgcb
dotnet tool install -g dotnet-mgcb-editor
mgcb-editor –register
```

Open the game engine project for Visual Studio, and you should be greeted by the following screen.

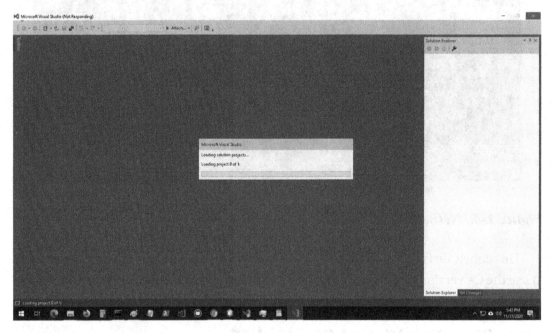

Figure 1-5. *Visual Studio IDE Install 2*

Double-check that the NuGet packages have all been installed.

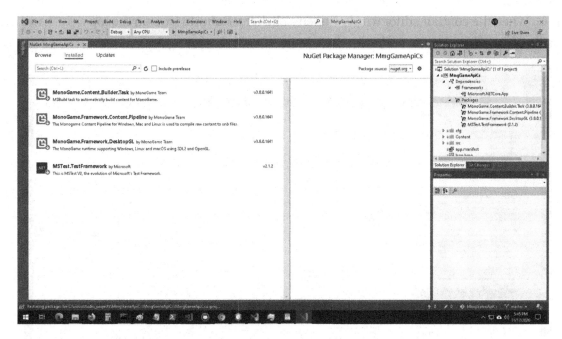

Figure 1-6. *Visual Studio IDE Install 3*

Expand the **Content** folder and select the **Content.mgcb** file. Right-click it and select **Open With** from the menu options. Select the **MGCB** editor as shown in the following and open the content file.

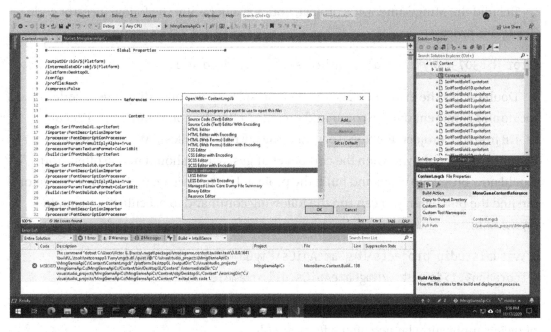

Figure 1-7. *Visual Studio IDE Install 4*

15

When the content editor window opens, click the **Rebuild** icon on the top right-hand side of the editor icon bar. Wait for the editor to finish compiling the content.

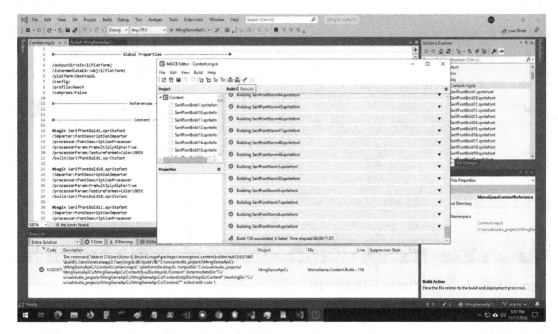

Figure 1-8. *Visual Studio IDE Install 5*

Rebuild the MmgGameApiCs project. You may encounter the following error code during this process:

```
Error MSB3073 any\mgcb.dll /quiet exited with code 1.
```

Double-click the error message to open the file with the offending line of code. Locate and comment out the command executed after the code comment "Execute MGCB from the project directory so we use the correct manifest." We can just run the compile step on our own when the content changes, which should not be often. You should now be able to clean and build the project. If you navigate to the project directory and find the bin folder, you can run the following command to execute the example application:

```
C:\visualstudio_projects\MmgGameApiCs\MmgGameApiCs\bin\Debug\
netcoreapp3.1>dotnet ./MmgGameApiCs.dll example
```

You'll have to adjust the path you use to match your environment. You should see the following application launch after a few seconds.

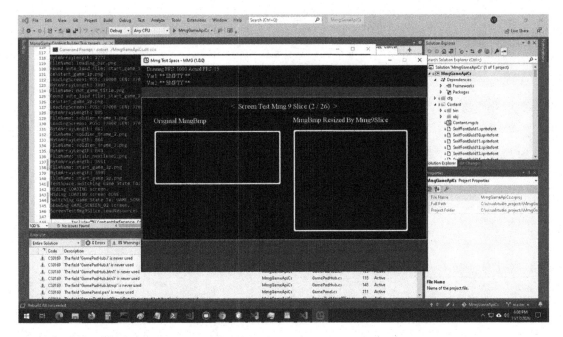

Figure 1-9. *Visual Studio IDE Install 6*

That brings us to the conclusion of this chapter. You should now be able to set up and run the game engine in either Java or C# or both!

CHAPTER 2

Base Classes

In this chapter, you'll review the base classes of the MmgBase API:

- MmgObj
- MmgColor
- MmgRect
- MmgFont
- MmgSound
- MmgPen
- MmgVector2
- MmgBmp

Classes are reviewed using the following standard review steps. If a class does not have anything to review for a particular step, the step will be omitted from the review process:

- Static class members
- Enumerations
- Class fields
- Support method details
- Main method details

The best way to learn the game engine software provided with this book is to follow along in Java or C#. However, the line numbers in C# will not match up perfectly with the Java code reviewed in this text. It is recommended you follow along in Java to get an understanding of the code and then look at it in C# so that you can see how to abstract framework-level classes from API classes and what aspects of the code are implemented in a different but functionally equivalent manner.

© Victor G Brusca 2021
V. G. Brusca, *Introduction to Video Game Engine Development*, https://doi.org/10.1007/978-1-4842-7039-4_2

Base Classes: MmgObj

The MmgObj class is the basis of all drawable objects in the game engine. Everything that you see on the screen implements this class in some way. This is a common theme in powerful game creation tools. You'll find that in any game engine, there are a set of classes that create a foundation that the rest of the engine is built on. In many cases, there is one class that is of primary importance with regard to the game engine's rendering routine. This is that class. It holds the main set of attributes necessary for the game engine to draw objects on the screen and forms the basis of all drawable objects in the API.

Class Fields

The first set of class fields we'll review are listed in the following.

Listing 2-1. MmgObj Class Fields 1

```
public MmgVector2 pos;
public int w;
public int h;
public boolean isVisible;
public MmgColor color;
```

Because we are reviewing the base classes for a 2D game engine, we should expect to see class fields that help us draw 2D images on the screen. Keep this concept in mind as we review different classes in the API. Think about the classes we review as models and try to come up with different ways they can be used together to create aspects of your game.

The pos field is an instance of the MmgVector2 class and is used to store the current position of the MmgObj on the screen. To do so for 2D space, we need to keep track of an X and a Y coordinate, which the MmgVector2 class helps us do. The w and h class fields are used to define the dimensions, width and height, of the MmgObj. This defines a rectangle that this MmgObj instance uses when drawn on the screen.

Note that with just three class fields, we've covered the core needs of just about all 2D drawing. Sure, we haven't talked about shapes and images, but all of those things have at least two properties in common, position and dimension. The next class field, isVisible, is used to control if this MmgObj is drawn on the screen. The color field is an instance of the MmgColor class and is used to represent the color of this object, although not all objects use the color attribute when drawn.

There is a design point I'd like to mention here. Notice that we could have just used the framework class directly in the API. Why introduce an API-level class to handle it? By using an API-level class to wrap the framework-level class, we introduce an abstraction layer that lets us translate features of the framework class, so they are better aligned with the API.

Listing 2-2. MmgObj Class Fields 2

```
private String version = "1.0.8";
public boolean hasParent;
public MmgObj parent;
public String name;
public String mmgUid;
```

The next set of class fields, listed in the preceding, starts with a private string that is used to store a version number. The version number represents the current API version code. The following two class fields, hasParent and parent, are used to track if this MmgObj instance belongs to another MmgObj instance and, if so, which one.

The name field is used to give this MmgObj instance a unique name and can be used to differentiate objects or types of objects. Lastly, the mmgUid is a class field that can be used to store a unique identifier. Again, this can be helpful when tracking and differentiating game objects.

Support Method Details

We won't go into detail when covering simple support methods. We just want to get an idea of what functionality is available so we can develop an idea of how the class functions and how it's used. The first set of support methods to review is listed in the following.

Listing 2-3. MmgObj Support Method Details 1

```
public String GetVersion() { ... }
public boolean GetIsVisible() { ... }
public void SetIsVisible(boolean bl) { ... }
public int GetWidth() { ... }
public void SetWidth(int W) { ... }
```

```
public int GetHeight() { ... }
public void SetHeight(int H) { ... }
public void SetPosition(MmgVector2 v) { ... }
public MmgVector2 GetPosition() { ... }
public MmgColor GetMmgColor() { ... }
public void SetMmgColor(MmgColor c) { ... }
```

Notice that you can choose to access class fields via get and set class methods or by direct class field access. In cases where you know the instance of the MmgObj doesn't have any advanced features that require using the class methods, you can use class fields and save some typing time. In general, I recommend using class methods and following good class encapsulation practices whenever possible.

Listing 2-4. MmgObj Support Method Details 2

```
public void SetX(int inX) { ... }
public int GetX() { ... }
public void SetY(int inY) { ... }
public int GetY() { ... }

public String GetName() { ... }
public void SetName(String n) { ... }
public String GetId() { ... }
public void SetId(String i) { ... }
public boolean GetHasParent() { ... }
public void SetHasParent(boolean b) { ... }
public MmgObj GetParent() { ... }
public void SetParent(MmgObj o) { ... }
```

The get and set methods for the X and Y coordinates are used to interact with the X and Y coordinate values directly. If you are frequently updating the position of an MmgObj, you should not use these methods and instead store a reference to the position vector returned by a call to GetPosition. This will save you many method calls, especially if the code is running as part of the update or drawing routine.

The last two methods I want to talk about are used to manage object parent membership. Two MmgObj instances can be related to each other by using the parent and hasParent class fields. This feature isn't used too much in the API – mainly in classes that are containers of child objects. You can however utilize this functionality to create different relationships between your game objects. It is important to note that the class field that indicates there is a parent and the actual parent work independently of each other, so care must be taken to set both class fields accordingly.

Main Method Details

We'll begin the MmgObj main method review with the methods listed in the following set.

Listing 2-5. MmgObj Main Method Details 1

```
public MmgObj(MmgVector2 v2, int W, int H, boolean isv, MmgColor c,
String n, String i) { ... }

public MmgObj(MmgObj obj) { ... }
public MmgObj Clone() { ... }
public MmgObj CloneTyped() { ... }
public void MmgDraw(MmgPen p) { ... }
public boolean MmgUpdate(int updateTick, long currentTimeMs, long
msSinceLastFrame) { ... }

public String ApiToString() { ... }
public boolean ApiEquals(MmgObj obj) { ... }
```

The first MmgObj constructor we'll review takes seven arguments and sets class fields to an initial value using either a default or argument value. Take note that the position is set by instantiating a new MmgVector2 class instance with the passed-in X and Y coordinates as arguments. Also, note that this constructor sets the hasParent Boolean to false and the parent field to null. This is a straightforward constructor. The next constructor we'll review is a little bit different.

The second MmgObj constructor takes an MmgObj instance as an argument. This is a specialized constructor that creates a new class instance based on the passed-in object. Almost all API objects are cloned to prevent shared references between the new object and the object it was based on.

The next set of main methods to review starts with the cloning methods. The implementation seems to be a little odd in that both the Clone and CloneTyped methods return a new MmgObj instance. This was a design decision to make cloning functionality standard across the API. For classes that extend the MmgObj class, the Clone method returns a new MmgObj instance, and the CloneTyped method returns a new instance of the extended class. In this case, the typed class is also MmgObj, so both methods return the same type of object. Typed cloning is only supported here for completeness.

The MmgUpdate method is part of the game engine drawing routine. The drawing routine consists of a set of standard methods that are called a certain number of times a second to maintain the desired frame rate. The updateTick argument is an index of the number of times the update method was called. In other words, if you run your game at 60 frames per second, then the updateTick argument will increase by roughly 60 each second.

The next method argument, currentTimeMs, is the time, in milliseconds, that the method was called. The last argument of the method, msSinceLastFrame, is the number of milliseconds since the last update method call. These arguments can be used to support timing control during game frames. Think of any temporary image change in any game. Timing is used to control that behavior. You can measure duration of time by storing the start time of the event and taking a measurement at the stop time of the event.

You could also aggregate the msSinceLastFrame value each update call and use that to measure how much time an event is taking. The next method to review, MmgDraw, is another drawing routine method. This method is passed an MmgPen object that wraps the framework drawing classes. The MmgDraw method is called by the drawing routine every game frame and always right after the update method call.

The ApiToString method is an API convention for providing a string representation of the class. The last main method we need to review for the MmgObj class is the ApiEquals method. Again, this is a convention that is carried throughout this API along with the ApiToString and cloning conventions. This method provides an API-level equality test.

Demonstration: MmgObj Class

The demonstration code review will not include a detailed review of the application and game screens used. A detailed review of this code can be found in Part 2 of this book where the MmgCore API is covered. We will however cover the pertinent blocks of code of the example game screen that demonstrates use of the MmgObj class. I recommend you run the example application to see the code you're reviewing in action.

Listing 2-6. MmgObj Class Demonstration 1

```
01 public void LoadResources() {
02     MmgHelper.wr("ScreenTestMmgObj.LoadResources");
03     pause = true;
04     SetHeight(MmgScreenData.GetGameHeight());
05     SetWidth(MmgScreenData.GetGameWidth());
06     SetPosition(MmgScreenData.GetPosition());
07
08     title = MmgFontData.CreateDefaultBoldMmgFontLg();
09     title.SetText("<  Screen Test Mmg Obj
       (21 / " + GamePanel.TOTAL_TESTS + ")  >");
10     MmgHelper.CenterHorAndTop(title);
11     title.SetY(title.GetY() + MmgHelper.ScaleValue(30));
12     AddObj(title);
13
14     int padding = MmgHelper.ScaleValue(20);
15     int objW = (GetWidth() - (padding * 4)) / 3;
16     int objH = MmgHelper.ScaleValue(150);
17     int objY = (GetHeight() - (objH + padding + MmgHelper.
       ScaleValue(10))) / 2 + GetY();
18     int objX = padding;
19
20     obj1 = new MmgObj();
21     obj1.SetPosition(objX, objY);
22     obj1.SetWidth(objW);
23     obj1.SetHeight(objH);
```

The example game screen is located in the ScreenTestMmgObj class of the
MmgTestSpace package, or namespace if you're using C#. Notice that the method line
numbers are relative to the method, not the entire file. The LoadResources method
is used by all example game screens and is responsible for initializing the drawable
objects used by the game screen. On line 3, we make sure the screen is paused so it
doesn't try to draw itself when not fully initialized. The width, height, and position of the
screen's drawable space are set from the MmgScreenData class' calculated values. The
MmgScreenData class determines the proper scaling based on the window's dimensions
and the desired game panel dimensions, lines 4–6.

25

The `title` for this game screen is set on lines 8–12. Notice that the font for the title is maintained by the class `MmgFontData`. This class is similar to the `MmgScreenData` class in that it handles scaling font sizes based on the screen's current scaling setup. Take notice of the scaling features. This 2D game API is meant to be automatically resizable in certain aspects, and two of those aspects are the screen size and the font size.

The text is set on line 9, and on line 10 we see the `MmgHelper` class in use. Thus far, we've seen a number of static support classes come in handy. The `MmgHelper` class is another handy support class that conveniently provides access to object positioning methods. Next, on line 11, we adjust the positioning slightly and move the title down by a scaled 30 pixels. The `ScaleValue` method is an easy-access static method that will scale a number based on the screen's scaling setup.

Every literal distance, position, or size value should be passed through the `MmgHelper` class' `ScaleValue` method. This will ensure your game can be run at different resolutions and all positioning, font, and screen dimensions will automatically be adjusted to accommodate the current resolution. The last line in that code block, line 12, adds the title `MmgFont` instance to the screen's collection of drawable objects. Because we extended the `MmgGameScreen` class for this game screen, we have some built-in functionality from that class.

Next up, on lines 14–18, we prepare the dimensions of the `MmgObj`'s we want to display on this screen. On line 14, we set the padding; again we are sure to scale our values. Line 15 stores the `MmgObj`'s desired width in the `objW` variable. The formula that initializes it simply calculates the width of three boxes spaced by the padding value and centered on the screen. On line 16, the desired height, `objH`, is set to the `ScaleValue` of 150. Then on lines 17 and 18, the Y coordinate for the `MmgObj` instance is calculated. The centered height takes into account the padding and height of the label font used.

Finally, the Y coordinate is increased by the Y offset of the screen. This is done in case the screen's Y coordinate is not zero. The variable `objX` is set to the value of the padding variable because this will be the start value of the X coordinate as the `MmgObj`'s are positioned across the screen. In the block of code on lines 20–23, we instantiate a new `MmgObj` and set its position and size.

Notice that we don't add the `MmgObj` instance to the screen's collection of drawable objects via the `AddObj` method. Can you guess why? It's because the `MmgObj` class by default does not have anything to draw. We work around this making the `MmgDraw` method explicitly draw the object instances in the example game screen with a direct call to the `MmgPen` class' `DrawRect` method that takes an `MmgObj` argument and uses it to draw a rectangle on the screen at the same position and with the same size as the object.

Base Classes: MmgColor

The MmgColor class is used to wrap the framework's color class and provide color support to the API. This is a very common setup in game engines, you will often see centralized classes that model color, position, and size. In following with the theme of using convenient static class methods, the MmgColor class provides a number of such methods for quick color access.

Static Class Members

The MmgColor class' static class methods listed here demonstrate creating a new MmgColor instance using four different techniques.

Listing 2-7. MmgColor Static Class Members 1

```
public static MmgColor GetYellow() { return new MmgColor(Color.YELLOW); }

public static MmgColor GetLimeGreen() { return new MmgColor(Color.
decode("#DAF7A6")); }

public static MmgColor GetDecodedColor(String htmlColor){return new
MmgColor(Color.decode(htmlColor));}

public static MmgColor GetTransparent() { return new MmgColor(new Color(0f,
0f, 0f, 1f)); }
```

The first method listed in the preceding demonstrates creating a new MmgColor instance from the static colors available in the framework's color class. The second method, GetLimeGreen, demonstrates creating a new MmgColor instance from a set HTML color code.

Third, we have the GetDecodeColor method, which is an example of creating a new MmgColor instance from a user-specified HTML color code. Lastly, we have a static class method that creates a new MmgColor instance from a set of four floating-point numbers. The GetTransparent method specifies the transparent color by setting the red, green, blue, and alpha channels to 0.

Class Fields

The MmgColor class has only one field we need to worry about, c. This field is an instance of the framework's color class. It is wrapped by the MmgColor class, which provides a standard way for the API to use colors.

Support Method Details

There are only two support methods to review in the MmgColor class. The class support methods, GetColor and SetColor, are just simple get and set methods for the color class' c field.

Main Method Details

We'll begin our main method review with the three constructors listed in the following set. They demonstrate creating a new MmgColor class with different arguments.

Listing 2-8. MmgColor Main Method Details 1

```
public MmgColor() { ... }
public MmgColor(MmgColor obj){ ... }
public MmgColor(Color C) { ... }
public MmgColor Clone() { ... }
public String ApiToString() { ... }
public boolean ApiEquals(MmgColor obj) { ... }
```

The first class constructor takes no arguments and defaults to the color white. The second class constructor listed takes an MmgColor class instance as an argument and uses its stored color to create a new MmgColor instance. The third and final constructor listed in the preceding takes a framework color instance as an argument. This color object is then used to create a new MmgColor instance.

The next main method to review is the Clone method. Take note that the MmgColor class does not extend the MmgObj class yet the ability to clone the class is available. The Clone method is very direct. It uses the specialized constructor we've reviewed to create a new instance of the MmgColor class with the same color. Lastly, the ApiEquals method provides a way to test for equality at the API level, and the ApiToString method is used to create a string representation of the object instance.

Demonstration: MmgColor Class

In this demonstration of the MmgColor class, we'll use the ScreenTestMmgColor screen as the basis of our example. You can find this class in the MmgTestSpace package, or namespace if you are following along in C#. Due to the repetition of code in the LoadResources method, I'll only list the pertinent lines in the following code block.

Listing 2-9. MmgColor Class Demonstration 1

```
01 public void LoadResources() {
02     MmgHelper.wr("ScreenTestMmgColor.LoadResources");
03     pause = true;
04     SetHeight(MmgScreenData.GetGameHeight());
05     SetWidth(MmgScreenData.GetGameWidth());
06     SetPosition(MmgScreenData.GetPosition());
07
08     title = MmgFontData.CreateDefaultBoldMmgFontLg();
09     title.SetText("<  Screen Test Mmg Color (11 / " + GamePanel.TOTAL_
       TESTS + ")  >");
10     MmgHelper.CenterHorAndTop(title);
11     title.SetY(title.GetY() + MmgHelper.ScaleValue(30));
12     AddObj(title);
13
14     int yDiff = MmgHelper.ScaleValue(40);
15     int yStrt = GetY() + MmgHelper.ScaleValue(140);
16     int xLeft = MmgHelper.ScaleValue(200);
17     int i = 0;
18
19     color1Label = MmgFontData.CreateDefaultBoldMmgFontLg();
20     color1Label.SetMmgColor(MmgColor.GetBlueGray());
21     color1Label.SetText("Color: BlueGray");
22     color1Label.SetX(xLeft);
23     color1Label.SetY(yStrt + (yDiff * i));
24     AddObj(color1Label);
25     i++;
```

The LoadResources method starts off in much the same way as the previous example game screen. A debug line is printed indicating which screen is loading resources, the pause flag is set to true, and the screen's dimensions and position are set based on values from the MmgScreenData class. You'll notice that all LoadResources methods in the example application are structured the same way and include very similar lines of code.

This is a good coding habit. Similar code is easier to read and understand. If you direct your attention to lines 8–12 in the code block listed in the preceding, you'll see standard title initialization code, customized for this particular screen, but similar to all example game screens. Notice that the title object is added to the screen using the AddObj method. If you look at the code on lines 14–17, you'll see the initialization of the positioning variables. Note that any literal numeric values are passed through the ScaleValue method. This ensures positioning values will scale with the screen.

Because all of the MmgColor examples are very similar, we'll only review one block of code, starting on line 19. We set the font using the MmgFontData class, which handles scaling the font based on the current screen scaling. On line 20, the actual example of setting the font's color can be seen. In this case, we're using the static helper method of the MmgColor class, the GetBlueGray method specifically.

The font entry will be drawn on the screen using this color. On line 21, we set the label font's text to the name of the color used. The positioning of the font entry is calculated based on the local variables we mentioned earlier. Line 24 is necessary to add the font to the game screen's list of drawable objects; and lastly, we increment a local variable, i, so the next font entry is drawn just below the current one. Be sure to check out this example game screen using the example application provided.

Base Classes: MmgRect

The MmgRect class is used to represent a simple rectangle in the MmgBase API. The rectangle class can be drawn to the screen to show size and position, it can be used in calculations like collision detection, and it can be used as a UI element such as a border or divider.

Static Class Members

The MmgRect class has one static class member, the GetUnitRect method. The GetUnitRect method is a convenient way to create a standardized MmgRect instance. The method creates a new MmgRect instance positioned at 0,0 and with dimensions both equal to 1.

Class Fields

The MmgRect class has only one class field we need to cover. The rect field is an instance of the framework's rectangle class. The MmgRect class wraps this framework and provides standardized rectangle support to the API.

Support Method Details

The first set of support methods to review are as follows.

Listing 2-10. MmgRect Support Method Details 1

```
public int GetLeft() { ... }
public int GetTop() { ... }
public int GetRight() { return ( ... }
public int GetBottom() { ... }

public int GetWidth() { ... }
public void SetWidth(int w){ ... }
public int GetHeight() { ... }
public void SetHeight(int h){ ... }
public Rectangle GetRect() { ... }
public void SetRect(Rectangle r) { ... }
```

The methods listed in the preceding are get and set methods that allow access to their associated class fields. The last two methods in the set allow access to the framework's rectangle class. While we want to limit interaction with the framework classes as much as possible by keeping them centralized and encapsulated within classes, we can't ignore that we are using them and do need to access them from time to time. With this in mind, you'll notice that we provide access to framework classes where it makes sense.

Main Method Details

The class' main methods start with a review of some of the available constructors.

Listing 2-11. MmgRect Main Method Details 1

```
public MmgRect() { ... }
public MmgRect(MmgRect obj) { ... }
public MmgRect(int left, int top, int bottom, int right) { ... }
```

The first constructor listed takes no arguments and creates a new MmgRect instance with height and width set to 1 and positioned at 0,0. The second constructor is a specialized constructor that creates a new MmgRect instance from an existing one. The last constructor listed in the preceding takes more granular data, left, top, bottom, right, values and uses them to create a new MmgRect object instance.

Listing 2-12. MmgRect Class Main Method Details 2

```
public void ShiftRect(int shiftLeftRight, int shiftUpDown) { ... }

public MmgRect ToShiftedRect(int shiftLeftRight, int shiftUpDown) { ... }

public MmgRect Clone() { ... }
```

The next two main methods we'll cover help you shift the rectangle object in different ways. The ShiftRect method shifts the current object instance in the left-right and up-down directions by the amounts specified in the method arguments. The next main method, ToShiftedRect, is similar; but it doesn't alter the current object instance. Instead, it creates and returns a new rectangle at the shifted position specified by the method arguments. These are convenient methods to use when you want to slightly adjust a rectangle or create a new one based on an existing instance.

The last method in the set is the Clone method. We've come across this method before. The MmgBase API supports cloning functionality across all classes where it makes sense. All cloning methods make use of the specialized class constructor.

Listing 2-13. MmgRect Main Method Details 3

```
public int GetDiffX(MmgRect inRect, int direction, boolean opposite,
boolean left2right) { ... }

public int GetDiffX(int x, int direction, boolean opposite) { ... }

public int GetDiffY(MmgRect inRect, int direction, boolean opposite,
boolean left2right) { ... }

public int GetDiffY(int y, int direction, boolean opposite) { ... }
public String ApiToString() { ... }
public boolean ApiEquals(MmgRect obj) { ... }
```

The GetDiffX methods are a set of main methods that quickly calculate the horizontal difference between two MmgRect objects. Using the method parameters for the first GetDiffX method, the entry that takes four arguments, you can compare rectangles using the left or right coordinate. You can also specify which object is used first in the comparison and the direction of the comparison itself. This gives you a lot of power on how to compare two rectangles. This method takes some experience. Take your time with it before you use it in your game.

The second GetDiffX method, the entry that takes three arguments, can be used to compare the current rectangle with an X coordinate. You can specify the rectangle coordinate you want to compare things with and the direction, left or right. You can also override the actual comparison by using the opposite argument. Again, this method takes some experience. Give yourself some time using it before you employ it in your game.

The next two main methods I want to mention are the GetDiffY methods. They are very similar to the methods we just reviewed. They perform the same operations except they are designed to work with Y coordinates and the up and down directions. I won't cover them in any detail here because they are so similar, but I recommend taking the time to look them over and make sure you understand how they work.

The last two main methods to review with regard to the MmgRect class are the ApiToString and ApiEquals methods. The ApiToString method is used to create a string representation of the MmgRect class. This is an API-level method for representing a class instance as a string. The ApiEquals method is an API-level comparison method. It defines equality as two MmgRect instances having the same position and dimensions.

Demonstration: MmgRect Class

In this section, we'll demonstrate use of the MmgRect class by looking at a few lines of code from the ScreenTestMmgRect class of the MmgTestSpace package, or namespace if you are following along in C#. We've seen a few LoadResources method reviews by now, so we'll skip over some of the common code and focus on the class-specific lines. Make sure to view this example screen in the example application.

Listing 2-14. MmgRect Class Demonstration 1

```
01    rect1 = new MmgRect(MmgHelper.ScaleValue(100), MmgHelper.
      ScaleValue(190), MmgHelper.ScaleValue(190) + GetHeight()/4,
      GetWidth() - MmgHelper.ScaleValue(100));
02    rect2 = new MmgRect(MmgHelper.ScaleValue(100), MmgHelper.
      ScaleValue(210) + GetHeight()/4, MmgHelper.ScaleValue(210)
      + GetHeight()/4 + GetHeight()/4, GetWidth() - MmgHelper.
      ScaleValue(100));
03    rect3 = new MmgRect(MmgHelper.ScaleValue(90), MmgHelper.
      ScaleValue(180), MmgHelper.ScaleValue(90) + GetHeight()/2 +
      GetHeight()/4 + MmgHelper.ScaleValue(28), GetWidth() - MmgHelper.
      ScaleValue(90));
```

In this example screen's LoadResources method, focus your attention on lines 1–3. These lines initialize and configure three MmgRect instances. Keep in mind that the MmgRect class does not extend the MmgObj class. This means that the MmgRect is not directly drawable by the game engine drawing routine. There is, however, support in the MmgPen class for drawing MmgRect instances. In this way, the MmgRect class sits on the fence between calculations and rendering.

Base Classes: MmgFont

The MmgFont class is used to wrap the framework's font class. Fonts are mainly created with the MmgFontData class' convenient, static methods. The MmgFontData class should always be used first, because it automatically scales font sizes based on the screen's current scaling, if any. This helps ensure that games can be scaled up or down in size and still maintain the positioning and size of game screen objects, including MmgFont objects.

The MmgFont class is the first class we've encountered that extends the MmgObj class. As such, it has built-in support for position and dimensions and receives update and drawing method calls when plugged into the game engine's drawing routine. Also note, because of a strict API design pattern, the MmgFont class supports cloning, typed cloning, and comparison functionality. Not too bad.

Enumerations

The MmgFont class has one associated enumeration that is important for us to review. The FontType enumeration is used by the MmgFont class to describe the style of font the class represents. For instance, if a bold font is loaded up, then the bold FontType would be used. It's important to note that the font type does not drive the way the font is rendered; it merely describes the font that is loaded.

Class Fields

The MmgFont class fields for us to review are listed in the following group.

Listing 2-15. MmgFont Class Fields 1

```
private Font font;
private String text;
private final FontRenderContext frc;
private int fontSize = -1;
private FontType fontType = FontType.NONE;
```

The first field listed in the preceding is the framework font class. In the C# version of MmgFont, the framework font class is the SpriteFont class. The MmgFont class wraps the underlying framework class and exposes a standard functionality for the MmgBase API. The text class field holds the text that is to be displayed by the MmgFont instance. The next field listed is a framework class used to describe the internal method used to render the font. This can be used to give us the dimensions of a rectangle that would fit the rendered font. Having accurate information on a font-rendered string's dimensions allows us to properly position the text on the screen.

Take a moment to think about the C# implementation and the SpriteFont framework class. Why does everything still work the same with regard to the MmgFont class and the API? This is because the font functionality that the API uses is defined by the MmgFont class and it's the same in any port of the game engine. It's the MmgFont class' responsibility to provide the functionality defined by its class using the framework classes available. The remaining two class fields, fontSize and fontType, are descriptive fields that should accurately reflect the type of font loaded by the class.

Support Method Details

The first set of support methods for us to review are listed in the following.

Listing 2-16. MmgFont Support Method Details 1

```
public String GetText() { ... }
public void SetText(String s) { ... }
public FontType GetFontType() { ... }
public void SetFontType(FontType ft) { ... }

public void SetFontSize(int sz) { ... }
public int GetFontSize() { ... }
public void SetFont(Font tf) { ... }
public Font GetFont() { ... }
```

The first two support methods we'll discuss are the get and set methods for the text class field. The GetText method just returns the text value. The SetText method, however, not only updates the text; it also updates the dimensions of the font. The size calculation turns out to be pretty accurate, but you'll notice positioning the font can feel a bit awkward. That's because the font actually draws from the vertical center of the specified position. Take this into account when working with fonts on a game screen.

The SetFontSize method is a bit different than some of the support methods we've seen thus far. It will resize the font when called. In turn, the GetFontSize method returns the size value from the actual font. The fontSize field is updated along with the resizing of the font. This field shadows the font's size when it is set. There are get and set methods for all important class fields. Make sure you familiarize yourself with them.

Main Method Details

First, we'll review the class constructors. Now, there are a few more constructors than the ones we'll review here; but in many ways, they are redundant, so we'll stick with those we have listed.

Listing 2-17. MmgFont Main Method Details 1

```
public MmgFont() { ... }
public MmgFont(MmgObj obj) { ... }
```

```
public MmgFont(Font tf, int fontSize, FontType fontType) { ... }

public MmgFont(MmgFont obj) { ... }
public MmgObj Clone() { ... }
public MmgFont CloneTyped() { ... }
public void MmgDraw(MmgPen p) { ... }
public boolean ApiEquals(MmgFont obj) { ... }
```

The first constructor I want to review takes three arguments, a font, a font size, and a font type. The constructor initializes each class field with either a default or argument value. Note that the font size argument does not set the font size; it represents the font size. The other constructor listed in the preceding is the specialized constructor used by the class' cloning methods. It takes an MmgFont object as an argument.

We've come across this type of constructor implementation before. This is a reinforced design pattern throughout the MmgBase API closely tied to cloning. In most cases, any class fields that are other API classes will need to be cloned to prevent shared references between the new object instance and the instance it was based on. All basic data types can just be set directly.

The next two main methods to talk about are cloning methods. You'll see these two particular class methods, Clone and CloneTyped, over and over again. Notice how we've created a reliable capability at the API level by implementing certain class functionality consistently. We could have chosen to implement the same thing using interfaces. That would create a more structured implementation, but we really value flexibility over rigid structure when building a game engine.

The MmgDraw method is called by the game engine's drawing routine when the object is part of a game screen's list of drawable objects by being passed to the AddObj method. You can also draw custom combinations of objects by adding code to the MmgDraw method directly. The ApiEquals method is something we've seen before. In this case, the ApiEquals method returns true if the two objects have the same font and text.

Demonstration: MmgFont Class

In this section, we'll demonstrate use of the MmgFont class by looking at specific methods of the ScreenTestMmgFont class from the MmgTestSpace package. There are a lot of font examples displayed on this screen; we'll only review a subset of them. Be sure to run the example application and view this example game screen in action.

Listing 2-18. MmgFont Class Demonstration 1

```
01    fontBoldLg = MmgFontData.CreateDefaultBoldMmgFontLg();
02    fontBoldLg.SetText("Font Bold Large");
03    fontBoldLg.SetY(GetY() + MmgHelper.ScaleValue(15) + (y * 1));
04    fontBoldLg.SetX(y);
05    AddObj(fontBoldLg);
06
07    fontBoldMd = MmgFontData.CreateDefaultBoldMmgFont(title.
      GetFontSize() - MmgHelper.ScaleValue(2));
08    fontBoldMd.SetText("Font Bold Medium");
09    fontBoldMd.SetY(GetY() + MmgHelper.ScaleValue(15) + (y * 2));
10    fontBoldMd.SetX(y);
11    AddObj(fontBoldMd);
12
13    fontBoldSm = MmgFontData.CreateDefaultBoldMmgFontSm();
14    fontBoldSm.SetText("Font Bold Small");
15    fontBoldSm.SetY(GetY() + MmgHelper.ScaleValue(15) + (y * 3));
16    fontBoldSm.SetX(y);
17    AddObj(fontBoldSm);
```

Our review begins with the code on line 1. This is an example of loading a scaled, large, bold, font and setting its position. Notice that on line 5 the MmgFont object, which extends the MmgObj class, is added to the game screen's default drawing routine via a call to the AddObj method. The remaining code blocks on lines 7–11 and 13–17 perform the same operations as the code we've just reviewed except for using different sized fonts. Make sure you take a moment to look over the different font entries, so you have an idea of how to create and use different fonts in your game.

Base Classes: MmgSound

The MmgSound class is used to wrap the framework's sound class and provides audio support to the MmgBase API. The MmgSound class is responsible for playing sound effects and background music. It's a bit different than other classes in that it's a resource but it isn't a drawable resource. The MmgSound class is designed to use a static, global value for the volume. There is also code in place for making sure that each MmgSound instance has a unique ID value. The class has cloning, string representation, and comparison functionality.

Static Class Members

The MmgSound class has some static class members for us to review.

Listing 2-19. MmgSound Static Class Members 1

```
private static int ID_SRC = 0;
public static float MMG_SOUND_GLOBAL_VOLUME = 0.65f;public static float
SetVolume(float f) { ... }
```

The first class field is a private field, ID_SRC, and it is used as part of the class constructor to set a unique ID for that instance of the class. The next static class field listed in the preceding is the volume field. It is used to set the volume of all MmgSound instances. The global volume is checked on each call to the sound's play method right before the sound is played.

The last static class member to review is the SetVolume method. This method is used to update the global volume value while applying a minimum and a maximum constraint. The SetVolume method returns the value of the volume field that it just updated. This ensures that the method caller is aware of any volume range constraints applied to the volume's value.

Class Fields

The MmgSound class has a few class fields that support sound resources, volume, and playback rate for us to discuss.

Listing 2-20. MmgSound Class Fields 1

```
private int id;
private String idStr;
private Clip sound;
private float usedVolume;
private float range;
```

The id field gets stamped with a unique value when the MmgSound object is created. The idStr field is similar except that it holds a string representation of the id field. The sound field is an instance of the framework's sound class. In the Java implementation of the game engine, the framework's sound class is the Clip class.

The usedVolume class field stores the volume applied to the sound. If the static class field, volume, changes after usedVolume is set, the volume of the sound will be automatically updated the next time it's played. The last entry in the set of fields listed in the preceding is the private class field range. This field is used to describe a volume range when applying a new volume to the current sound.

Listing 2-21. MmgSound Class Fields 2

```
private float gain;
private FloatControl vol;
private float currentVolume;
private float currentRate;
```

The private class field gain is a calculated adjustment used to alter the sound's volume. The FloatControl instance vol is a Java-specific implementation used to set the volume and rate of the sound. It is a control class used to manage attributes of the sound clip.

Support Method Details

Let's take a look at the first set of support methods to review.

Listing 2-22. MmgSound Support Method Details 1

```
public void ApplyVolume() { ... }
public void ApplyRate(float rate) { ... }
public float GetCurrentRate() { ... }
public float GetCurrentVolume() { ... }
public String GetIdStr() { ... }
```

The ApplyVolume support method is used to update the volume of the sound and the usedVolume class field. The method uses Java framework classes to set the gain of the sound clip based on the available volume range and the global volume value. The currentVolume class field is also updated by this method to reflect the volume used.

The next support method to review is the ApplyRate method. This method is used to set the playback rate of the sound if it's supported. The sample rate is not controlled by a global static value like the way the volume is controlled. Each MmgSound instance can have its own playback rate. This method also updates the currentRate field. As you can see, the currentVolume and currentRate fields are descriptive and shadow the values used by the sound object.

The next two support methods, GetCurrentRate and GetCurrentVolume, are just simple get methods that return the current value of their associated fields. The last entry in this set of methods is the GetIdStr method. This method returns the value of the idStr field, which is a string representation of the class' id field.

Listing 2-23. MmgSound Support Method Details 2

```
public int GetId() { ... }
private void SetId() { ... }
public Clip GetSound() { ... }
public void SetSound(Clip snd) { ... }
```

The GetId method is your typical field access method; however, the SetId method is not your typical set method. The SetId method is private, and it's used internally by the class to assign a value to the id field of each new class instance. The remaining two support methods provide access to the sound field allowing you to set or get the framework class that the MmgSound class wraps.

Main Method Details

We'll begin the MmgSound class main method review with the constructors listed in the following group.

Listing 2-24. MmgSound Main Method Details 1

```
public MmgSound(Clip se) { ... }
public MmgSound(MmgSound obj) { ... }
public MmgSound Clone() { ... }
```

The first constructor takes a framework sound class as an argument. In the Java implementation, this is the Clip class. In the C# implementation, the SoundEffect class is used. The global volume is applied to the new sound instance via the ApplyVolume method call. The constructor also calls the SetId method giving the new class instance a unique identity. The second constructor listed is a specialized constructor that takes an MmgSound instance as an argument and uses it to create a new, unique MmgSound object from the existing one.

Listing 2-25. MmgSound Main Method Details 2

```
public void Play() { ... }
public void Play(int loop, float rate) { ... }
public void Stop() { ... }
public String ApiToString() { ... }
public boolean ApiEquals(MmgSound obj) { ... }
```

The class provides two ways to play the sound resource. The first way, listed in the preceding, takes no arguments and is a direct way to play a sound. The sound is reset for playback, and it is configured not to loop. This method is for quickly playing sound effects and shorter sounds that don't need looping.

The second Play method takes two arguments and can be used to set the loop count and the playback rate before playing the sound. This method is convenient for longer-duration sounds like background music. Notice that we set the loop number for the sound's playback, meaning the sound will play in full that many times before stopping.

The final main method left to review is the Stop method. The sound is stopped, and the volume is synced to the global value before the method returns. Notice that both play methods and the stop method all ensure that the sound object's volume matches the global volume. It makes sense because in a game we could have a number of different sounds playing and available to play. The class is configured to automatically keep all sound object instances synchronized to the global volume.

The remaining two main methods I'd like to discuss are the ApiToString method and the ApiEquals method. We've seen both of these methods before, but I'll briefly cover them again here. The ApiToString method is used to create a string representation of the MmgSound class. The method is useful in debugging and logging situations. The ApiEquals method is used to compare two MmgSound instances and determine their equality.

Demonstration: MmgSound Class

In this section, we'll demonstrate use of the MmgSound class by looking at specific methods of the ScreenTestMmgSound class from the MmgTestSpace package, or namespace in C#. This demonstration uses input events, so I'll cover some input handling basics here as well. There is also some sound playback, so we'll cover a little resource loading too.

Listing 2-26. MmgSound Class Demonstration 1

```
01 sound1 = MmgHelper.GetBasicCachedSound("jump1.wav");
02 sound2 = MmgHelper.GetBasicCachedSound("jump2.wav");
03
04 soundLabel1 = MmgFontData.CreateDefaultBoldMmgFontLg();
05 soundLabel1.SetText("MmgSound Example");
06 MmgHelper.CenterHorAndVert(soundLabel1);
07 soundLabel1.SetY(soundLabel1.GetY() - MmgHelper.ScaleValue(20));
08 AddObj(soundLabel1);
09
10 soundLabel2 = MmgFontData.CreateDefaultBoldMmgFontLg();
11 soundLabel2.SetText("Press Enter or Space to Play a Sound");
12 MmgHelper.CenterHorAndVert(soundLabel2);
13 soundLabel2.SetY(soundLabel2.GetY() + MmgHelper.ScaleValue(20));
14 AddObj(soundLabel2);
```

The LoadResuorces method is very similar to previous versions we've reviewed. On lines 1 and 2, we have some resource preparation code that sets the sound1 and sound2 class fields. Notice that the fields are set using the static method GetBasicCachedSound of the MmgHelper class. There are a few ways resources can be loaded into the game using the API. For the most part, resource loading is a higher-level action to be performed by the game implementation's MmgCore library.

However, with the way the MmgBase API is structured, images and sounds can be loaded automatically based on where the game is running and what the game is named in the code and settings. In this case, the MmgTestScreens application is run out of the MmgTestSpace package. In the case of the C# implementation, the MmgGameApiCs project has a similar MmgTestScreens class in the MmgTestSpace namespace. The Java project has the following directory structure:

Listing 2-27. MmgGameApiJava Project Directory Structure

```
MmgGameApiJava
|-> src (Source Code Directory)
|-> dist (Executable Directory)
```

```
|-> cfg (Resource and Configuration Directory)
    |-> playable
        |-> MmgTestSpace
             |-> jump2.wav
        |-> auto_load
             |-> jump1.wav
```

As the game starts up, code from the MmgCore API, essentially the game engine runtime, checks to see if some default folders exist in the project directory. Because the Java version of the project was developed in the NetBeans IDE, we have the IDE project configured to compile to the dist folder. If there is a directory named cfg in the same directory as the dist folder, it is treated as the configuration directory and is scanned for subfolders and files.

One such special subfolder is the playable folder found in the cfg directory of the project. Notice the MmgTestSpace and auto_load subfolders. If a subfolder is found that has the same name as the project's NAME static field, found in the game's GameSettings class, that folder is scanned for audio files. Any audio files found are loaded into the game engine's audio resource cache by file name.

To demonstrate playing the sound, we tap into the input handling methods that are called by the GamePanel class for the current game screen. This will be covered in more detail during the MmgCore API review. The ProcessKeyClick method is fired when a keyboard key is pressed. It is passed a character and an integer representation of the keyboard key. In this case, pressing Enter or the space bar will play a sound. We can use the character representation to check for Enter "\n" or space " ". When the Enter key is pressed, sound1 is played; and when the space bar is pressed, sound2 is played.

Base Classes: MmgPen

The MmgPen class wraps the framework's drawing class. In the Java/Swing implementation, the MmgPen class wraps the Graphics class. In the C#/MonoGame implementation, the MmgPen class wraps the SpriteBatch class. The MmgPen class provides drawing support to the MmgBase API and allows for drawing images, text, and rectangles to the screen.

The MmgPen class is designed to be flexible and allow the user to call the drawing method that best suits the needs of the given situation. You'll notice that this class does not present the same cloning and comparison functionality as other classes we've seen.

Why do you think this is? It has to do with how the MmgPen class is used. It is always used in a data-driven way, drawing the specified object. Therefore, it has almost no internal state and nothing that requires cloning. As such, the class has no cloning methods.

Static Class Members

The first class field for us to review, FONT_NORMALIZE_POSITION, is a special flag that when enabled alters the way fonts are rendered. If the field is set to true, then the MmgPen class will call the NormalizeFontPosition method for the X and Y coordinates of its position. This allows the developer to adjust the render position of fonts based on the type and size of the font. This comes in handy when you are trying to normalize the way fonts are positioned between different fonts on different platforms.

The next entry, ADV_RENDER_HINTS, is a Boolean flag that when enabled, on the Java version of the game engine, forces the game engine to configure several rendering settings. The C# implementation has the same capabilities but doesn't have to run any code. It's ready for games out of the box. The hints provide some indication of how to handle certain 2D rendering events like scaling and rotating 2D images. The remaining static field, TRANSPARENT, is a convenient way to access the transparent color value. This can come in handy with certain games and certain drawing scenarios.

Listing 2-28. MmgPen Static Class Members 3

```
public static Image CreateColorTile(int w, int h, MmgColor c) { ... }

public static Image RotateImageStatic(int width, int height, Image img, int
angle, int originX, int originY) { ... }

public static Image ScaleImageStatic(Image img, MmgVector2 scale) { ... }

public static Image ScaleImageStatic(Image img, double scaleX, double
scaleY) { ... }
```

The CreateColorTile static method uses framework classes to create an image, a colored square, with the specified dimensions.

The RotateImageStatic method is a static method that rotates an image by the specified angle in degrees. The method still requires proper image dimensions and a rotation origin be configured. Notice that if either originX or originY is set to –1, the method calculates the origin of rotation as the center of the image. A copy of the original image is drawn to the new buffered image while applying the rotation transform.

The first `ScaleImageStatic` method has a convenient overload that takes an `MmgVector2` argument to define the horizontal and vertical scaling. The second `ScaleImageStatic` method takes three arguments, an image and a scale value for each coordinate, X and Y. The new image's dimensions are based on the scaling values passed in as arguments.

Class Fields

The `MmgPen` class has a few important class fields for us to cover. Let's look at some code!

Listing 2-29. MmgPen Class Fields 1

```
private Graphics pen;
private Color color;
private boolean cacheOn;
```

The first field in the set is an instance of the `Graphics` class. The `Graphics` object, pen, is the framework class that the `MmgPen` class wraps. The next field, `color`, is the framework class for representing colors. Be mindful how you use this class field; it may not reflect the color that is being used by the pen. I'll cover this in more detail when we review the `MmgPen` class' methods.

The last class field in this set has a bit of a story to it. The MmgBase API, at one time, had a focus on being able to draw scaled images on the fly. To help speed this up, the `MmgPen` class had special support added to it so that certain image drawing methods would cache an image that was scaled or rotated on the fly so the same transformations wouldn't have to be performed again.

There is even special support in the `MmgBmp` class for accessing the scaled and unscaled image dimensions. As it turns out, this is not the best practice for a 2D game. If you are planning to do on-the-fly scaling and rotation, think about setting up the images you need ahead of time during resource loading. This way they are already in memory and the work is only done once. The `cacheOn` field should remain false unless you are experimenting with the image transform cache.

Support Method Details

The first set of support methods we'll review here are your standard get and set support methods.

Listing 2-30. MmgPen Support Method Details 2

```
public boolean GetCacheOn() { ... }
public void SetCacheOn(boolean b) { ... }
public boolean IsEmptyColor(Color c) { ... }
public Graphics GetSpriteBatch() { ... }
public void SetSpriteBatch(Graphics sp) { ... }
public Graphics GetGraphics() { ... }
public void SetGraphics(Graphics sp) { ... }
public Color GetColor() { ... }
public void SetColor(Color c) { ... }
public Color GetGraphicsColor() { ... }
public void SetGraphicsColor(Color c) { ... }
```

The first two methods to discuss are get and set methods for the cacheOn class field. We recommend leaving the MmgPen's caching system off unless you're very experienced with the API. The next method, IsEmptyColor, just checks to see if the color argument is null or not returning a Boolean value indicating the result.

The next two support methods, GetSpriteBatch and SetSpriteBatch, have a bit of history to them. These two methods entered into the API during a port to Microsoft's XNA framework. The methods are essentially the same as the GetGraphics and SetGraphics methods. They act as a pass-through to the sprite batch methods. They're also named to reflect the drawing class in the Java implementation of the API. The GetColor and SetColor methods allow you access to the class' color field. Note, these methods do not change the current color of the pen. In order to do that, you need to use the GetGraphicsColor and SetGraphicsColor methods. They will adjust the color directly on the pen.

Listing 2-31. MmgPen Support Method Details 2

```
public Image ScaleImage(Image img, double scaleX, double scaleY) { ... }

public Image RotateImage(int width, int height, Image img, int angle, int
originY, int originY) { ... }
```

Notice that the two support methods, listed in the preceding set, act as a nonstatic pass-through to the class' static method. This is implemented for convenience to allow access to scaling and rotation methods from nonstatic class methods. The last group of support methods we have to review are the drawing methods. There are many more methods than those covered here; however, in the interest of efficiency, we won't cover every method and instead focus on a few key examples.

Listing 2-32. MmgPen Support Method Details 3

```
public void DrawText(MmgFont f, MmgVector2 pos) { ... }

public void DrawBmpBasic(String idStr, MmgVector2 position) { ... }

public void DrawBmpFromCache(MmgBmp b) { ... }
public void DrawBmp(MmgBmp b) { ... }
public void DrawRect(MmgObj obj) { ... }
public void DrawRect(MmgRect r) { ... }
public void DrawRect(int x, int y, int w, int h) { ... }
```

The first method in the set of drawing methods listed in the preceding is the DrawText method. This method is overloaded, but we'll focus on the version that takes an MmgFont instance and an MmgVector2 instance as arguments. If the FONT_NORMALIZE_ POSITION flag is set to true, then the text is drawn using adjusted positioning; otherwise, it is drawn using the specified coordinate values. The method resets the original color and font of the pen before returning. This is something you should make a habit of doing.

The next method to cover is the DrawBmpBasic method. This method is designed to be a simple image drawing method that doesn't perform transformations or complex logic of any kind. Up next, the DrawBmpFromCache method is a pass-through to the DrawBmpBasic method we just looked at. Notice that the MmgBmp instance's ID string is used to locate the desired image in the resource cache.

This method is a slightly more concise way to draw an image from the image cache if the MmgBmp instance has the correct ID and position set. The last method in the set is a generic MmgBmp drawing method, DrawBmp. Note that this method calls a more complicated version of the DrawBmp class that uses rendering options like origin, scaling, and rotation.

Main Method Details

We'll begin the main method review section by looking at some class constructors.

Listing 2-33. MmgPen Main Method Details 1

```
public MmgPen(Graphics p) { ... }
public MmgPen(Graphics p, Color c) { ... }
```

The two constructors I want to review are straightforward. The first constructor takes a Graphics object as an argument and uses it to set the pen class field. The next constructor, listed in the preceding, takes a Graphics object and a Color object as arguments. Note that the color argument is not used to change the graphics object's color field. It is only used to update the MmgPen's color field. In both constructors, the cacheOn class field is set to false. Remember, we don't activate that feature unless we explicitly want to experiment with it.

Demonstration: MmgPen Class

There isn't an example game screen specific to the MmgPen class. Rather, just about every game screen in the example application uses the MmgPen class in some way. We'll take a look at an MmgDraw method to demonstrate how to use the MmgPen class in an actual game.

Listing 2-34. MmgPen Class Demonstration 1

```
01 public void MmgDraw(MmgPen p) {
02     if (pause == false && isVisible == true) {
03         if (background != null) {
04             background.MmgDraw(p);
05         }
06
07         if (header != null) {
08             header.MmgDraw(p);
09         }
10
```

```
11            if (footer != null) {
12                 footer.MmgDraw(p);
13            }
14
15            if (message != null) {
16                 message.MmgDraw(p);
17            }
18
19            if (objects != null) {
20                 objects.MmgDraw(p);
21            }
22
23            if (menuOn == true) {
24                 DrawMenu(p);
25            }
26
27            if (foreground != null) {
28                 foreground.MmgDraw(p);
29            }
30        }
31 }
```

The MmgDraw method listed in the preceding is from the MmgGameScreen class of the MmgBase API. This is the method that gets called in the example screen classes when you see the super class' MmgDraw method being called. In the C# version, the method will call the base class' MmgDraw method. This is an example of the drawing routine that is built into the game engine and is responsible for drawing different types of objects on the screen.

This specific implementation supports drawing a background image, a header, a footer, a screen message, a set of drawable objects, a menu, and a foreground image. The MmgDraw method of the MmgGameScreen class is called by the game engine's drawing routine originating in the GamePanel class of the MmgCore API.

Base Classes: MmgVector2

The MmgVector2 class is used to model position information for objects drawn by the game engine. Of course, there are other uses for the vector class, but that's the main one. The class is commonly used to represent data that has an X and/or a Y component to it. For instance, an MmgVector2 object can be used to hold X,Y scaling data or X,Y offset data, and the most common use is for X,Y position data.

The MmgVector2 class does not extend the MmgObj class so it's not part of the drawable subset of API classes. It does, however, implement cloning, comparison, and string representation in the same way we've seen with previous classes. One other design detail to note is that the MmgVector2 class was designed to be flexible and allow for the use of float, double, or integer values for the X and Y components of the vector.

Static Class Members

There are two static class methods that I want to quickly review. The first static class member is the method GetOriginVec. This method is used to return a new, unique, MmgVector2 instance that points to the origin, 0,0. Similarly, the next static method, GetUnitVec, returns a new, unique instance that points to the unit vector, 1,1.

Class Fields

The MmgVector2 class has only one class field to speak of. Don't you wish they were all this simple? The only class field for us to review is an array of doubles named vec. This array will be initialized to a length of two, representing X and Y components. The class is designed to hold either an integer, float, or double pair of values. In most cases, and for all drawing-related purposes, using integer values makes the most sense because the screen coordinates will always be integer values.

Support Method Details

The MmgVector2 class has a number of get and set support methods. These simple methods are really important because they define an interaction with the MmgVector2 class that uses integers, floats, or doubles. This gives you a lot of flexibility in how you decide to use the class.

Listing 2-35. MmgVector2 Support Method Details 1

```
public double[] GetVector() { ... }
public void SetVector(double[] v) { ... }

public int GetX() { ... }
public void SetX(int x) { ... }
public float GetXFloat() { ... }

public void SetX(float x) { ... }
public double GetXDouble() { ... }
public void SetX(double x) { ... }
```

The first two entries listed in the preceding are get and set methods for the class' vector array. This lets you quickly and easily set a vector object's value using an array of doubles. The next six methods are all get and set methods for the X and Y component values. In each case, the get method is designed to return the X component value in a specific data type. The class supports double, float, and integer representations of the X component value.

Similarly, you can set the X component value using a version of the set method that takes an argument of the desired type, double, float, or integer. Both types of methods work together to create three distinct ways to interact with the X component's value. The next set of support methods provide similar functionality for the Y component value.

Listing 2-36. MmgVector2 Support Method Details 2

```
public int GetY() { ... }
public void SetY(int y { ... }
public float GetYFloat() { ... }

public void SetY(float y) { ... }
public double GetYDouble() { ... }
public void SetY(double y) { ... }
```

This concludes the "Support Method Details" section of the class review. Up next, we'll look at some of the class' main methods.

Main Method Details

This section of the MmgVector2 class starts with a set of constructors that demonstrate the flexibility of the class.

Listing 2-37. MmgVector2 Main Method Details 1

```
public MmgVector2() { ... }
public MmgVector2(MmgVector2 v) { ... }
public MmgVector2(double[] v) { ... }
public MmgVector2(double x, double y) { ... }
public MmgVector2(float x, float y) { ... }
public MmgVector2(int x, int y) { ... }

public MmgVector2 Clone() { ... }
public MmgVector2 CloneFloat() { ... }
public MmgVector2 CloneDouble() { ... }
public MmgVector2 CloneInt() { ... }
```

The constructors listed in the preceding demonstrate support for initializing the class with integers, floats, and doubles. There is a constructor for each case listed and even a few more that aren't listed here. The next set of main methods for us to review are cloning methods. While each cloning method returns an MmgVector2 instance, each method is a little unique. For instance, in all of the type-explicit cloning methods, CloneInt, CloneFloat, and CloneDouble, a new object instance is created using values cast to the specified data type. The generic Clone method creates a new object instance but uses the array entries for the component values to do so.

The final set of main methods left to review contains the ApiToString and ApiEquals methods. The ApiToString method is an API-level method for representing the given MmgVector2 instance as a string. It simply reports the X and Y component values as doubles printed in a string description of the object. The ApiEquals method is like the previous API comparison methods we've seen. It's an API-level method used by the MmgBase API for comparing class instances.

Demonstration: MmgVector2 Class

There isn't an example game screen just for the MmgVector2 class specifically, but the class is used on every single example game screen in the MmgTestSpace library. Let's take a look at one way the MmgVector2 class is used.

Listing 2-38. MmgVector2 Class Demonstration 1

```
1 pause = true;
2 SetHeight(MmgScreenData.GetGameHeight());
3 SetWidth(MmgScreenData.GetGameWidth());
4 SetPosition(MmgScreenData.GetPosition());
```

In the LoadResources method of any game screen in the MmgTestSpace library, the code listed in the preceding can be found. The SetPosition method, line 4, is used to position the game screen to the correct offsets specified by the MmgScreenData class. The offset information is stored as an MmgVector2 instance because it has X and Y component values.

Base Classes: MmgBmp

The MmgBmp class is the last base class we have to review. It extends the MmgObj class and is a member of the subset of drawable classes. Every time you see an image on the screen, an MmgBmp instance is being used. The MmgBmp class has some particular design details I'd like to talk about. The MmgBmp class has a drawing mode feature. This should only be used if you know what you're doing; if not, use the default mode. What this feature does is it controls how the MmgBmp class uses drawing methods from the MmgPen class.

The basic, default mode is the most efficient and uses the fewest method calls. The full mode is slightly less efficient than the basic mode, but it supports more method calls, so more drawing features are supported. For instance, when setting up an MmgLoadingBar class instance, you need to provide a background image that will be used to fill the loading bar. This image must have its draw mode set to full so that it can take advantage of some more advanced image rendering techniques.

Lastly, there is a cached mode. This mode utilizes the image resource cache to pull a reference to the image that is drawn at the specified position. The MmgBmp class also supports cloning, comparison, and string representation as we've seen in many other API classes.

Static Class Members

The MmgBmp class has one static class member for us to review. It's similar to a class field we saw in the MmgSound class. Can you guess which one? Give up? The ID_SRC field. The ID_SRC static class field is used to give each new MmgBmp instance a unique ID. Each new MmgBmp instance gets its id field set to the value of the ID_SRC static class field. Then the ID_SRC field is incremented so it's ready for the next object instance.

Enumerations

The MmgBmp class has one enumeration to cover. The MmgBmpDrawMode enumeration is used to control how the MmgBmp class is drawn when the class' MmgDraw method is called. The simplest and most efficient strategy in most cases is to use the DRAW_BMP_BASIC drawing mode.

Class Fields

The MmgBmp class fields wrap the values necessary to perform different drawing operations like scaling and rotation.

Listing 2-39. MmgBmp Class Fields 1

```
private MmgVector2 origin;
private MmgVector2 scaling;
private MmgRect srcRect;
private MmgRect dstRect;
private Image b;
```

The first set of class fields to review are used to hold drawing information for the given MmgBmp image. It's important to mention that this information might not be used by the MmgPen class when drawing the image. It depends on what method is used to draw the image object. For instance, using the default drawing mode, DRAW_BMP_BASIC, results in a call to the MmgPen class' DrawBmpBasic method.

As you can see in the method, only the position information is taken into consideration when drawing the image. What does this mean? This means that the MmgBmp class is set up for simplicity and efficiency. In general, we shouldn't really be performing image transformations that often, so the API is set up expecting most image drawing operations to be basic.

This also means if you want to do more advanced image drawing that takes into account transformations like rotation and scaling, you'll need to make sure that the correct MmgPen drawing method is used. Be sure to take the complexity of drawing images using more advanced techniques into consideration when planning your game. Again, it's always better to perform image transformations during resource loading once, rather than over multiple game frames, if possible.

With regard to the fields listed in the preceding, the origin vector is used to describe the image's rotation origin. The scaling vector is used to describe scaling values in the X and Y directions. The next two class fields, srcRect and dstRect, are used to describe a source and destination drawing rectangle.

Listing 2-40. MmgBmp Class Fields 2

```
private float rotation;
private String idStr;
private int id;
public MmgBmpDrawMode DRAW_MODE = MmgBmpDrawMode.DRAW_BMP_BASIC;
```

The next set of class fields for us to review starts off with some image transformation information, the rotation angle. The next two fields are like those we've seen in the MmgSound class. The id and idStr class fields are unique identifiers assigned to the class instance when it's created. The ID fields are part of the caching system. I wouldn't recommend adjusting this functionality until you have enough experience working with the drawing routine. Lastly, the DRAW_MODE field is used to adjust how the MmgBmp class' MmgDraw method interacts with the MmgPen argument as we've detailed earlier.

Support Method Details

The first set of support methods begins with get and set methods for the framework's image class.

Listing 2-41. MmgBmp Support Method Details 1

```
public Image GetTexture2D() { ... }
public void SetTexture2D(Image d) { ... }
public Image GetImage() { ... }
public void SetImage(Image d) { ... }
```

There is a bit of legacy code in here from the original XNA implementation of this class. You'll notice that there are two ways to interface with the image class field. The GetTexture2D and SetTexture2D pair of methods refers to the C#/MonoGame framework class Texture2D, while the GetImage and SetImage methods refer to the Java/Swing framework class Image. Either pair of methods will update the class' image field.

Listing 2-42. MmgBmp Support Method Details 2

```
public MmgRect GetSrcRect() { ... }
public void SetSrcRect(MmgRect r) { ... }
public MmgRect GetDstRect() { ... }
public void SetDstRect(MmgRect r) { ... }
public float GetRotation() { ... }
public void SetRotation(float r) { ... }
```

The second set of support methods we have to review are also get and set methods for key class fields. They are direct and simple. Read them over and make sure you understand them.

Listing 2-43. MmgBmp Support Method Details 3

```
public MmgVector2 GetOrigin() { ... }
public void SetOrigin(MmgVector2 v) { ... }
public MmgVector2 GetScaling() { ... }
public void SetScaling(MmgVector2 v) { ... }
public int GetHeight() { ... }
public int GetWidth() { ... }
```

The third and final set of support methods, listed in the preceding, allow access to the origin and scaling vectors. Because rotation can be performed around different points, changing the resulting transformation, you have to specify what coordinates you want to use as the center of rotation. The scaling field is an MmgVector2 instance that holds floating-point values describing how much to scale an image in the X and Y directions.

Because the MmgBmp class has support for on-the-fly transformations, the class supports handling scaled image dimensions. Things can get a little complicated when working with images that are transformed as part of the drawing routine. I highly recommend preparing the image, applying transformations, and then saving a copy of the resulting image for future use.

Main Method Details

The first set of main methods for us to review for the MmgBmp class are a group of class constructors. There are more constructors available than we'll review here, so be sure to look over the class' code and familiarize yourself with any other constructors you find interesting.

Listing 2-44. MmgBmp Main Method Details 1

```
public MmgBmp(MmgObj obj) { ... }
public MmgBmp(MmgBmp obj) { ... }
public MmgBmp(Image t) { ... }

public MmgBmp(Image t, MmgRect Src, MmgRect Dst,
MmgVector2 Origin, MmgVector2 Scaling, float Rotation) { ... }

public MmgObj Clone() { ... }
public MmgBmp CloneTyped() { ... }
```

The first class constructor we'll review is listed in the preceding group. It takes an MmgObj as an argument and uses it to initialize an empty MmgBmp instance.

This is an example of a bare-bones constructor. The MmgBmp instance created by this constructor is not ready for use. You'll have to set an image and double-check the dimensions at the very least. The next main method to review is a specialized constructor that takes an MmgBmp instance as an argument and uses it to create a new, unique copy of the object. Note that the SetBmpId method is called in every constructor, ensuring a unique ID for each class instance.

The next set of main methods to review contains two class constructors that take framework class instances to set the image and related class fields. Let's take a look at the constructor that takes only an Image instance as an argument. In the C# implementation, it would take a Texture2D instance as an argument.

This constructor sets up a basic MmgBmp implementation to use with the game engine's drawing routine. Make sure you review and understand the different MmgBmp constructors available to you. The next set of main methods to review include the class' cloning methods. The ability to clone an MmgBmp instance is provided by the Clone and CloneTyped main methods.

The Clone method returns a reference to the super class, base class in C#, of the MmgBmp class by casting the object instance before returning it. Similarly, the CloneTyped method returns an MmgBmp instance that is a clone of the current class. Notice that both cloning methods use the specialized constructor we reviewed earlier to create a new class instance to return.

Listing 2-45. MmgBmp Class Method Details 2

```
public boolean ApiEquals(MmgBmp obj) { ... }
public void MmgDraw(MmgPen p) { ... }
```

The last remaining methods to review are the ApiEquals method and the class' drawing method, MmgDraw. The ApiEquals method compares certain class properties of two class instances and makes a determination about the equality of those class instances. The last main method left to review is the MmgDraw method. We've seen this method before; it's used by the MmgPen class as part of the underlying drawing routine. Note that the drawing mode controls which MmgPen drawing method is used. The reason for this functionality is efficiency. If we want to draw a simple MmgBmp instance, then we don't want to worry about configuring the scaling, rotation, and origin fields.

In this case, we would set the drawing mode to DRAW_BMP_BASIC. This will force efficient, simple, MmgBmp rendering. For more complex drawing that requires rotation, scaling, or source and destination rectangles, use the DRAW_MODE_FULL setting. The DRAW_BMP_BASIC_CACHE setting should be avoided unless you are an advanced user.

Demonstration: MmgBmp Class

The example screen for the MmgBmp class can be found in the MmgTestSpace package, namespace in C#, in the ScreenTestMmgBmp class. I will sometimes refer to namespaces, packages, and APIs loosely as libraries. I won't focus on game screen–specific code and will try to focus on the code that utilizes the MmgBmp class.

Listing 2-46. MmgBmp Class Demonstration 1

```
14    bmpCache = MmgHelper.GetBasicCachedBmp("soldier_frame_1.png");
15    bmpCache.SetY(GetY() + MmgHelper.ScaleValue(90));
16    bmpCache.SetX(MmgHelper.ScaleValue(220));
17    AddObj(bmpCache);
18
```

```
19    bmpCacheLabel = MmgFontData.CreateDefaultBoldMmgFontLg();
20    bmpCacheLabel.SetText("MmgBmp From Auto Load Cache");
21    bmpCacheLabel.SetPosition(MmgHelper.ScaleValue(50), GetY() +
      MmgHelper.ScaleValue(70));
22    AddObj(bmpCacheLabel);
23
24    bmpFile = MmgHelper.GetBasicCachedBmp("../cfg/drawable/loading_
      bar.png", "loading_bar.png");
25    bmpFile.SetY(GetY() + MmgHelper.ScaleValue(90));
26    bmpFile.SetX(MmgHelper.ScaleValue(560));
27    AddObj(bmpFile);
28
29    bmpFileLabel = MmgFontData.CreateDefaultBoldMmgFontLg();
30    bmpFileLabel.SetText("MmgBmp From Path");
31    bmpFileLabel.SetPosition(MmgHelper.ScaleValue(545), GetY() +
      MmgHelper.ScaleValue(70));
32    AddObj(bmpFileLabel);
33
34    bmpCustomFill = MmgHelper.CreateFilledBmp(MmgHelper.ScaleValue(50),
      MmgHelper.ScaleValue(50), MmgColor.GetCalmBlue());
35    bmpCustomFill.SetY(GetY() + MmgHelper.ScaleValue(210));
36    bmpCustomFill.SetX(MmgHelper.ScaleValue(205));
37    AddObj(bmpCustomFill);
38
39    bmpCustomFillLabel = MmgFontData.CreateDefaultBoldMmgFontLg();
40    bmpCustomFillLabel.SetText("MmgBmp Created Custom with Fill");
41    bmpCustomFillLabel.SetPosition(MmgHelper.ScaleValue(45), GetY() +
      MmgHelper.ScaleValue(190));
42    AddObj(bmpCustomFillLabel);
43
44    bmpSet = MmgHelper.CreateDrawableBmpSet(bmpCache.GetWidth()/2,
      bmpCache.GetHeight()/2, true);
45    srcRect = new MmgRect(0, 0, bmpCache.GetHeight()/2, bmpCache.
      GetWidth()/2);
46    dstRect = new MmgRect(0, 0, bmpCache.GetHeight()/2, bmpCache.
      GetWidth()/2);
```

```
47    bmpSet.p.DrawBmp(bmpCache, srcRect, dstRect);
48
49    bmpSet.img.SetY(GetY() + MmgHelper.ScaleValue(210));
50    bmpSet.img.SetX(MmgHelper.ScaleValue(650));
51    AddObj(bmpSet.img);
52
53    bmpPartialCopyLabel = MmgFontData.CreateDefaultBoldMmgFontLg();
54    bmpPartialCopyLabel.SetText("MmgBmp Custom with Copy");
55    bmpPartialCopyLabel.SetPosition(MmgHelper.ScaleValue(505), GetY() +
      MmgHelper.ScaleValue(190));
56    AddObj(bmpPartialCopyLabel);
```

Let's take a look at the LoadResources method listed in the preceding. This method is responsible for setting up a variety of MmgBmp use cases for demonstration on the ScreenTestMmgBmp game screen. The first example demonstrates creating an MmgBmp object from an already loaded image resource entry, line 14. All we need to access the image we want to use is the file name of the image.

This is how the auto loading image resource cache works. You can, however, load an image into the cache using your own key. In that case, use your key instead of the file name as shown in the example. Lines 15 to 17 show you how to position the MmgBmp object and add it into the drawing routine.

The next use of the MmgBmp class we'll review loads an image into the image cache with the specified key, line 24. The key can be any string, but in this example, we stick to the auto loaded resource technique of using the file name. You can use this approach to load image resources directly from the file system and ensure that they are cached for future use.

On line 34, we have an example of creating an MmgBmp object that is a custom rectangle filled with the specified color. This can come in handy in a number of situations from background fills to game-level features and so on. In the next example to review, we'll see how to create a new MmgBmp object by drawing a portion of an existing MmgBmp object into a new image. Take a look at line 44 of the method. We call the CreateDrawableBmpSet method with a width and height and a Boolean indicating if we want transparency supported.

The result of this call is an MmgDrawableBmpSet object that contains the framework and API classes needed to draw on a new MmgBmp object. We define the source and destination drawing rectangles on lines 45 and 46. On line 47, we call a special drawing method of the MmgPen class that draws on the new MmgBmp instance. This call will draw the pixels in the source rectangle from the source image to the destination rectangle on the destination image.

Chapter Conclusion

In this chapter, we completed a very detailed review of the base classes of the game engine's MmgBase API. If you take a close look at the classes we've covered, you can see that you almost have enough there to start making a game. That's not by accident. The base classes we've reviewed here are foundational to the game engine's design and implementation.

I want to step back from the code we've looked at and work on developing the larger picture. We're working on defining the classes necessary to power a general 2D game engine. In doing so, we've covered the following classes:

- MmgObj: Super class, or base class in C#, of the entire MmgBase API. Models an object in 2D space that has position, dimensions, and color.

- MmgColor: An API class for representing color.

- MmgRect: An API class for representing a rectangle with position and dimensions.

- MmgFont: An API class that extends the MmgObj class and is used to represent font-rendered text when drawn to the screen.

- MmgSound: An API class that represents a sound resource for the MmgBase API.

- MmgPen: An API class that handles all drawing for the API.

- MmgVector2: An API class that models a two-component vector of double, float, or integer precision for API positioning support.

- MmgBmp: An API class that extends the MmgObj class and is used to represent images for the API.

You may notice that while we've covered a lot of code, there isn't really a comprehensive structure or capability arising in the API that we can see. You won't start to see the structure you're looking for until you begin to review the MmgCore API in Part 2 and you see how everything ties together.

That being said, there is a reason for this. We're reviewing the code that powers a game engine, not a game. What that means is that the code is general in nature. There aren't a lot of hardwired connections between classes. There are a lot of potential connections, but nothing that is enforced. This is because we're reviewing the code for a general 2D game engine that draws images on the screen. It doesn't care how that happens, single screen, scrolling screen, isometric, or top-down. All the engine is concerned with is drawing the current set of drawable objects to the screen as quickly as possible.

That is the power that a game engine has over a single game. It's designed to be a general processor of 2D drawable objects as opposed to a specific processor of 2D drawable objects. In the coming chapters, we'll cover more of the MmgBase API, and you'll begin to see more and more connections between classes that could exist to create different aspects of your next game.

CHAPTER 3

Helper Classes

In this chapter, you'll review the helper classes of the MmgBase API. Helper classes are usually simple to initialize, use static methods to expose functionality, and provide support for different features of the API. We'll encounter the following classes during this review:

- MmgApiUtils
- MmgHelper
- MmgScreenData
- MmgFontData
- MmgDebug
- MmgBmpScaler
- MmgMediaTracker

Helper Classes: MmgApiUtils

The MmgApiUtils class is a simple helper class that provides centralized logging support for the MmgBase API. The MmgApiUtils class was implemented to be a convenient helper class, and as such it only has static class members to review.

Static Class Members

The logging class field is used to control the output of the class. If the Boolean field is set to false, no logs are generated. The field is a public field that can be set from a game engine config file. This allows you to turn off logging when the game is no longer in development, in a data-driven way. Next, we'll take a look at the class' static methods.

© Victor G Brusca 2021

V. G. Brusca, *Introduction to Video Game Engine Development*, https://doi.org/10.1007/978-1-4842-7039-4_3

Listing 3-1. MmgApiUtils Static Class Members 1

```
public static void wr(String s) { ... }
public static void wrErr(Exception e) { ... }
public static void wrErr(String s) { ... }
```

The first method we'll cover, wr, provides basic logging support for the API. It takes only a string as an argument and, if logging is enabled, writes it to standard output. The next two methods to review, wrErr, are designed to help log error messages.

The first wrErr method takes an Exception instance as an argument and uses the object to print information about the exception to standard error. The method will print out the exception's message and loop over the stack trace printing out information about each entry. The second wrErr method takes a string argument and prints it to standard error.

Demonstration: MmgApiUtils Class

The MmgApiUtils class is used mainly as a level 1 logging class. An example of its usage can be found in the MmgDebug class. Let's take a look at some code!

Listing 3-2. MmgApiUtils Class Demonstration 1

```
1 public static void wr(String key, String s) {
2     if (DEBUGGING_ON == true) {
3         MmgApiUtils.wr(key + ": " + s);
4     }
5 }
```

The method listed in the preceding is a level 2 logging method because it has its own logging control field and it calls methods from the MmgApiUtils class. This means that the logging can be turned off at this level for, say, all game screen logging and at the MmgApiUtils level, say, for all MmgCore application logging.

That completes our review of the MmgApiUtils class. I hope you don't overlook the importance of the class not only in its simple and direct logging capability but also as a center point for new API-level code that will make your next game project that much easier to write.

Helper Classes: MmgHelper

The MmgHelper class is a helper class that provides high-level functionality to the MmgBase API via static methods. This class provides positioning methods, resource cache management methods, logging methods, image transformation methods, and more. The MmgHelper class is a vital class that provides assistance in many different aspects of game development.

Static Class Members

The MmgHelper class has a few static class fields listed in the following. The fields are used as Boolean flags that control logging and resource caching functionality.

Listing 3-3. MmgHelper Static Class Members 1

```
public static boolean LOGGING = true;
public static boolean BMP_CACHE_ON = true;
public static boolean SND_CACHE_ON = true;
private static Random rando = new Random(System.currentTimeMillis());
```

The first entry in the static class fields listed in the preceding is the LOGGING field. This is a Boolean flag similar to what we've seen in the MmgApiUtils class. The flag controls the logging output of this class and can be used to turn off all logging. As you've seen, there are a few different logging channels supported by the API. This may seem redundant at first, but it actually comes in handy when you want separate logging channels for certain information.

The next two static class fields listed in the preceding control the resource cache for image and sound resources, respectively. If these Boolean flags are set to false, then resources that would normally be stored in a cache won't be. The last entry in the list is a random number generator that is initialized with the current time in milliseconds. That should provide a good, dynamic seed for the random number generator. You can use the rando field any time you need access to a random number. Let's move on and take a look at some static class methods.

Listing 3-4. MmgHelper Static Class Members 2

```
public static boolean WriteClassConfigFile(String file, MmgCfgFileEntry[]
data) { ... }

public static boolean WriteClassConfigFile(String file, Hashtable<String,
MmgCfgFileEntry> data) { ... }

public static Hashtable<String, MmgCfgFileEntry> ReadClassConfigFile(String
file) { ... }

public static Hashtable<String, MmgCfgFileEntry> ReadClassConfigFile(String
file) { ... }
```

The first two static class methods are used to write out class configuration data passed into them as an argument. The first WriteClassConfigFile method takes a string and an array of data as arguments. The array contains MmgCfgFileEntry objects. A class config file is a text file that contains data in the form of key-value pairs. The data can be used to configure the fields of a class dynamically as part of the class' resource loading process.

This is particularly useful when combined with game screens because it allows you to data drive the layout of the game screen. In this way, you can test changes to a game screen's layout by altering the class config file without having to recompile the game.

I should mention that when a class config file is written with a call to these methods, comments and the original order of the data may be lost. The data in each MmgCfgFileEntry instance is written to the class config file. Each key-value pair in the config file is represented by an MmgCfgFileEntry instance.

The second implementation of the WriteClassConfigFile method is similar except that it receives data in the form of a Hashtable, or Dictionary if you're looking at the C# implementation, instead of an array. The data structure's keys are sorted alphabetically, and the data is written out just like in the first version of the method. Now let's take a look at the other side of the coin, the class config read method.

The next class config helper method we'll review is the ReadClassConfigFile method. This method parses the specified class config text file and stores the key-value pairs as MmgCfgFileEntry entries in a Hashtable. The class config read method has built-in support for detecting and loading screen resolution–specific class config files.

This allows you to automatically load data based on the current game screen size if a screen resolution–specific class config file exists. If not, we try to open the originally specified file. If we have found a class config file to read, we open it and iterate over the lines. Comments in a class config file are prefixed with the # character. These lines are ignored when parsing the file.

The data read in from the class config file can be one of two types, numeric or alphanumeric. To denote a number, use the "=" character in between the key and value. To denote a string, use a "->" in between the key and value. Numeric values can be retrieved as integers, floats, or doubles. The following listing shows the contents of a simple class config file.

Listing 3-5. MmgHelper Static Class Members 3

```
1 bmpLogo->logo_large.jpg
2 splashScreenDisplayTimeMs=2000.0
3 splashLogoScale=1.0
4 #splashLogoOffsetX=0
5 #splashLogoOffsetY=0
6 #splashLogoPosX=0
7 #splashLogoPosY=0
```

Notice that a different key-value pair separator is used when the data represented is a string, line 1, than when it is numeric, lines 2 and 3. Let's move on to the next few methods to review. Up next, we have a pair of CreateDrawableBitmapSet methods. These helper methods are used to create a set of objects, framework and MmgBase API objects, that are all configured for drawing onto a new MmgBmp instance.

The first version of the method takes dimensions, width and height, and a Boolean transparency indicator as arguments. The second CreateDrawableBmpSet method is actually an extension of the first. This version takes an additional color argument that is then used to fill the new image.

Listing 3-6. MmgHelper Static Class Members 4

```
public static MmgBmp CreateFilledBmp(int width, int height, MmgColor color)
{ ... }

public static int AbsDistance(int x1, int x2, int y1, int y2) { ... }

public static int GetRandomInt(int exclusiveUpperBound) { ... }

public static void ListCacheEntries() { ... }
```

```
public static MmgDrawableBmpSet CreateDrawableBmpSet(int width, int height,
boolean alpha) { ... }
```

```
public static MmgDrawableBmpSet CreateDrawableBmpSet(int width, int height,
boolean alpha, MmgColor color) { ... }
```

The next set of helper methods we have to cover are a bit of a random bunch. Let's get to it, shall we? The first method is the `CreateFilledBmp` method. The `CreateFilledBmp` method continues from the previous set of methods reviewed. The method calls the version of the `CreateDrawableBmpSet` method that takes a color argument. The resulting `MmgDrawableBmpSet` is discarded, save for the `MmgBmp` instance, `img`, of the set. This implementation allows you to just grab the image you need and discard the rest of the set. It is very useful for quickly creating color tiles.

The `AbsDistance` method is a helper method that returns an absolute distance calculated from two pairs of coordinates, `x1,y1` and `x2,y2`. The `GetRandomInt` method uses the `rando` static class field we reviewed earlier. It returns a new random number between 0 and the `exclusiveUpperBound`. Obviously, the range excludes the upper bound. The next method to look at is the `ListCacheEntries` method, listed in the preceding. This method is used to report the contents of the resource caches including image and sound resources.

The next set of static methods we're going to cover are positioning methods, and they are extremely useful. You'll see these methods in use all over the MmgBase API.

Listing 3-7. MmgHelper Static Class Members 5

```
public static MmgObj CenterHor(MmgObj obj) { ... }
```

```
public static MmgObj CenterHorAndBot(MmgObj obj) { ... }
```

```
public static MmgObj CenterHorAndMid(MmgObj obj) { ... }
```

```
public static MmgObj CenterHorAndTop(MmgObj obj) { ... }
```

```
public static MmgObj CenterHorAndVert(MmgObj obj) { ... }
```

The next set of helper methods to review are all about centering objects. The first method listed in the preceding, `CenterHor`, centers the given `MmgObj` instance horizontally. Note that these methods take `MmgObj` arguments. That means these methods rely on fields of the `MmgObj` class and screen dimension data from the

MmgScreenData class. You'll find that you can easily use them to position any drawable object, since any drawable object extends the MmgObj class. The power of a general model can be seen in how useful these positioning methods are.

The CenterHorAndBot method centers the object horizontally and positions the object at the bottom of the screen. The CenterHorAndMid method is just an alias for the CenterHorAndVert method, and it places the object at the center of the screen both horizontally and vertically. The CenterHorAndTop is similar to the other methods except that it positions the object at the screen's horizontal center and at the top of the screen. The last method listed in the preceding, CenterHorAndVert, will center the MmgObj instance both horizontally and vertically. Keep these methods in mind; they will come in handy time and time again.

Listing 3-8. MmgHelper Static Class Members 6

```
public static MmgBmp GetBasicBmp(String src) { ... }

public static MmgSound GetBasicSound(String src) { ... }

public static MmgMenuItem GetBasicMenuItem(MmgEventHandler handler, String
name, int eventId, int eventType, MmgBmp img) { ... }
```

The next set of helper methods to cover are a bit sorted but mainly have to do with resource loading. These helper methods provide high-level code in a convenient, encapsulated way. You should always use the game engine's resource loading system, and you should always use resource loading methods that store data in the resource cache.

The first helper method, GetBasicBmp, is an image resource loading method that takes a file path string as an argument. This method is very useful on game screens that display before the resource load completes because you can point directly to an image resource on the file system.

The next method in the set is a helper method that is used with the menu system built into the API. The GetBasicMenuItem method is a convenience method that prepares a new MmgMenuItem instance in a quick and uniform way. The next method to review is used to load sound resources, GetBasicSound.

This method is similar to the GetBasicBmp method we just reviewed. Both are basic resource loading methods. Be sure you read over and understand how these resource loading methods work. There are a couple of different methods that can be used; so make sure you understand which methods use the resource cache, which methods scale the loaded image, and what different arguments they require.

Listing 3-9. MmgHelper Static Class Members 7

```
public static MmgBmp GetBasicCachedBmp(String path, String imgId) { ... }

public static MmgBmp GetBasicCachedBmp(byte[] data, String imgId) { ... }

public static MmgBmp GetBasicCachedBmp(String imgId) { ... }

public static MmgSound GetBasicCachedSound(String path, String sndId) { ... }

public static MmgSound GetBasicCachedSound(byte[] data, String sndId) { ... }

public static MmgSound GetBasicCachedSound(String sndId) { ... }

public static MmgBmp GetImageCacheBmp(Image b) { ... }

public static int ScaleValue(int val) { ... }
public static float ScaleValue(float val) { ... }
public static float ScaleValue(double val) { ... }
```

The next set of static helper methods we'll review deal mostly with loading resources from the image or sound resource cache. The first method in the list, GetBasicCachedBmp, takes a string argument with the path to the image resource and a string argument that represents the key for the associated image data. If the imgId exists, then the image associated with that entry is retrieved from the cache and returned.

If no entry can be found in the image cache, the image is loaded from the file using the GetBasicBmp method. The resulting image is added to the image cache using the provided imgId as the key. Note that if image caching is turned off, the image is loaded from the file every time the method is called. Obviously, enabling caching makes resource loading much more efficient.

The second GetBasicCachedBmp method takes only the image key, imgId, as an argument. This version of the method is similar to the first except that this version is only able to load an image from the image cache. If an image is found for the given key, it is retrieved and returned.

The next support methods, GetBasicCachedSound, are very similar to their image counterparts. The same exact functionality is expressed by these methods, so I won't go over them in any detail. Take a look at them and make sure you understand the code and how the methods work with the sound cache.

The last method I want to mention is the GetImageCacheBmp method. This is a legacy method, and it doesn't actually interact with the image cache. The name is just a bit misleading, don't you think? You should also note that it doesn't do any scaling to match the image to the current screen scaling. This method just converts a framework image class into an MmgBase API image class, MmgBmp. So be careful. You've been warned about the pitfalls of this method!

I should mention there are a number of positioning methods. We took a look at the set of methods that center objects, but there are also methods for positioning an object on the left- and right-hand sides of the screen. Another set of methods that are subtle but are of vital importance are the scale value methods listed in the preceding. These methods scale numeric values to match the screen's scaling, if any. You should use these methods any time you are using a literal distance or size value.

Listing 3-10. MmgHelper Static Class Members 8

```
public static boolean RectCollision(int x, int y, MmgRect r)

public static boolean RectCollision(int r1x, int r1y, int w, int h, MmgRect r)

public static boolean RectCollision(MmgRect src, MmgRect dest)

public static boolean RectCollision(MmgObj src, MmgObj dest)

public static boolean RectCollision(MmgVector2 src, int sW, int sH,
MmgVector2 dest, int dW, int dH)

public static boolean RectCollision(int r1x, int r1y, int r1w, int r1h, int
r2x, int r2y, int r2w, int r2h)
```

Just when you thought it wouldn't end, we come to the last set of helper methods to review. As you can see, the MmgHelper class is awesome. It has something for just about every occasion – from logging to positioning, collision detection, and resource loading. The final set of methods to review are all collision detection methods. These methods are designed to find collisions between rectangles and points taking different types of data as arguments.

They are simple methods. I won't go into much detail about them here. In each case, the method returns true if it determines there is an overlap between the objects compared. Be sure to familiarize yourself with the complete set of collision detection methods; they come in handy often during 2D game development. That wraps up the MmgHelper class review. We didn't cover every method, but I tried to give you good exposure to some of the key features and functionality provided by the class.

Demonstration: MmgHelper Class

There is a ton of powerful, convenient functionality contained in the MmgHelper class. It would take a lot of time to write up an example for each method set we've reviewed. This example is from the ScreenTestMmgColor class of the MmgTestSpace package, or namespace if you're following along in C#.

Listing 3-11. MmgHelper Class Demonstration 1

```
1 title.SetY(title.GetY() + MmgHelper.ScaleValue(30));
2 AddObj(title);
3
4 int yDiff = MmgHelper.ScaleValue(40);
5 int yStrt = GetY() + MmgHelper.ScaleValue(140);
```

The first block of demonstration code shows the use of perhaps one of the most important methods, the ScaleValue method. This example shows using the ScaleValue method to wrap a constant value used to position a drawable object. The second type of use case shown here on lines 4 and 5 is using the method when instantiating variables that are used to position, scale, and size an object.

Listing 3-12. MmgHelper Class Demonstration 2

```
1 title = MmgFontData.CreateDefaultBoldMmgFontLg();
2 title.SetText("<  Screen Test Mmg Color (11 / " +
  GamePanel.TOTAL_TESTS + ")  >");
3 MmgHelper.CenterHorAndTop(title);
4 title.SetY(title.GetY() + MmgHelper.ScaleValue(30));
```

In this next block of demonstration code, we can see how to use the MmgHelper class' positioning methods. In this example, the title is centered horizontally and placed at the top of the game screen. A subtle point here is how the position is refined after the CenterHorAndTop method is called. The subsequent line of code adjusts the positioning slightly by moving the title down a few pixels.

This is a very important class with a lot of functionality and features. Make sure to take the time to review and understand the class methods that we didn't cover here.

Helper Classes: MmgScreenData

The MmgScreenData class is designed to hold data about the game's display context. For instance, this class holds important data about the desired game panel and window dimensions. This class is a key feature of the MmgBase API and is used in many places where screen dimensions are taken into consideration.

Static Class Members

The MmgScreenData static class members we'll review start with a set of class fields that describe the game's dimensions.

Listing 3-13. MmgScreenData Static Class Members 1

```
public static int DEFAULT_WIDTH = 1024;
public static int DEFAULT_HEIGHT = 768;
private static int gameWidth;
private static int gameHeight;
private static int gameLeft;
private static int gameTop;
private static int screenWidth;
private static int screenHeight;
```

The first two static class fields listed in the preceding are default values for the width and height of the game panel and screen. The next two class fields hold data about the desired dimensions of the game, gameWidth and gameHeight. The gameLeft and gameTop static class fields may seem a little odd at first.

Normally you would expect them to both always be zero, but in our case, the game engine has the ability to display a development header with frame rate information and some variable debugging. This pushes down the game's panel, so we need the ability to set the panel's offset. The last two fields in the set are the screenWidth and screenHeight entries.

Note that the game screen only has dimension data, while the renderable area of the screen, the game panel, has dimension and position data. Why do you think that is? This is because the renderable area of the screen may be smaller than the window itself and so the game panel would be rendered at offset gameLeft and gameTop.

Listing 3-14. MmgScreenData Static Class Members 2

```
private static double scaleX;
private static double scaleY;
private static boolean scaleXOn;
private static boolean scaleYOn;
private static MmgVector2 scaleVec = MmgVector2.GetUnitVec();
private static MmgVector2 posVec;
```

The next set of static class fields begins with two scaling fields. The scaleX and scaleY fields hold data about the scaling needed to present the game panel inside the dimensions of the game window. For instance, if the desired game dimensions are larger than the game window, the game dimensions will be scaled down to fit, centered, inside the game window. The scaleX and scaleY static class fields will hold the scaling values needed to accomplish this.

The scaleXOn and scaleYOn static class fields are Boolean flags indicating that scaling is required on the X and/or the Y axis. Lastly, the scaleVec and posVec static class fields are convenience fields that hold scaling and position data for the X and Y coordinates.

Listing 3-15. MmgScreenData Static Class Members 3

```
private static int origGameWidth;
private static int origGameHeight;

GRAPHICS_CONFIG = GraphicsEnvironment.getLocalGraphicsEnvironment().
getDefaultScreenDevice().getDefaultConfiguration();

public static ScalingMode scalingMode = ScalingMode.AXIS_X_AND_Y;
```

The last set of static class fields is listed in the preceding. The first two entries are fields that track the initially specified game dimensions. If the game needs to be scaled to fit inside the game window, then these fields will have the original game dimensions. The GRAPHICS_CONFIG static class field is an important one; it holds information about the current graphics context.

In other words, it holds information about the current graphics capabilities like screen dimensions, bit depth of each pixel, and so on. The final entry in the list of fields in the preceding is the scalingMode class field. This field is used to track what type of scaling was used to adjust the game panel. Next, we'll take a look at some of the MmgScreenData class' static methods.

Listing 3-16. MmgScreenData Static Class Members 4

```
private static void CalculateLeft() { ... }
private static void CalculateTop() { ... }
public static void CalculateScaleAndOffset() { ... }
private static void CalculateScaleX(boolean agg) { ... }

private static void CalculateScaleY(boolean agg) { ... }
```

The first two static methods for us to review, CalculateLeft and CalculateTop, have only one line each, and they are used as part of the game configuration process to set the gameLeft and gameTop class fields. The next method, CalculateScaleAndOffset, is also part of the configuration process and is used to prepare any scaling on the X and Y axes. If scaling is not needed, we set the scaleX and scaleY class fields to 1.0 or 100%. This means that no scaling is necessary.

If we do need to do some scaling, we have to decide if we should support X axis scaling, Y axis scaling, or both. In our case, the method is locked to using both the X and Y axes. This causes the CalculateScaleX method to get called first and CalculateScaleY to get called subsequently if necessary. The next two methods up for review, CalculateScaleX and CalculateScaleY, are used to detect the necessary scaling value to correctly resize the game panel.

These methods perform a series of loop iterations. In each iteration, a new scaling test is performed and checked to see that the scaling results are as close to an integer as possible. It does this by making tiny increments in the scaling amount. Because we don't know if we'll be able to find an adequate scaling value, we need another way to escape the while loop. In this case, if the number of loop iterations reaches the value of the panic variable, which is set to 5000, the loop exits.

Once the loop is complete, the prctDiffX variable is used to set a number of static class fields. The scaling we're trying to do here is uniform, so we end up scaling both the X and Y axes even though we're only working with the X axis. Both scaleX and scaleY are set to the newly determined scaling value.

If, after horizontal scaling is performed, the vertical size is still an issue, we then call the CalculateScaleY method to determine the best scaling value to use that now, also, takes into account the current scaling results. The CalculateScaleX and

CalculateScaleY methods are very similar, so we won't cover it again here. Make sure you read and understand these methods. The goal here isn't to have a robust game screen scaling implementation; it's just to have a simple, direct way to fit the game panel into the game window's dimensions.

Take note that this class is meant to hold centralized data about the dimensions of the game panel and window as well as information about the current scaling of the screen. If you recall, we encountered image scaling calls in the MmgHelper class that used the scaling values determined here. This is a safe operation because the default expectation is that the scaling is uniform. The while loop is simply trying to determine a scaling value that results in near-integer values, so image scaling is smooth.

The last set of methods we have to review are the GetGameRight and GetGameBottom methods. These methods are used to calculate the right and bottom positions of the game panel based on its dimensions and current offset. Take a moment to review any methods we didn't get a chance to cover here.

Enumerations

The MmgScreenData class has one associated enumeration for us to review. The ScalingMode enumeration is used to describe the type of scaling that was determined to be necessary by the MmgScreenData class. A value from this enumeration is used to set the scalingMode class field.

Main Method Details

The main method details for this particular class consist of constructors.

Listing 3-17. MmgScreenData Main Method Details 1

```
public MmgScreenData() { ... }
public MmgScreenData(int w, int h) { ... }
public MmgScreenData(int ScreenWidth, int ScreenHeight, int GameWidth, int
GameHeight) { ... }
```

The first constructor we'll look at takes no arguments and is used to prepare the class' static fields. Because the MmgScreenData class is primarily a static helper class, it mainly exposes static methods and fields that hold data about the game's dimensions, position, and scaling. Notice that each constructor overload attempts to set the static class fields to provided argument values, when available. If not, default values are used instead of calculated values.

The proper way to use this class is to provide the game panel and window dimensions to the overloaded constructor. This results in static class fields being set and the CalculateScaleAndOffset static class method being called. Take notice that the other constructors listed don't call the scaling calculation method because default values are used instead.

Demonstration: MmgScreenData Class

The MmgScreenData class is a centralized helper class, and as such it is used a lot by other classes.

Listing 3-18. MmgScreenData Class Demonstration 1

```
screenData = new MmgScreenData(winWidth, winHeight, GamePanel.GAME_WIDTH,
GamePanel.GAME_HEIGHT);
```

The preceding line of code is from the MmgCore package's GamePanel class. This line is really important to the game engine and demonstrates how the MmgScreenData class is prepared. All static class fields and methods should work just fine once the class is instantiated and properly configured.

Helper Classes: MmgFontData

The MmgFontData class is designed to hold data about fonts, styles, and sizes. Its main focus is to provide easy access to MmgFont instances configured with different styles and sizes. The MmgFontData class follows, to a certain extent, the design and implementation of the MmgScreenData class in that although the class is used as a static helper class, it still requires preparation before it can be used. However, once the class is properly initialized, it provides access to a variety of different MmgFont instances.

Static Class Members

The MmgFontData class has a number of static class members. We'll begin this section of the class review with the static class fields listed in the following.

Listing 3-19. MmgFontData Static Class Members 1

```
public static String DEFAULT_FONT_FAMILY = Font.SERIF;

public static int DEFAULT_FONT_TYPE = Font.PLAIN;
private static int fontSize = 18;
private static int targetPixelHeight = 22;
private static int targetPixelHeightScaled = 22;
```

The first set of static class fields listed in the preceding prepares default values for some important font metrics. The first two entries listed set default values for the font family and type. The next three fields are used to store font size information. They are initialized to values that define a reasonable, normal-sized font.

The fontSize field is defaulted to 18, and the targetPixelHeight and targetPixelHeightScaled class fields are defaulted to 22. These two fields will be used to synchronize the font height, in pixels, with information from the MmgScreenData class. This is done so font sizes automatically scale with the screen.

The second set of static class fields is used to set up default instances of the framework's font class and the MmgFont class. There are also static class fields that hold default instances of the MmgFont class in normal, bold, and italic font styles.

These class instances are based on the framework font instances fontNorm, fontBold, and fontItalic. There are a number of methods for working with framework fonts and MmgFont objects, specifically for creating different font sizes and styles.

Listing 3-20. MmgFontData Static Class Members 2

```
public static Font CreateDefaultBoldFont(int sz) { ... }

public static Font CreateDefaultBoldFontLg() { ... }
public static Font CreateDefaultBoldFontSm() { ... }
```

The set of methods listed in the preceding are used to instantiate a new framework font object of a specific type and size. I've only listed a few of them here. These methods have a name similar to CreateDefaultBoldFont and return a framework Font instance. Notice that all the methods that take a size argument check to make sure the font size is not larger than the maximum allowed font size of 50.

These methods are designed to work with the default font family and either a specified font size and style or the default font size and style. Keep in mind they are used to create framework font objects. Next, we'll see how we can create MmgFont objects.

Listing 3-21. MmgFontData Static Class Members 3

```
public static MmgFont CreateDefaultBoldMmgFont(int sz) { ... }

public static MmgFont CreateDefaultBoldMmgFontLg() { ... }

public static MmgFont CreateDefaultBoldMmgFontSm() { ... }

public static void CalculateScale() { ... }
```

The next set of static methods should be immediately familiar. For each method that returned a framework font object, in the previous set of methods we've reviewed, there is a corresponding method that returns a new MmgFont object. As you can see, there is a lot of flexibility as to how you can set up a font. I recommend sticking with the default values at first until you get the hang of things. The remaining class methods are get and set methods for the static class fields we reviewed earlier. I won't list them here, but take a moment to review them on your own and understand exactly how they work.

The last method we'll review in this section is the CalculateScale method. This method is very similar to the scale calculation methods found in the MmgScreenData class. Ultimately, we're going to measure the pixel height of the MmgFont instance and adjust its size until the font's height matches the scaled target pixel height. If the font height is off, the font point size is adjusted by 1 until a good font size is found or the maximum number of iterations has been reached.

All of the default font static fields are updated to reflect the new font size. In this way, the game engine can synchronize the scaling of the screen through the MmgScreenData class, fonts through the MmgFontData class, and image resources through the use of the MmgHelper class' loading methods.

Main Method Details

The only main method we have to review for this class is the class constructor. Much like the MmgScreenData class, the MmgFontData class requires an instantiation before the class can configure itself and be available for use to the API. What is more, the MmgFontData class configuration has to occur after the MmgScreenData class because it relies on scaling values calculated by the MmgScreenData class.

The class constructor is a pass-through to call the static configuration methods. You don't have to use the class this way. You could just call the static methods directly, but I tend to use the constructor and keep a reference to the MmgFontData class around at a high level in the code.

Demonstration: MmgFontData Class

In demonstrating the MmgFontData class, we'll take a look at how the class is initialized in the MmgCore API as part of the game's startup code.

Listing 3-22. MmgFontData Class Demonstration 1

```
01 screenData = new MmgScreenData(winWidth, winHeight, GamePanel.GAME_
   WIDTH, GamePanel.GAME_HEIGHT);
02 MmgHelper.wr("");
03 MmgHelper.wr("--- MmgScreenData ---");
04 MmgHelper.wr(MmgScreenData.ApiToString());
05
06 fontData = new MmgFontData();
07 MmgHelper.wr("");
08 MmgHelper.wr("--- MmgFontData ---");
09 MmgHelper.wr(MmgFontData.ApiToString());
10 debugFont = MmgFontData.CreateDefaultFontSm();
11 mmgDebugFont = new MmgFont(debugFont, "Test", 0, 0, MmgColor.
   GetWhite());
```

The code snippet listed in the preceding is from the MmgCore API's GamePanel class, specifically the class constructor. As you can see on line 1, the MmgScreenData class is initialized with the game dimensions passed in from the static main entry point. Notice that simply initializing the class is all we need to do to prep it.

On line 6, the MmgFontData class is initialized; and as we just mentioned, the class constructor calls the scaling calculation method and gets our font sizes all prepped. On line 9, debugging information about the current font metrics is displayed. Take a moment to look at these debugging lines when you're building your games. They can really help you track down little issues with the game dimensions and font sizes. One example of how you can use the class to create new fonts can be found on lines 10 and 11.

Helper Classes: MmgDebug

The `MmgDebug` class is similar to the `MmgApiUtils` class in that it is an easy-access class that provides logging features. Again, we've seen similar functionality in the `MmgApiUtils` and `MmgHelper` classes. So why do we need another logging helper class? Well, in this case, having multiple logging classes is not the worst thing; it's even kind of helpful. The idea here is that you can use the different logging classes to provide output from different parts of your game independently from one another.

Static Class Members

The `MmgDebug` class has only two static fields for us to review.

Listing 3-23. MmgDebug Static Class Member 1

```
public static boolean DEBUGGING_ON = true;
public static String appName = "MmgApi.MmgDebug";
```

The first entry listed in the preceding, `DEBUGGING_ON`, is used to control the logging generated by this class. Similar to other logging classes, you can turn off all logging generated by setting this field to false. The second entry listed is a log prefix. Use this to insert a string before each log entry generated. Up next, we'll take a look at some static class methods.

Listing 3-24. MmgDebug Static Class Member 2

```
public static void wr(String s)
public static void wr(String key, String s)
public static void wrTs(String s)
```

There are three simple logging methods we have to cover listed in the preceding. They differ slightly from previous logging methods we've reviewed in that these methods prefix the log with a key. The first method, `wr`, uses the default prefix text, while the overloaded version of the method takes both a prefix string and text to log. Lastly, the `wrTs` method includes a timestamp in the logged text. This can be very helpful when tracing bugs that have to do with timing and animation.

Helper Classes: MmgBmpScaler

The MmgBmpScaler class is another static helper class that is structured in a similar fashion to some of the helper classes we've already looked at. The main use of this class is to transform images by resizing or rotating them. All of the class' functionality can be accessed via static methods without having to create a class instance.

Static Class Members

The MmgBmpScaler class has a few static class methods that we'll review next.

Listing 3-25. MmgBmpScaler Static Class Member 1

```
01 public static MmgBmp ScaleMmgBmpToGameScreen(MmgBmp subj, boolean alpha)
{ ... }

public static MmgBmp ScaleMmgBmpToGameScreen(MmgBmp subj, boolean alpha)
{ ... }

public static MmgBmp ScaleMmgBmp(MmgBmp subj, MmgVector2 newSize, boolean
alpha) { ... }

public static MmgBmp ScaleMmgBmp(MmgBmp subj, boolean useScreenDataScaleX,
boolean alpha) { ... }

public static MmgBmp ScaleMmgBmp(MmgBmp subj, double scale, boolean alpha)
{ ... }

public static MmgBmp RotateMmgBmp(MmgBmp subj, int angle, boolean alpha)
{ ... }
```

The set of methods we'll review first contains the MmgBmp scaling methods. The first method listed in the preceding, ScaleMmgBmpToGameScreen, is designed to scale an MmgBmp image to match the screen's scaling, if any. The next entry is the ScaleMmgBmp method. It takes an MmgBmp, an MmgVector2, and a Boolean as arguments. This method is almost identical to the previously reviewed method. The only difference is that the dimensions of the new image are determined by the passed-in MmgVector2 instance.

There are two more versions of the ScaleMmgBmp method. These versions provide you with different ways to define how the image is scaled. In one overloaded version of the method, you can specify either the X or Y axis as the source of the scaling percentage. And in the other method entry, you can scale the specified image by a set scaling amount. This class gives you a lot of flexibility with regard to resizing images. Let's take a look at the last remaining method in the class, which can be used for image rotation transformations.

The last method left for us to review in the MmgBmpScaler class has nothing to do with image scaling. Instead, we have another type of image transformation method, rotation. The RotateMmgBmp static class method has a similar setup to the scaling methods we just reviewed but is designed to provide image rotation functionality.

Demonstration: MmgBmpScaler Class

The demonstration code listed in the following can be found in the LoadResources method of the ScreenTestMmgBmp class in the MmgTestSpace package, or namespace if you are following along in C#.

Listing 3-26. MmgBmpScaler Class Demonstration 1

```
1 bmpScaled = MmgBmpScaler.ScaleMmgBmp(bmpCache, 1.50, true);
2 bmpScaled.SetPosition(MmgHelper.ScaleValue(213), GetY() + MmgHelper.
  ScaleValue(330));
3 AddObj(bmpScaled);
4
5 bmpRotate = MmgBmpScaler.RotateMmgBmp(bmpCache, 90, true);
6 bmpRotate.SetPosition(MmgHelper.ScaleValue(645), GetY() + MmgHelper.
  ScaleValue(330));
7 AddObj(bmpRotate);
```

The example code listed in the preceding uses the methods we just reviewed to create a scaled and rotated version of an MmgBmp object. The first entry in the code, lines 1–3, is used to create a new version of an existing image that is scaled 150%. The second block of code, lines 5–7, is an example of using the MmgBmpScaler class to rotate an MmgBmp object by 90 degrees.

This concludes the review of the MmgBmpScaler class. Make sure you read and understand the code completely as it's a useful helper class that will certainly come in handy.

Helper Classes: MmgMediaTracker

The MmgMediaTracker class is, you guessed it, another helper class that is implemented in the same easy-access static method style we've seen before. If you've noticed, the helper classes employ static methods and fields because it creates a centralization of functionality that can be accessed with little to no preparation.

For instance, when you set a logging control Boolean to false, it turns off logging everywhere those logging methods are used. The MmgMediaTracker class is a centralized repository for storing and retrieving image and sound resources.

The MmgMediaTracker class is implemented using static methods and fields. It contains methods for managing image and sound resources in one, central location. The class is used heavily by the game engine's resource loading code via some of the MmgHelper class' static methods that we've reviewed earlier.

Static Class Members

The first set of static class members for us to review consists of three static class fields.

Listing 3-27. MmgMediaTracker Static Class Members 1

```
public static Hashtable<String, Image> cacheBmp = new Hashtable<String,
Image>();

public static Hashtable<String, Clip> cacheSound = new Hashtable<String,
Clip>();

public static boolean REMOVE_EXISTING = true;
```

The first two entries listed in the preceding are data structures that store data in key-value pairs. If you are following along with the C# version of the code, you'll notice that the framework class for this type of data structure is the Dictionary class. In the Java implementation of the game engine, the framework class for this type of data is the Hashtable.

The two data structures act as resource caches with the ability to store image data in the cacheBmp field and sound data in the cacheSound field. Recall that the MmgHelper class has a number of methods that interact with the MmgMediaTracker class' caches. This is an example of how API classes are designed to work together but also provide functionality independently. The REMOVE_EXISTING Boolean flag is used to indicate if we should clean a resource cache before adding to it.

Listing 3-28. MmgMediaTracker Static Class Members 2

```
public static void CacheImage(String key, Image val) { ... }

public static void CacheSound(String key, Clip val) { ... }

public static boolean HasBmpKey(String key) { ... }
public static boolean HasSoundKey(String key) { ... }
public static boolean HasBmpValue(Image img) { ... }
public static boolean HasSoundValue(Clip snd) { ... }

public static boolean RemoveBmpByKey(String key) { ... }

public static boolean RemoveBmpByKeyValue(String key, Image img) { ... }

public static boolean RemoveSoundByKey(String key) { ... }

public static boolean RemoveSoundByKeyValue(String key, Clip snd) { ... }
```

The first set of methods for us to review allow you to store images and sounds in independent caches, query the size of a cache, and retrieve resources from either cache. Note that deleting a cache entry before adding it to the cache is controlled by the REMOVE_EXISTING static class field in both the CacheImage and CacheSound methods.

The next set of methods to review are simple utility methods that check if a key exists in either the image or sound cache. You can also check to see if a value exists in either cache. These methods are very helpful when interacting with the MmgMediaTracker's caches. Make sure you read and understand how these methods are used.

The last set of static class methods listed in the preceding are cache removal methods for image and sound resources. You can remove items by key or by key and value. That rounds out the available methods giving you the ability to easily add, remove, and query for cached resources. That's pretty much everything you need to manage a resource cache! Let's take a look at some example code.

Demonstration: MmgMediaTracker Class

The snippet of demonstration code listed in the following is the GetBasicCachedSound method from the MmgHelper class.

Listing 3-29. MmgMediaTracker Class Demonstration 1

```
01 public static MmgSound GetBasicCachedSound(String path, String sndId) {
02     MmgSound lval = null;
03     if (SND_CACHE_ON == true) {
04         if (MmgMediaTracker.HasSoundKey(sndId) == true) {
05             lval = new MmgSound(MmgMediaTracker.GetSoundValue(sndId));
06         } else {
07             lval = MmgHelper.GetBasicSound(path);
08             MmgMediaTracker.CacheSound(sndId, lval.GetSound());
09         }
10     } else {
11         lval = MmgHelper.GetBasicSound(path);
12     }
13     return lval;
14 }
```

The MmgMediaTracker class is used by the auto loading functionality contained in the MmgCore library. One example of its use is in the GetBasicCachedSound method. Notice how easy it is to connect static helper classes to create even more useful methods. We have essentially created an interface in code for working with the cache. Can you think of some other interfaces we've defined through different classes? Well, a simple logging interface might be one answer. I'll let you ponder the question and see if you can come up with any more.

Chapter Conclusion

In this chapter, we completed a review of the MmgBase API's helper classes. If you stop and think about the code we've reviewed in this chapter, the one thing that should stand out the most is the idea of easy-access classes with static methods providing high-level, encapsulated functionality.

The classes we've reviewed here are very different from the base classes we covered in Chapter 1. These classes aren't directly part of the game engine in a foundational sense. They are, however, very high-level, easy-to-use classes that help with a lot of tasks necessary in game development. For instance, the API as we've covered it now has fully integrated resource loading and retrieval using the MmgCore application-level code and the MmgMediaTracker and MmgHelper classes.

I want to step back from the code we've looked at and work on developing the larger picture. We're working on defining the classes necessary to support a general 2D game engine. In doing so, we've covered the following classes:

- MmgApiUtils: A helper class that provides logging support with centralized logging control.

- MmgHelper: A very important support class that provides static methods that help with positioning objects, logging, loading resources, class config file reading/writing, creating drawable image surfaces, rectangle collision, and value scaling. The list says it all.

- MmgScreenData: A helper class that provides information about the game panel and window dimensions. Provides support for scaling the game panel to fit within the dimensions of the game screen.

- MmgFontData: A helper class that provides support for scaling the font to match the screen's scaling, if any. It also has a number of static methods that provide access to different preconfigured fonts. This class is very useful to say the least.

- MmgDebug: A helper class that provides logging support that is tied to the MmgApiUtils logging creating a two-layer logging system with independent logging controls.

- MmgBmpScaler: A helper class that provides support for scaling and rotating images.

- MmgMediaTracker: A very important part of the game engine that is responsible for caching game resources.

We've seen our tool chest increase in size dramatically. We now have a set of classes that multiply the capabilities defined by the game engine's base classes outlined in Chapter 1. For instance, we have the foundation of a resource management system that is easy to use from any class in a game. We have helper classes that load resources for us, position objects, and much, much more.

One other thing you should notice is that we're still missing an overall structure. I'll remind you to be patient. We won't be able to see the entire picture until Part 2 when we review the MmgCore library. The main take-away should be that we have a good set of tools for making a game at this point. In upcoming chapters, we define more powerful tools that use multiple API classes in different ways to solve problems like sprite loading and animation.

CHAPTER 4

Other Classes

In this chapter, you'll review the "other" classes of the MmgBase API. These are classes that don't quite fit into your typical categories, so we gave them their own. We'll look at the following classes during this review:

- MmgCfgFileEntry
- MmgEvent
- MmgEventHandler

Other Classes: MmgCfgFileEntry

The MmgCfgFileEntry class is used to hold data when reading and writing config files. It's a small class, but I think it's important to review it because class config automation is such a useful feature when setting up game screens. The MmgCfgFileEntry class is designed to hold numeric or string data in the form of key-value pairs loaded from a special text file, a class config file.

Enumerations

There is one enumeration that is associated with the MmgCfgFileEntry class, the CfgEntryType enumeration. It has three different values, TYPE_DOUBLE, TYPE_STRING, and NONE. The first two values are used to indicate the type of data stored in the config entry. The NONE value is used to indicate an uninitialized state.

© Victor G Brusca 2021

V. G. Brusca, *Introduction to Video Game Engine Development*, https://doi.org/10.1007/978-1-4842-7039-4_4

Class Fields

The MmgCfgFileEntry has a few descriptive fields I've listed in the following.

Listing 4-1. MmgCfgFileEntry Class Fields 1

```
public CfgEntryType cfgType = CfgEntryType.NONE;
public Double number;
public String str;
public String name;
```

The first entry is an instance of the CfgEntryType enumeration we just reviewed. It is used to keep track of the type of data that is stored in this object. The next two class fields, number and str, are used to hold the actual data read in from the class config file. The last field is the name field. It's used to store the key string associated with the line of data in the class config file.

Support Method Details

Due to the simple nature of the class, there aren't any get and set support methods. That gives us only two methods to review.

Listing 4-2. MmgCfgFileEntry Support Method Details 1

```
public String ApiToString() { ... }
public int compare(MmgCfgFileEntry o1, MmgCfgFileEntry o2) { ... }
```

The first of the two entries for us to review is an API-to-string method. We've come across this before, so I won't spend more time on it here. The compare method is a framework comparison method used to sort the config file entries before writing them.

Main Method Details

The MmgCfgFileEntry class has some standard main methods for us to review.

Listing 4-3. MmgCfgFileEntry Main Method Details 1

```
public MmgCfgFileEntry() { ... }
public MmgCfgFileEntry(MmgCfgFileEntry obj) { ... }
public MmgCfgFileEntry Clone() { ... }
public boolean ApiEquals(MmgCfgFileEntry obj) { ... }
```

The first main method is a simple constructor that takes no arguments. This is very useful for quickly instantiating an object and then configuring it later on. The second constructor is a specialized constructor that takes an MmgCfgFileEntry as an argument and uses it to create a new, unique, class instance.

The Clone method is used to make a new unique copy of the class. It uses the specialized constructor to do this. The last entry in the preceding list is the ApiEquals method, which is an API-level comparison method. That wraps up the main methods I wanted to review. Let's take a look at the class in action!

Demonstration: MmgCfgFileEntry Class

The snippet of example code listed in the following shows the MmgCfgFileEntry class in use as part of a class config implementation.

Listing 4-4. MmgCfgFileEntry Class Demonstration 1

```
01 classConfig = MmgHelper.ReadClassConfigFile(GameSettings.CLASS_CONFIG_
DIR + "screen_splash.txt");

...

02 key = "splashScreenDisplayTimeMs";
03 if(classConfig.containsKey(key)) {
04 super.SetDisplayTime(classConfig.get(key).number.intValue());
05 }
06
07 key = "bmpLogo";
08 if(classConfig.containsKey(key)) {
09     file = classConfig.get(key).str;
10 } else {
11     file = "logo_large.jpg";
12 }
```

The code snippet listed in the preceding is from the LoadResources method of the SplashScreen class from the MmgTestSpace library. The first line of code demonstrates loading a class config file. On lines 2–5, we can see how to access the data from a config file entry. Note that we know ahead of time what type of data to expect for the given key. On line 4, the display time field is set based on the config file entry's numeric value.

The next block of example code on lines 7–12 demonstrates using a config file entry object to retrieve a string value. Notice on line 9 the config file entry object is located by its key and the str field is used. That completes the demonstration code I wanted to review for this class.

Other Classes: MmgEvent

The MmgEvent class and its counterpart, the MmgEventHandler class, create a generic event handling system that you can use to send and receive events. We'll cover the MmgEventHandler class after this class review. The MmgEvent class has a simple implementation. The only thing I should mention is that there are some preset event IDs for handling menu navigation.

Static Class Members

The MmgEvent class has a number of class fields that are default static values for different events. These presets were mainly designed to be used with a menu system allowing the user to move around to the different menu options.

Listing 4-5. MmgEvent Static Class Members 1

```
public static int EVENT_ID_UP = 0;
public static int EVENT_ID_DOWN = 1;
public static int EVENT_ID_LEFT = 2;
public static int EVENT_ID_RIGHT = 3;
public static int EVENT_ID_ENTER = 4;
public static int EVENT_ID_SPACE = 5;
public static int EVENT_ID_BACK = 6;
public static int EVENT_ID_ESC = 7;
```

The static class fields of the MmgEvent class are preset event IDs meant to represent keyboard or gamepad input. An input can be mapped to one of these static IDs indicating directional pad input, enter or space bar input, or back or escape input.

It's important to note that the event ID is really only important in the context of the event and the event handler. You could choose to use the preset IDs to indicate something entirely different than a keyboard event. It's really up to you.

Class Fields

The class fields listed in the following define the payload for the event and the handler for the event. The MmgEvent class is implemented in a general way allowing you the flexibility to use it however you want.

Listing 4-6. MmgEvent Class Fields 1

```
private MmgEventHandler parentHandler;
private String message;
private int id;
private int type;
private MmgEventHandler targetHandler;
private Object extra;
private MmgEvent prevEvent;
```

The MmgEvent class supports different associations between events and event handlers. The first field can be used to assign a parent event handler. You can ignore this or use it to create parent-child events. The next class field is the message field. This can optionally be used to add information about the event or event payload data if the string data type is useful. The next two class fields, id and type, are used to identify and respond to the event when being processed by the event handler. The id and type combination should be unique for a given event and event handler setup.

The targetHandler field is the handler that receives the event when it triggers. The extra field is an event payload that can be used to store objects and data associated with the event. Last but not least, we have the prevEvent field, which is an instance of the MmgEvent class. This field can be used to store a reference to a previous event. You can use this feature to create chains of events.

Support Method Details

The MmgEvent class has the following support methods.

Listing 4-7. MmgEvent Support Method Details 1

```
public MmgEvent GetPrevEvent() { ... }
public void SetPrevEvent(MmgEvent p) { ... }
public void SetParentEventHandler(MmgEventHandler e) { ... }

public MmgEventHandler GetParentEventHandler() { ... }

public void SetTargetEventHandler(MmgEventHandler e) { ... }

public MmgEventHandler GetTargetEventHandler() { ... }

public String GetMessage() { ... }
public void SetMessage(String s) { ... }
public int GetEventId() { ... }
public void SetEventId(int s) { ... }
public int GetEventType() { ... }
public void SetEventType(int s) { ... }
public Object GetExtra() { ... }
public void SetExtra(Object obj) { ... }
```

The support methods listed in the preceding are just simple get and set methods for the various class fields. I won't cover them in any detail here, but make sure to look over them and make sure you understand them.

Main Method Details

The MmgEvent class has a few main methods for us to look at.

Listing 4-8. MmgEvent Main Method Details 1

```
public MmgEvent(MmgEventHandler ParentHandler, String Msg, int Id, int
Type, MmgEventHandler TargetHandler, Object Ex) { ... }

public void Fire() { ... }
public String ApiToString() { ... }
```

The first method in the preceding listing is the class constructor. It takes an argument for each of the class' pertinent fields. Note that you don't need to provide an object for each argument if you don't plan to use that field. For instance, the ParentHandler argument can be set to null if you don't have an event hierarchy.

The next two main methods for us to look at are the Fire and ApiToString methods. The Fire method is called when the MmgEvent should trigger. If the targetHandler is defined, then it's called, and the current MmgEvent object is passed as an argument. The ApiToString method returns a string representation of the event.

Demonstration: MmgEvent Class

As a demonstration of the MmgEvent class, we'll take a look at creating and firing an event.

Listing 4-9. MmgEvent Class Demonstration 1

```
1 private MmgEvent clickScreen = new MmgEvent(null, "vert_click_screen",
MmgScrollVert.SCROLL_VERT_CLICK_EVENT_ID, MmgScrollVert.SCROLL_VERT_CLICK_
EVENT_TYPE, null, null);
```

The first line of example code shows us how to instantiate a new MmgEvent object. This line of code is from the class field section of the MmgScrollVert class, in the MmgBase package, or namespace in C#. Notice that the parent handler, target handler, and previous event fields are all set to null. In this example, we are prepping the event with the correct id and type, but we aren't specifying an event handler just yet. In this case, the event handler is set a little later on in the configuration of the MmgScrollVert class.

Listing 4-10. MmgEvent Class Demonstration 2

```
1 if(clickScreen != null) {
2     clickScreen.SetExtra(new MmgVector2(x, y));
3     clickScreen.Fire();
4 }
```

In the second snippet of example code, we can see how to properly trigger the click screen event of the MmgScrollVert class. In response to receiving a mouse click event, the clickScreen field, if defined, will be fired. Notice the use of the extra field to store information about the event. In this case, we are sending the screen click coordinates, as an MmgVector2 object, along with the click event.

Other Classes: MmgEventHandler

The MmgEventHandler is an interface that a class can implement so that it can handle certain MmgEvent objects. The MmgEventHandler class is implemented as an interface so that any class can implement it and register to handle events.

Class Review

Because the MmgEventHandler interface does not have the same features as a regular class, we'll just print out the code and talk about it directly.

Listing 4-11. MmgEventHandler Class Review 1

```
1 public interface MmgEventHandler {
2     public void MmgHandleEvent(MmgEvent e);
3 }
```

The MmgEventHandler interface defines one method signature, MmgHandleEvent. When a class implements the interface, it must define the MmgHandleEvent method and in doing so can receive registered events. It's really that simple.

Demonstration: MmgEventHandler Class

For this class' demonstration, we'll take a look at three snippets of code that show you how to set up an MmgEvent and handler.

Listing 4-12. MmgEventHandler Class Demonstration 1

```
//MmgScrollVert
01 public void SetEventHandler(MmgEventHandler e) {
02     clickScreen.SetTargetEventHandler(e);
03     clickUp.SetTargetEventHandler(e);
04     clickDown.SetTargetEventHandler(e);
05 }
```

```
//ScreenTestMmgScrollVert.LoadResources
01 scrollVert = new MmgScrollVert(vPort, sPane, sBarColor, sBarSldrColor,
sBarWidth, sBarSldrHeight, interval);
```

```
02 scrollVert.SetIsVisible(true);
03 scrollVert.SetWidth(sWidth + scrollVert.GetScrollBarWidth());
04 scrollVert.SetHeight(sHeight);
05 scrollVert.SetEventHandler(this);

//ScreenTestMmgScrollVert
01 public void MmgHandleEvent(MmgEvent e) {
02      if(e.GetEventId() == MmgScrollVert.SCROLL_VERT_CLICK_EVENT_ID
        || e.GetEventId() == MmgScrollHor.SCROLL_HOR_CLICK_EVENT_ID ||
        e.GetEventId() == MmgScrollHorVert.SCROLL_BOTH_CLICK_EVENT_ID) {
03          MmgVector2 v2 = (MmgVector2)e.GetExtra();
04          event.SetText("Event: Id: " + e.GetEventId() + " Type: " +
            e.GetEventType() + " Pos: " + v2.ApiToString() + " Msg: " +
            e.GetMessage() + " " + System.currentTimeMillis());
05
06      } else {
07          event.SetText("Event: Id: " + e.GetEventId() + " Type: " +
            e.GetEventType() + " Msg: " + e.GetMessage() + " " + System.
            currentTimeMillis());
08
09      }
10
11      MmgHelper.CenterHor(event);
12 }
```

The first snippet of code listed in the preceding shows the SetEventHandler method of the MmgScrollVert class. This method is used to register event handlers for the different events supported by the class. Notice that each event supported by the class has its event handler set, lines 2–4. The next snippet of code is from the ScreenTestMmgScrollVert class' LoadResources method from the MmgTestSpace library. In this code block, a new instance of the MmgScrollVert class is initialized. Notice that on line 5 the event handler for the scroll pane widget is set to the game screen.

That brings us to the last piece of the puzzle – the event handler method from the game screen class, ScreenTestMmgScrollVert. On line 2, we check to see if the event received is an event we can process by looking at the id and type fields of the received object. If we can process the event, an MmgVector2 object is cast from the extra field, line 3. In this case, we use the click information to update an MmgFont instance's text.

Chapter Conclusion

In this chapter, we completed a review of the "other" classes. The classes we covered are very useful, and I'll summarize them as follows:

- MmgCfgFileEntry: A class that models a line of data in a class config file. This class is used to store data from a class config file line and use it to set up a game screen.

- MmgEvent: A general event class that provides basic event support to the API.

- MmgEventHandler: An event handler interface. This interface is used to set up an event handler to receive registered events. When used in combination with the MmgEvent class, the two classes constitute a simple event system.

There is subtle power in these classes. Take a minute to think about the event system configuration. Notice how general it is. Like most of the functionality we're building up to support the game engine, we have a generalized event system that you can use in your next game. When working with events, be sure not to abuse them. Think about using events when one class needs to notify another class about something that happened. Use that as a guide when implementing events.

CHAPTER 5

Advanced Classes

In this chapter, you'll review the advanced classes of the MmgBase API.

Advanced classes are a general group of classes that use multiple base classes to create more powerful tools. We'll look at the following classes during this chapter's review:

- Mmg9Slice
- MmgContainer
- MmgLabelValuePair
- MmgLoadingBar
- MmgSprite
- MmgDrawableBmpSet

Advanced Classes: Mmg9Slice

The Mmg9Slice class is a more advanced class than we've previously seen. This class is designed to slice an MmgBmp image in nine locations so that the image can be resized without distortion. Mainly this feature is used for rectangular images like buttons, frames, and window backgrounds. The image is sliced and resized so that the corners are maintained and the straight edges between corners are scaled to meet the resizing requirements.

© Victor G Brusca 2021

V. G. Brusca, *Introduction to Video Game Engine Development*, https://doi.org/10.1007/978-1-4842-7039-4_5

Class Fields

The Mmg9Slice has a few class fields, listed in the following group. We'll review these next.

Listing 5-1. Mmg9Slice Class Fields 1

```
private int offset;
private MmgBmp src;
private MmgBmp dest;
```

There are only three fields we need to review for this class. The first field is the offset field. This field is used in the image slicing process. Essentially the value of the offset field is the position from the nearest corner where the image will be sliced. This slicing approach preserves the corner, preventing stretching and distortion during scaling. The next field, dest, is an MmgBmp that will hold the resulting scaled image.

Support Method Details

The Mmg9Slice class has a few support methods we'll review here. It's important to mention that you need to have experience using these methods when working with more advanced classes. They might not have the result that you expect. For instance, altering the src field won't change the destination field unless the object is reinitialized.

Listing 5-2. Mmg9Slice Support Method Details 1

```
public void SetOffset(int i) { ... }
public int GetOffset() { ... }
public void SetSrc(MmgBmp b) { ... }
public MmgBmp GetSrc() { ... }
public void SetDest(MmgBmp b) { ... }
public MmgBmp GetDest() { ... }
```

The support methods we have to review are get and set methods for the class fields we reviewed earlier. These methods are straightforward, so I won't cover them in any detail here. Make sure to look them over and make sure you understand their use.

Main Method Details

The Mmg9Slice class has a set of main methods that include constructors, class preparation, cloning, and comparison.

Listing 5-3. Mmg9slice Main Method Details 1

```
public Mmg9Slice(int Offset, MmgBmp Src, int w, int h) { ... }

public Mmg9Slice(int Offset, MmgBmp Src, int w, int h, MmgVector2 Pos)
{ ... }

public Mmg9Slice(Mmg9Slice obj) { ... }
public void MmgDraw(MmgPen p) { ... }
```

The first set of main methods to review begins with three constructors and the MmgDraw method. Notice that the first two constructors are essentially the same, save that the second constructor takes an MmgVector2 position argument. The offset, source image, width, and height are set before the destination image is created. Once the destination image is ready, the position and visibility are set. The first two constructor overloads use this pattern.

The Mmg9Slice class supports cloning functionality. As such, there is a specialized constructor that takes an Mmg9Slice object as an argument. This constructor follows the same general pattern as the first two except that all values come from the argument object. The last method in this set is the MmgDraw method. This method is simple and just draws the resized, destination image if visible.

Listing 5-4. Mmg9Slice Main Method Details 2

```
public MmgObj Clone() { ... }
public Mmg9Slice CloneTyped() { ... }
public boolean ApiEquals(Mmg9Slice obj) { ... }
public void DrawDest() { ... }
```

The second set of main methods begins with the Clone method. Notice how the Clone method uses the constructor overload that takes an Mmg9Slice object to create a new, unique copy. The first Clone method returns an MmgObj as argument. The second version of the Clone method, CloneTyped, returns an Mmg9Slice object. The ApiEquals method is an API-level comparison method for testing equality between two Mmg9Slice instances.

The last method we have to review is the DrawDest method. This method is responsible for performing the nine-slice operation on the source image. If you change certain class fields, you will need to rerun this method to update the destination image. Keep that in mind when working with this class.

Demonstration: Mmg9Slice Class

This code example is from the LoadResources method of the ScreenTestMmg9Slice class. Because the Mmg9Slice class is more advanced than previous classes, we need to load up an image resource to use as a source MmgBmp image. Make sure you follow along by running the example application and viewing this demonstration screen.

Listing 5-5. Mmg9Slice Class Demonstration 1

```
01 bground = MmgHelper.GetBasicCachedBmp("popup_window_base.png");
02 MmgHelper.CenterHorAndVert(bground);
03 bground.SetX(bground.GetX() - MmgHelper.ScaleValue(200));
04 bground.SetY(bground.GetY() - MmgHelper.ScaleValue(32));
05 AddObj(bground);
06
07 bgroundLabel = MmgFontData.CreateDefaultBoldMmgFontLg();
08 bgroundLabel.SetText("Original MmgBmp");
09 bgroundLabel.SetPosition(bground.GetPosition().Clone());
10 bgroundLabel.SetY(bgroundLabel.GetY() - bgroundLabel.GetHeight());
11 AddObj(bgroundLabel);
12
13 menuBground = new Mmg9Slice(MmgHelper.ScaleValue(16), bground,
   width, height);
14 menuBground.SetPosition(MmgVector2.GetOriginVec());
15 menuBground.SetWidth(width);
16 menuBground.SetHeight(height);
17 MmgHelper.CenterHorAndVert(menuBground);
18 menuBground.SetX(menuBground.GetX() + MmgHelper.ScaleValue(200));
19 menuBground.SetY(menuBground.GetY() + MmgHelper.ScaleValue(36));
20 AddObj(menuBground);
```

In the example snippet listed in the preceding, the source image is loaded on lines 1–5. The MmgBmp image instance is loaded from a call to the GetBasicCachedBmp method with the file name as the image resource key. This will pull the specified image from the resource cache if it exists. This particular image is part of the default image set so it is always loaded and ready to use. On line 13, a new Mmg9Slice object is created using the source image, bground, and specifying a new width and height to scale the source image to.

Notice that on lines 15 and 16, the dimensions of the Mmg9Slice object are reinforced. The object is added to the list of drawable objects for the current example game screen on line 20; this plugs the nine-slice object into the default drawing routine. That's all it takes to use an Mmg9Slice class to resize a popup window's background image and display it on the screen.

Advanced Classes: MmgContainer

The MmgContainer class is, as its name suggests, a container that holds MmgObj instances. This includes objects that extend the MmgObj class. You can start to see the power of the general game engine we've built thus far. For instance, an MmgContainer could hold all the MmgBmp objects needed to draw a game's information HUD. Then you could make the entire set of images invisible by setting the isVisible field to false on the container object.

The MmgContainer class is designed to hold other objects, but it does not have a concept of dimension or position with regard to its children. It does extend the MmgObj class, so you can assign the container dimensions and a position to help add structure to the container's use. Note, these settings don't affect how the container's contents are drawn.

Static Class Member

There is one static class field I'd like to discuss quickly. The INITIAL_SIZE static class field is used to control the initial sizing of the MmgContainer's internal data structure. If your game requires having containers with lots of objects, you may want to increase the value of this field.

Enumerations

The MmgContainer class has two important enumerations we need to cover. First is the ChildAction enumeration. This enumeration is used to define the type of action performed on the set of child objects. It has two values, STAMP and UNSTAMP, and is used to tell the UpdateAllChildren method how to process the child objects. Stamping a child object marks this container as the parent and sets the hasParent field to true. Unstamping a child reverses this and clears parent membership, setting hasParent to false.

The second enumeration that is important to the class is the RenderMode enumeration. This enumeration controls how the class renders itself. It has two values, RENDER_ALWAYS and RENDER_ONLY_WHEN_DIRTY. If the render mode is set to always, then the container class will always call the update method of its child objects. If the mode is set to render only when dirty, the container will only update its child objects if the class field isDirty is set to true.

Class Fields

There are only two pertinent class fields that we should discuss.

Listing 5-6. MmgContainer Class Fields 1

```
private ArrayList<MmgObj> container;
private boolean isDirty;
private RenderMode mode = RenderMode.RENDER_ALWAYS;
```

The first field is the class' internal data structure. This is where all the child objects are stored. Notice the container is designed to take MmgObj instances. This includes all classes that extend the MmgObj class. The next field, isDirty, is an important one. If this field is true, then the container is marked as being dirty. In this case, on the next update call, the class will update each of its children. It's important to control this field.

Only allowing the children to update when something has changed will make your game more efficient. In the case where a child object is constantly changing, the isDirty field will need to be set to false to force the child objects to receive an update call from the game engine's drawing routine. Remember the game engine drawing routine starts in the game panel class that the current game screen plugs into.

This causes the game screen to receive update and draw method calls, which in turn means its child objects receive update and draw method calls. In the case where a child object is a container, this process repeats one more time for all the container's child objects. The preceding last entry is the mode field. This field controls whether the container automatically updates all its child objects every update call or only when the isDirty flag is set to true.

Support Method Details

Let's take a look at the MmgContainer class' support methods. These methods allow us to access and manage the class' child objects.

Listing 5-7. MmgContainer Support Method Details 1

```
//Add objects
public void Add(MmgObj obj) { ... }
public void AddAt(int idx, MmgObj obj) { ... }

//Remove Objects
public void Remove(MmgObj obj) { ... }
public MmgObj RemoveAt(int idx) { ... }

//Access objects
public int GetCount() { ... }
public MmgObj[] GetArray() { ... }
public MmgObj GetAt(int idx) { ... }
public MmgObj GetChildAt(int idx) { ... }
public MmgVector2 GetChildPosAbsolute(int idx) { ... }

public MmgVector2 GetChildPosRelative(int idx) { ... }


//Clean array of objects
public void Clear() { ... }
public void Reset() { ... }
```

The first set of methods listed in the preceding provide management capabilities to the MmgContainer class. The first two methods allow you to add a new object to the container. You can add the object to the end of the current list of objects or insert the object into a specific position in the list of objects. The next two methods allow you to remove objects from the container.

In the "Access objects" section of the main methods listed in the preceding group, you have methods that allow you to get the total count of child objects, GetCount. The GetArray method returns an array representation of the child objects. The GetAt and GetChildAt methods are overloaded and provide the same functionality, returning a child object, at the specified index, from the container. The next two methods GetChildPosAbsolute and GetChildPosRelative are used to return child objects from the container and adjust their positioning to be relative to the container or relative to the game panel.

Lastly, we have two methods that are used to reset the container's contents. The two methods perform similar tasks, but there are some subtle differences between them. The Clear method unstamps all child objects before clearing the container's contents. The Reset method is similar, but it doesn't unstamp its child objects and it doesn't clear the current container; it instantiates a new data structure. These are subtle but important differences you should keep in mind when using this class.

Listing 5-8. MmgContainer Support Method Details 2

```
public ArrayList<MmgObj> GetContainer() { ... }
public void SetContainer(ArrayList<MmgObj> aTmp) { ... }

public void SetIsDirty(boolean b) { ... }
public boolean GetIsDirty() { ... }
public void SetMode(RenderMode m) { ... }
public RenderMode GetMode() { ... }
```

The second set of support methods for us to review are just standard get and set methods for the class' fields. Be mindful when adjusting fields if the object is being used by the game engine's drawing routine. You can end up with exceptions or unexpected screen rendering if you aren't careful.

Main Method Details

The main methods we have to review consist of constructors, child-parent association, and update and draw methods.

Listing 5-9. MmgContainer Main Method Details 1

```
//Constructors
public MmgContainer() { ... }
public MmgContainer(MmgContainer obj) { ... }
public MmgContainer(ArrayList<MmgObj> objects) { ... }

//Parent-Child association
private void StampChild(MmgObj obj) { ... }
private void UnstampChild(MmgObj obj) { ... }
private void UpdateAllChildren(ChildAction act) { ... }

//Drawing routine
public void MmgDraw(MmgPen p) { ... }
public boolean MmgUpdate(int updateTicks, long currentTimeMs, long
msSinceLastFrame) { ... }
```

The first set of main methods for us to review are the class' constructors. The first constructor creates a new empty MmgContainer object with the container data structure set to the default initial size. The second constructor listed is a specialized constructor used in the class' cloning functionality. It creates a new container object from an existing one. It will also make a clone of all of its child objects as part of the cloning process.

The last constructor listed takes a data structure of child objects used to initialize its contents. Note that this constructor doesn't stamp the child objects. Managing parent/child relationships is going to be your responsibility. The game engine doesn't enforce any default behavior in this regard.

The next three methods are used to manage the parent/child relationship of the container and its children. The StampChild and UnstampChild methods are used to set the child object's parent as the container or to remove that association. The UpdateAllChildren method takes a ChildAction instance as an argument and will run the StampChild or UnstampChild method for each child object. That brings us to the end of the main method review. Up next, we'll take a look at some example code demonstrating how to use the MmgContainer class.

Demonstration: MmgContainer Class

The example code for this demonstration section comes from the LoadResources method of the ScreenTestMmgContainer class in the MmgTestSpace package, or namespace in C#. Let's take a look at some code!

Listing 5-10. MmgContainer Class Demonstration 1

```
01 frame2 = MmgHelper.GetBasicCachedBmp("soldier_frame_2.png");
02 frame2 = MmgBmpScaler.ScaleMmgBmp(frame2, 2.0f, true);
03 MmgHelper.CenterHorAndVert(frame2);
04 frame2.SetY(frame2.GetY() - 0);
05
06 frame3 = MmgHelper.GetBasicCachedBmp("soldier_frame_3.png");
07 frame3 = MmgBmpScaler.ScaleMmgBmp(frame3, 2.0f, true);
08 MmgHelper.CenterHorAndVert(frame3);
09 frame3.SetY(frame2.GetY() + MmgHelper.ScaleValue(80));
10
11 holder = new MmgContainer();
12 holder.Add(frame2);
13 holder.Add(frame3);
14 holder.SetWidth(frame1.GetWidth());
15 holder.SetHeight(MmgHelper.ScaleValue(160));
16 MmgHelper.CenterHorAndVert(holder);
17 AddObj(holder);
```

The first two sections of code, lines 1–4 and lines 6–9, load up two images, animation frames, using the image resource cache. Each frame is scaled and positioned to align vertically in the center of the screen. The third section of code shows the initialization of an MmgContainer object that adds the frame1 and frame2 variables as child objects.

Notice that even though the MmgContainer itself doesn't display on the screen, we make sure to set the container dimensions on lines 14 and 15. The container is added to the game engine's drawing routine on line 17. This ensures the container's children are drawn to the screen via the MmgContainer class' MmgDraw method.

Advanced Classes: MmgLabelValuePair

The MmgLabelValuePair class is used to hold label and value text for display on game screens. Think settings entries, game options, and in-game HUD. The class provides a quick way to set up fonts, text, and positioning for the label and value text displayed.

Static Cass Members

The only static class member we have to review is an X axis positioning value, DEFAULT_ PADDING_X. This is the default value to use for padding the space between the label and value text. There are no pertinent enumerations to review for this class, so we'll skip that section of the review process and move on to the class' field review.

Class Fields

There are only four class fields for us to review with regard to the MmgLabelValuePair class. I've listed them in the following group.

Listing 5-11. MmgLabelValuePair Class Fields 1

```
private MmgFont lbl;
private MmgFont val;
private int paddingX;
private boolean skipReset;
```

The first field in the list is an MmgFont instance that is used to display the label text. The second field is also an MmgFont instance, and it's used to display the value text of the label-value pair. The paddingX field is used to hold a horizontal padding value so that the label and value text have some separation between them. The last field in the set is a Boolean flag used to indicate that we should skip repositioning the label and value objects.

The class will automatically prep itself after certain class fields are changed. We don't always want the class to prep itself. We can control this aspect of the class using the skipReset field. If set to false, it will skip the automatic class preparation step. Keep in mind you should make sure the class is properly prepared before using it in your game screen.

Support Method Details

The MmgLabelValuePair class has support methods that help you control different aspects of the class and how it displays on the screen.

Listing 5-12. MmgLabelValuePair Support Method Details 1

```
//Value methods
public MmgFont GetValue() { ... }
public void SetValue(MmgFont ft) { ... }
public String GetValueText() { ... }
public void SetValueText(String s) { ... }
public Font GetValueFont() { ... }
public void SetValueFont(Font ft) { ... }

//Font methods
public MmgFont GetLabel() { ... }
public void SetLabel(MmgFont ft) { ... }
public String GetLabelText() { ... }
public void SetLabelText(String s) { ... }
public Font GetLabelFont() { ... }
public void SetLabelFont(Font ft) { ... }

//Attribute methods
public void SetFontSize(int sz) { ... }
public int GetFontSize() { ... }
public void SetMmgColor(MmgColor c) { ... }
public boolean GetSkipReset() { ... }
public void SetSkipReset(boolean b) { ... }

//Positioning
public void SetPosition(MmgVector2 v) { ... }
public void SetPosition(int x, int y) { ... }
public void SetX(int x) { ... }
public void SetY(int y) { ... }
public int GetPaddingX() { ... }
```

```
public void SetPaddingX(int p) { ... }

//Other Methods
private void Reset() { ... }
```

The first set of support methods listed in the preceding helps you manage the value field. You can access the value field using get and set methods. You can also specify the text to be displayed and the font to be used. The same set of methods exist for the class' label field. This gives you a great amount of control over the text and fonts used to render the class.

The next set of methods allow you to control attributes of both the label and value fields. You can use the GetFontSize method to pull the font size of the label. Because the label and value fields are independent of each other, you could potentially have two different font sizes set. The GetFontSize method won't try to make a determination of which font size to use, label or value; it will always return the label's font size.

The SetFontSize method is similar in nature. You can use this method to update the font size of both the label and value objects. This method, and many other methods that change the properties of the label and value, will attempt to prep the class and align the text for display. If you don't want the class preparation step to run, set the skipReset class field to true before calling the support method.

The next method in this set is the SetMmgColor method. While this may seem to be a simple set method, it's not. This method will set the color attributes of the container and the label and value fields. The last set of methods listed in the preceding is for positioning the MmgLabelValuePair class either by setting its location, adjusting the horizontal offset, or resetting the positioning of the label and value objects.

The positioning methods, SetPosition, SetX, and SetY, are used to adjust the position of the label-value pair. Note that using these methods will only update the label object. The positioning methods will call the class' Reset method once the label's position is set. The Reset method will take care of aligning the label and value text. If you don't want the class to prep automatically, make sure to set the skipReset field to true. Always remember to call the Reset method when you're done modifying the class if it doesn't run automatically.

Main Method Details

The main methods of the MmgLabelValuePair class include constructors, cloning methods, and drawing and class preparation methods. The list of methods to review in the following only has three constructors, but the class has a few more. Make sure to read them over and understand how they work.

Listing 5-13. MmgLabelValuePair Main Method Details 1

```
public MmgLabelValuePair() { ... }
public MmgLabelValuePair(MmgFont fontLbl, MmgFont fontVal) { ... }

public MmgLabelValuePair(MmgLabelValuePair obj) { ... }

public MmgObj Clone() { ... }
public MmgLabelValuePair CloneTyped() { ... }

public void MmgDraw(MmgPen p) { ... }
```

The first constructor takes no arguments and sets default values for the label and value fonts as well as padding and dimensions. This constructor doesn't set any text values for the MmgFont instances. The class dimensions are set to zero before a call to the Reset method. The Reset method will calculate the dimensions of the object and adjust the positioning of the label and value fonts based on their size.

The second constructor listed in the preceding takes two MmgFont arguments, one for the label and one for the value. This is probably the most common use case, passing in prepared MmgFont objects with text, style, and size already configured. The last constructor listed should look familiar. This is the specialized constructor that takes an MmgLabelValuePair object as an argument and uses it to create a new, unique copy of the object.

That brings us to the class' cloning methods. The Clone and CloneTyped methods, as we've seen before, use the specialized constructor to create a new object and return it either casted to an MmgObj object or as an MmgLabelValuePair instance. The next method in the list is the Reset method. This method is very important to the class' functionality. It's designed to be called after any support method that changes the label MmgFont, value MmgFont, or the object's position. Last but not least, the MmgDraw method is responsible for drawing the label and value to the screen as part of the game engine's drawing routine.

Demonstration: MmgLabelValuePair Class

The snippet of example code listed in the following is from the LoadResources method of the ScreenTestMmgLabelValuePair class in the MmgTestSpace package, or namespace in C#. The demonstration shows you how to initialize an MmgLabelValuePair object properly.

Listing 5-14. MmgLabelValuePair Class Demonstration 1

```
01 labelFont = MmgFontData.CreateDefaultBoldMmgFontLg();
02 labelFont.SetMmgColor(MmgColor.GetGrayWolf());
03 labelFont.SetText("Label1:");
04
05 valueFont = MmgFontData.CreateDefaultBoldMmgFontSm();
06 valueFont.SetMmgColor(MmgColor.GetBlueGray());
07 valueFont.SetText("Value1");
08
09 lvPair1 = new MmgLabelValuePair(labelFont, valueFont);
10 MmgHelper.CenterHorAndVert(lvPair1);
11 lvPair1.SetY(lvPair1.GetY() - MmgHelper.ScaleValue(30));
12 AddObj(lvPair1);
```

In the first block of code, a new MmgFont object is created with the text and color specified on lines 2 and 3. Notice that on line 1 the large font instance is created from a static helper method of the MmgHelper class. The second block of code, lines 5–7, creates and configures the value MmgFont instance. The last block of code, lines 9–12, shows the instantiation of a new MmgLabelValuePair object using the two MmgFont objects we just created.

Notice that all we need to do is call the constructor with the label and value objects. As we've seen before, the constructor takes care of prepping the class via the inherent call to the Reset method. In the next two lines of code, lines 10 and 11, the object is centered horizontally and positioned vertically before being added to the game engine's drawing routine with a call to the AddObj method.

Advanced Classes: MmgLoadingBar

The MmgLoadingBar class is an advanced class that uses MmgBmp objects to create a new loading bar. The loading bar is used by the MmgLoadingScreen class as part of the resource loading process. You may find loading bars useful not only during the game's startup process but as a UI element. For instance, you could use the class as a health bar or charge meter.

Class Fields

The MmgLoadingBar's class fields are listed in the following. There are only seven fields, and they are used to hold a foreground image, a background image, positioning, and loading bar fill properties.

Listing 5-15. MmgLoadingBar Class Fields 1

```
//Loading bar images
private MmgBmp loadingBarBack;
private MmgBmp loadingBarFront;

//Padding methods
private int xPadding;
private int yPadding;

//Loading bar fill methods
private float fillAmt;
private int fillHeight;
private int fillWidth;
```

The first class field, loadingBarBack, is used to draw the background image of the loading bar. In most cases, you'll want to use a solid color for the loading bar's back image. This image will be resized to indicate the loading progress, health, or charge bar level. The following class field, loadingBarFront, is also an MmgBmp object; and it's used as the foreground of the loading bar. This is the image that covers the actual bar. It's usually a rectangle- or pill-shaped image with the center cut out to allow for the background, progress bar, image to be visible.

The second set of class fields are used to provide a padding adjustment to the position of the loadingBarBack image. You can adjust the xPadding and yPadding to get the loading bar to fit nicely in the cut-out window of the loadingBarFront image. The last set of fields are used to describe the height, width, and fill amount used to resize the loadingBarBack image to match the loading bar's progress. The fillAmt field holds a value that ranges from 0.0 to 1.0. This value is used to calculate the proper width of the loadingBarBack image. In this way, the image's width reflects the progress percentage stored in the fillAmt class field.

Support Method Details

The support methods for the MmgLoadingBar class listed in the following allow you to control the background and foreground images, control the fill image's size and padding, and reposition the loading bar.

Listing 5-16. MmgLoadingBar Support Method Details 1

```
//Loading bar back methods
public MmgBmp GetLoadingBarFront() { ... }
public void SetLoadingBarFront(MmgBmp f) { ... }
public MmgBmp GetLoadingBarBack() { ... }
public void SetLoadingBarBack(MmgBmp b) { ... }

//Loading bar fill methods
public float GetFillAmt() { ... }
public void SetFillAmt(float f) { ... }
public int GetFillWidth() { ... }
public void SetFillWidth(int w) { ... }
public int GetFillHeight() { ... }
public void SetFillHeight(int h) { ... }

//Padding methods
public int GetPaddingY() { ... }
public void SetPaddingY(int py) { ... }
public int GetPaddingX() { ... }
public void SetPaddingX(int px) { ... }
```

```
//Positioning methods
public void SetPosition(MmgVector2 pos) { ... }
public void SetPosition(int x, int y) { ... }
public void SetX(int inX) { ... }
public void SetY(int inY) { ... }
```

The first set of support methods provide access to the background and foreground images. I should mention that the fill amount, scaling value, is cleared when the SetLoadingBarBack method is called. This is done to ensure that there isn't any scaling applied to the background image. In general, the loading bar class will control the scaling of the background image.

The second set of methods provide access to the fillAmt, fillWidth, and fillHeight fields. The fillWidth and fillHeight fields describe the dimensions of the loading bar foreground image's cut-out. The fillAmt, the percentage complete, is multiplied by the fillWidth field to determine how wide the background image should be. The third set of methods are just simple get and set methods for the class' padding fields.

The final set of support methods listed in the preceding help you reposition the loading bar on the screen. Because this is an advanced class, it has multiple internal objects that are drawn to the screen. This poses a challenge when trying to reposition the object because we have to reposition multiple objects and often have to recalculate their relative positioning.

The main method for overcoming this complication is to override the set position and set coordinate methods. This gives us an abstraction point where we can run code to handle issues like this. In this case, when the object's position is changed using these methods, we can update the base class, background image, and foreground image positions all at once.

Main Method Details

The main methods listed in the following are class constructors, cloning methods, and the game engine draw method. Notice that the cloning functionality is present and that this class extends the MmgObj class, which makes it a member of the set of drawable objects.

Listing 5-17. MmgLoadingBar Main Method Details 1

```
public MmgLoadingBar() { ... }
public MmgLoadingBar(MmgLoadingBar obj) { ... }
public MmgLoadingBar(MmgBmp LoadingBarBack, MmgBmp LoadingBarFront) { ... }

public MmgObj Clone() { ... }
public MmgLoadingBar CloneTyped() { ... }

public void MmgDraw(MmgPen p) { ... }
```

The first set of main methods to review begins, as we expect, with a set of class constructors. The base constructor takes no arguments and initializes the class with some placeholder values. This constructor does not put the class into a state that is fit for use. You'll need to call some support methods to configure the class properly.

The next constructor is a specialized constructor that takes an MmgLoadingBar instance as an argument and uses it to create a new, unique MmgLoadingBar object. The remaining constructor takes two MmgBmp arguments. It follows almost the same implementation as that of the constructor we just reviewed, save that this constructor overload sets the loading bar front and back images from the provided arguments.

The next set of main methods to review are the class' cloning methods. As we've seen before, there are two types of cloning method. The first, Clone, will create a new, unique copy of this class and return it cast up to the super class, MmgObj. The second cloning method, CloneTyped, performs the same actions but doesn't cast the returned object so the method returns an MmgLoadingBar instance.

The last method we have left to review is the MmgDraw method. Note that the method draws the back image first and that it sets the color as well as the source and destination drawing rectangles needed to scale the image on each game frame. The source and destination rectangles are used to scale the background image to the proper size with regard to the foreground image and the fillAmt field.

Demonstration: MmgLoadingBar Class

The example code used to demonstrate the MmgLoadingBar class in action is from the ScreenLoading class of the MmgBase library. These snippets demonstrate setting up the MmgLoadingBar class and show how to use event-driven data on the progress of the resource load.

Listing 5-18. MmgLoadingBar Class Demonstration 1

```
01 key = "imgLoadingBar";
02 if(classConfig.containsKey(key)) {
03     file = classConfig.get(key).str;
04 } else {
05     file = "loading_bar.png";
06 }
07
08 tB = MmgHelper.GetBasicBmp(GameSettings.IMAGE_LOAD_DIR + file);
09
10 key = "imgLoadingBarFill";
11 if(classConfig.containsKey(key)) {
12     file = classConfig.get(key).str;
13 } else {
14     file = "blue_square.png";
15 }
16
17 tB1 = MmgHelper.GetBasicBmp(GameSettings.IMAGE_LOAD_DIR + file);
18 if (tB1 != null) {
19     tB1.DRAW_MODE = MmgBmpDrawMode.DRAW_BMP_FULL;
20 }
21
22 if (tB != null && tB1 != null) {
23     lb = new MmgLoadingBar(tB1, tB);
24     lb.SetMmgColor(null);
25     lb.SetWidth(tB.GetWidth() - MmgHelper.ScaleValue(10));
26     lb.SetHeight(tB.GetHeight() - MmgHelper.ScaleValue(12));
27     lb.SetFillAmt(0.0f);
28     lb.SetPaddingX(MmgHelper.ScaleValue(8));
29     lb.SetPaddingY(MmgHelper.ScaleValue(4));
30     lb.SetFillHeight(tB.GetHeight() - MmgHelper.ScaleValue(10));
31     lb.SetFillWidth(tB.GetWidth() - MmgHelper.ScaleValue(12));
32     super.SetLoadingBar(lb, lbOffSet);
```

The first few lines of code, lines 1–6, are used to load the location of the loading bar foreground image from the local class config object. If no class config key is found, a default resource is used. The image is loaded on line 8. The next block of code on lines 10–15 performs a similar function to the code we just reviewed but, with regard to the loading bar's background image.

Recall that we intend to scale the loading bar's background image, and to do so we need to make sure the image has support for scaling. To make sure the image can be resized, we set the drawing mode to DRAW_BMP_FULL so that source and destination rectangles can be taken into consideration when rendering the MmgBmp image, lines 17–20.

The next lines of code, lines 22–32, detail the proper way to set up the MmgLoadingBar object for use. Notice that the constructor is used to set the loading bar's background and foreground images. The color is set to null, and the width and height of the MmgLoadingBar object are set on lines 25 and 26. The fillAmt field is set to 0, and padding values are set to 8 and 4 pixels for the X and Y axes, respectively, lines 27–29. On lines 30 and 31, the fill height and width are set. Notice that the fill width and height are based on the dimensions of the loading bar's foreground image and the class' padding values. Take the time on your own to trace how the loading bar's value get's updated. Make sure you understand the process.

Advanced Classes: MmgSprite

The MmgSprite class is an advanced class that models a sprite image. A sprite in 2D game development is a multiframe 2D image that animates as it's drawn. As such, the MmgSprite class is designed to handle an array of MmgBmp objects that represent the frames of the sprite object.

Static Class Members

The MmgSprite class has three static class fields for us to take a look at, listed in the following set.

Listing 5-19. MmgSprite Static Class Members 1

```
public static int DEFAULT_MS_PER_FRAME = 100;
public static int MMG_SPRITE_FRAME_CHANGE = 0;
public static int MMG_SPRITE_FRAME_CHANGE_TYPE = 0;
```

The first field is the default value for the number of milliseconds to wait on each frame of the sprite animation. Now, 100 ms is a fairly long time to wait when it comes to 2D image animations, but this is a default value and is set to be slow, so you don't miss any frames. The remaining two static class fields are ID values used during sprite animation frame change events.

Class Fields

The first set of class fields for us to look at are listed in the following group. These fields control advanced rendering of each frame, hold the frames of the animation, and track the start and stop frames of the sprite animation.

Listing 5-20. MmgSprite Class Fields 1

```
private MmgVector2 origin;
private MmgVector2 scaling;
private MmgRect srcRect;
private MmgRect dstRect;
private MmgBmp[] b;
private float rotation;
private int frameStart;
private int frameStop;
```

The preceding first entry contains fields that are used in frame scaling and rotation operations. The origin field is an MmgVector2 object that stores the coordinates of the center point to be used for rotation transformations. Similarly, the scaling, srcRect, and dstRect class fields are used in animation frame scaling transformations. You guessed it. The MmgSprite class has the ability to scale or rotate any sprite frame on the fly.

The actual animation frames are stored in the MmgBmp array class field b. The rotation field is used to store a rotation angle in degrees to be used during image rotation. The next two class fields are deceptively powerful. Using the frameStart and frameStop fields, you can animate over only a section of the sprite's frames. This last point is really important. You can have animations that only run over a subset of the sprite's frames.

Listing 5-21. MmgSprite Class Fields 2

```
private long frameTime = -1;
private long prevFrameTime = -1;
private int frameIdx;
private long msPerFrame;
private boolean simpleRendering;
private MmgEventHandler onFrameChange;
private boolean timerOnly;
private MmgEvent frameChange = new MmgEvent(null, "frame_changed",
MmgSprite.MMG_SPRITE_FRAME_CHANGE, MmgSprite.MMG_SPRITE_FRAME_CHANGE_TYPE,
null, null);
```

The second set of class fields starts with two time-tracking fields, frameTime and prevFrameTime. These fields are used to measure frame duration. The frameIdx field tracks the current frame by its array index. The msPerFrame field is used to determine how long to stay on each animation frame. The simpleRendering Boolean flag is used to force simple MmgBmp rendering making the draw method more efficient by performing fewer operations.

In this case, there are fewer checks to determine which drawing routine to use. The onFrameChange field is an event handler that triggers when the frame being rendered changes. The timerOnly Boolean flag will cause the timing mechanism that tracks frame changes to work as a timer for the current frame only. The frame index doesn't increment in this case. Lastly, the frameChange event is the event template for handling frame change events.

Support Method Details

The classes we're reviewing are becoming more and more complex. As such, we sometimes encounter long lists of get and set methods. I'll try and break the methods up into groups that make sense. Let's take a look at the first set of methods to review, listed in the following group.

Listing 5-22. MmgSprite Support Method Details 1

```
//Frame timing methods
public long GetFrameTime() { ... }
public void SetFrameTime(long l) { ... }
public long GetPrevFrameTime() { ... }
public void SetPrevFrameTime(long l) { ... }
public long GetMsPerFrame() { ... ]
public void SetMsPerFrame(long f) { ... }

//Frame event methods
public void SetFrameChangeEventId(int i) { ... }
public MmgEventHandler GetOnFrameChange() { ... }
public void SetOnFrameChange(MmgEventHandler e) { ... }

//Frame methods
public boolean GetSimpleRendering() { ... }
public void SetSimpleRendering(boolean s) { ... }
public boolean GetTimerOnly() { ... }
public void SetTimerOnly(boolean b) { ... }
public MmgBmp GetCurrentFrame() { ... }
public void SetCurrentFrame(MmgBmp bmp) { ... }
public MmgBmp[] GetBmpArray()  { ... }
public void SetBmpArray(MmgBmp[] d)  { ... }
```

The first set of methods for us to review are the support methods that handle frame timing. There are get and set methods for setting the current frame time, the previous frame time, and the number of milliseconds to wait before changing frames. The second set of methods allow access to the class' events. You can customize the ID of the event fired when the animation's frame changes. The next two methods in the set allow you to access the event handler for the class' on frame change event.

The last set of support methods listed in the preceding provide you with the capability to control the sprite's animation frames and rendering. The first two methods, GetSimpleRendering and SetSimpleRendering, give you access to the simple rendering field. If set to true, the class will only use basic rendering on the sprite animation's frames. The next two methods listed are access methods for the timerOnly field. If the timerOnly flag is set to true, the timing mechanism that tracks frame changes will work as a timer for the current frame only. The animation frame doesn't automatically increment in this case.

The remaining four methods allow you to get or set the current animation frame and to access the MmgBmp array that controls the sprite class' frames. Setting the MmgBmp array will cause the sprite object's dimensions and the frame indexes to be reset.

Listing 5-23. MmgSprite Support Method Details 2

```
//Frame rendering methods
public MmgRect GetSrcRect() { ... }
public void SetSrcRect(MmgRect r) { ... }
public MmgRect GetDstRect() { ... }
public void SetDstRect(MmgRect r) { ... }
public float GetRotation() { ... }
public void SetRotation(float r) { ... }
public MmgVector2 GetOrigin() { ... }
public void SetOrigin(MmgVector2 v) { ... }
public MmgVector2 GetScaling() { ... }
public void SetScaling(MmgVector2 v) { ... }

//Frame index methods
public boolean IsFrameNull(int i) { ... }
public int GetFrameIdx() { ... }
public void SetFrameIdx(int f) { ... }
public int GetFrameStart() { ... }
public void SetFrameStart(int f) { ... }
public int GetFrameStop() { ... }
public void SetFrameStop(int f) { ... }
```

The next block of methods for us to look at consists of two sets, frame rendering methods and frame index methods. The frame rendering methods give you access to all of the advanced rendering fields necessary to support scaling and/or rotation of the MmgSprite's current frame. The frame index methods are simple get and set methods for the class' animation frame index fields. You can control the current frame index and the animation's start and stop frame indexes using these methods. That brings us to the conclusion of the MmgSprite class' support method review. Up next, we'll take a look at the class' main methods.

Main Method Details

The class' main methods are listed in the following in three groups. There are the usual class constructors; this MmgSprite class has more constructors than those we have listed here. Please take the time to review and understand them before moving on. We'll also review cloning, comparison, and rendering methods here.

Listing 5-24. MmgSprite Main Method Details 1

```
//Class constructors
public MmgSprite(MmgBmp[] t, MmgVector2 Position) { ... }

public MmgSprite(MmgBmp[] t) { ... }
public MmgSprite(MmgSprite obj) { ... }

//Cloning methods
public MmgObj Clone() { ... }
public MmgSprite CloneTyped() { ... }

//Draw, update, and comparison methods
public void MmgDraw(MmgPen p) { ... }
public boolean MmgUpdate(int updateTick, long currentTimeMs, long
msSinceLastFrame) { ... }

public boolean ApiEquals(MmgSprite obj) { ... }
```

The first set of methods we'll look at are the class' constructors. The first entry takes an array of MmgBmp objects representing the sprite's animation frames and an MmgVector2 object that holds the current position of the frames. This constructor will set the animation frames and position the sprite. The second constructor is similar, but it only takes animation frames as an argument. Last but not least, the specialized constructor takes an MmgSprite object as an argument and uses it to create a new, unique, class instance.

The next set of methods are cloning methods. We've seen this implementation many times before, so I won't go into too much detail here. The two cloning methods use the specialized constructor to create a new, unique copy of the class and return it cast to the specified class type. The last set of main methods to review are also methods we've seen before. The game engine's default drawing routine will call the class' update and draw methods.

The update method is responsible for handling timing, animating the frames, and events, firing an event when the frame changes. The class' drawing method can handle more advanced rendering features if enabled or just a simple direct rendering of the sprite's current animation frame. The last entry in the set is the ApiEquals method. This is an API-level method used to compare two MmgSprite objects for equality.

Demonstration: MmgSprite Class

The demonstration code listed in the following is from the LoadResources method of the ScreenTestMmgSprite class. Also listed are the game engine drawing routine methods for the game screen class' MmgUpdate and MmgDraw methods.

Listing 5-25. MmgSprite Class Demonstration 1

```
//ScreenTestMmgSprite.LoadResources
01 frame1 = MmgHelper.GetBasicCachedBmp("soldier_frame_1.png");
02 frame1 = MmgBmpScaler.ScaleMmgBmp(frame1, 2.0f, true);
03 MmgHelper.CenterHorAndVert(frame1);
04
05 frame2 = MmgHelper.GetBasicCachedBmp("soldier_frame_2.png");
06 frame2 = MmgBmpScaler.ScaleMmgBmp(frame2, 2.0f, true);
07 MmgHelper.CenterHorAndVert(frame2);
08
09 frame3 = MmgHelper.GetBasicCachedBmp("soldier_frame_3.png");
10 frame3 = MmgBmpScaler.ScaleMmgBmp(frame3, 2.0f, true);
11 MmgHelper.CenterHorAndVert(frame3);
12
13 frames1 = new MmgBmp[4];
14 frames1[0] = frame1;
15 frames1[1] = frame2;
16 frames1[2] = frame3;
17 frames1[3] = frame2;
18
19 frames2 = new MmgBmp[4];
20 frames2[0] = frame1.CloneTyped();
21 frames2[1] = frame2.CloneTyped();
```

```
22 frames2[2] = frame3.CloneTyped();
23 frames2[3] = frame2.CloneTyped();
24
25 MmgVector2 tmpPos = frame1.GetPosition().Clone();
26 tmpPos.SetY(tmpPos.GetY() - MmgHelper.ScaleValue(30));
27 sprite1 = new MmgSprite(frames1, tmpPos);
28 sprite1.SetMsPerFrame(200l);
29 AddObj(sprite1);
```

```
//Game engine drawing routine
01 public boolean MmgUpdate(int updateTick, long currentTimeMs, long
   msSinceLastFrame) {
02     lret = false;
03
04     if (pause == false && isVisible == true) {
05         //always run this update
06         sprite1.MmgUpdate(updateTick, currentTimeMs, msSinceLastFrame);
07         sprite2.MmgUpdate(updateTick, currentTimeMs, msSinceLastFrame);
08     }
09
10     return lret;
11 }
```

```
01 public void MmgDraw(MmgPen p) {
02     if (pause == false && isVisible == true) {
03         super.MmgDraw(p);
04     }
05 }
```

The first snippet of code on lines 1–23 of the LoadResources method shows us how to configure a simple MmgSprite object and draw it to the screen. On lines 1–3, an animation frame is loaded from the key, "soldier_frame_1.png". You can tell that this is a cached image resource because it's being loaded by key only. Most likely, this image was auto loaded from the test application's project resource folder.

The image is scaled up a bit on line 2, and its position is centered, line 3. The same steps are performed for two more animation frames so that we have a total of three frames loaded. On line 13, an array of MmgBmp objects is instantiated to hold the frames we just loaded. Now the nature of the animation is such that we don't want to go from frame 3 to frame 1; we want to return to frame 2 first. As such, we create an array of length 4 and store the frames in the correct order. On lines 25 and 26, we prepare the position of the MmgSprite object.

Look carefully at the positioning code. Notice that we clone the position used by frame1 and adjust it down slightly – about 15 pixels. A new MmgSprite object is created on line 27 using the MmgBmp array, frames, and position. Note that the frames have a different position than the sprite object. Recall the animation frames are drawn at the position of the sprite.

On line 28, the frame time is set to a large number, 200 ms, so that it can be easily observed. Because the MmgSprite class extends the MmgObj class, it can be added to the game screen's set of drawable objects with a call to AddObj. The next section of code to review in this demonstration snippet is the MmgUpdate method. Notice that on lines 6 and 7 the update methods of the sprite object are called if the game screen is visible and is not paused. This example code shows us how to update other objects in the update method and how to make more complex classes update themselves. Lastly, the MmgDraw method shows us that the sprite object is drawn via the default drawing routine just like any other MmgObj on the screen.

Advanced Classes: MmgDrawableBmpSet

The MmgDrawableBmpSet class is used to create a set of framework and MmgBase API classes that are preconfigured to work together. The classes are set up such that the MmgPen object draws on the MmgBmp object. The framework classes that support this functionality are included as part of the MmgDrawableBmpSet object's fields.

For the most part, the C# implementation of the game engine is very similar to the Java implementation. The API is identical, but the implementation differs naturally due to the differing frameworks they're based on.

Class Fields

In the following, I've listed the Java and C# versions of the MmgDrawableBmpSet class. You can use these classes as a reminder of how the framework classes align. A Java BufferedImage roughly equates to C#'s RenderTarget2D. Similarly, the Java Graphics2D class is roughly equivalent to C#'s SpriteBatch class.

Listing 5-26. MmgDrawableBmpSet Class Fields Java

```
public BufferedImage buffImg;
public Graphics2D graphics;
public MmgPen p;
public MmgBmp img;
```

Listing 5-27. MmgDrawableBmpSet Class Fields C#

```
public RenderTarget2D buffImg;
public SpriteBatch graphics;
public MmgPen p;
public MmgBmp img;
```

The first field, buffImg, is used to hold a framework implementation of a drawable image. The graphics field is a framework class that draws on surfaces including images. The API-level classes are used as fields to support the class' ability to draw on the target MmgBmp image, img, using the MmgPen field, p.

Demonstration: MmgDrawableBmpSet Class

The first snippet of code is the CreateDrawableBmpSet method from the MmgBase API's MmgHelper class. The second snippet is from the ScreenTestMmgBmp class' LoadResources method. Be sure to check out this game screen in action by running the example application.

Listing 5-28. MmgDrawableBmpSet Class Demonstration 1

```
//MmgHelper.CreateDrawableBmpSet
01 public static MmgDrawableBmpSet CreateDrawableBmpSet(int width, int
   height, boolean alpha) {
02     MmgDrawableBmpSet dBmpSet = new MmgDrawableBmpSet();
03     dBmpSet.buffImg = MmgScreenData.GRAPHICS_CONFIG.
       createCompatibleImage(width, height, alpha ? Transparency.
       TRANSLUCENT : Transparency.OPAQUE);
04     dBmpSet.graphics = (Graphics2D)dBmpSet.buffImg.getGraphics();
05     dBmpSet.p = new MmgPen();
06     dBmpSet.p.SetGraphics(dBmpSet.graphics);
```

```
07      dBmpSet.p.SetAdvRenderHints();
08      dBmpSet.img = new MmgBmp(dBmpSet.buffImg);
09      return dBmpSet;
10 }
```

```
//ScreenTestMmgBmp.LoadResources
01 bmpSet = MmgHelper.CreateDrawableBmpSet(bmpCache.GetWidth()/2,
   bmpCache.GetHeight()/2, true);
02 srcRect = new MmgRect(0, 0, bmpCache.GetHeight()/2, bmpCache.
   GetWidth()/2);
03 dstRect = new MmgRect(0, 0, bmpCache.GetHeight()/2, bmpCache.
   GetWidth()/2);
04 bmpSet.p.DrawBmp(bmpCache, srcRect, dstRect);
05
06 bmpSet.img.SetY(GetY() + MmgHelper.ScaleValue(210));
07 bmpSet.img.SetX(MmgHelper.ScaleValue(650));
08 AddObj(bmpSet.img);
```

The first block of code listed in the preceding shows the standard way one might initialize an MmgDrawableBmpSet object by hand. Also, the CreateDrawableBmpSet is a great convenience method for doing just that. This method is important because it shows the core interaction between the classes involved.

First, a buffered image is created with the specified dimensions and opacity, line 3. A reference to the buffered image's graphics object is created on line 4. A new MmgPen object is initialized with the graphics object of the buffered image, lines 5–7. Lastly, the MmgBmp instance, img, is set to a newly created MmgBmp object based on the loaded buffered image.

The second block of demonstration code shows the class in use. On lines 1–4, a new drawable bmp set is created with dimensions one-half that of the original image. The source rectangle is the top-left square, one-half the width and height. The destination is a new image with the same dimensions, so the srcRect and the dstRect are the same. On line 4, using the MmgPen instance, p, the top-left square is drawn onto the new image, img. The position of the image is adjusted, and it's added into the default drawing routine, lines 6–8.

Chapter Conclusion

In this chapter, we completed a review of the MmgBase API's advanced classes. The classes we covered are starting to use base classes in new combinations to solve different problems. We have a bunch of new tools in our toolbox. Let's take a look at a summary of them:

- Mmg9Slice: A scaling class that uses a nine-slice technique to resize rectangular images, UI frames, borders, and other images without distortion.

- MmgContainer: An API class for representing a group of MmgObj instances for the API.

- MmgLabelValuePair: A UI class that displays text in a label and value pair format. Provides more advanced text support geared toward game HUDs and other game stats UI.

- MmgLoadingBar: An API class for representing a loading bar or progress for the API.

- MmgSprite: An advanced class that uses an array of MmgBmp objects to create an animated 2D game object for the API.

- MmgDrawableBmpSet: An advanced class that contains a set of fields needed to draw on a new MmgBmp object. The class contains all the framework and API-level classes to accomplish the configuration.

These classes are starting to show the emergence that occurs when you start adding layers of functionality on top of a solid foundation of classes. We have access to some very powerful functionality in the classes we've reviewed here. Be sure to include them when you're planning out your next great game.

CHAPTER 6

Widget Classes

In this chapter, we'll review the UI widget classes of the MmgBase API. These are advanced classes similar to those we've reviewed before, but they are designed to work as part of a game menu, a settings screen, or other types of configuration screen. These classes greatly simplify the work needed to get a game screen that takes user input up and running. They also provide solid support for scroll panes and large text blocks:

- MmgTextField
- MmgTextBlock
- MmgScrollVert/MmgScrollHor/MmgScrollHorVert
- MmgMenuContainer
- MmgMenuItem

Widget Classes: MmgTextField

The MmgTextField class is part of the group of UI widget classes. It's a simple text field widget much like you might see on a web form. The class is designed to provide basic support for reading in values from the user.

Static Class Members

The set of static class fields listed in the following are the only static class members we need to review for the MmgTextField class. The static fields listed here are used to control some aspects of how the class is rendered and describe the class' error event ID and type.

© Victor G Brusca 2021
V. G. Brusca, *Introduction to Video Game Engine Development*, https://doi.org/10.1007/978-1-4842-7039-4_6

Listing 6-1. MmgTextField Static Class Members 1

```
public static int DEFAULT_MAX_LENGTH = 20;
public static int TEXT_FIELD_9_SLICE_OFFSET = MmgHelper.ScaleValue(16);

public static String TEXT_FIELD_CURSOR = "_";
public static long TEXT_FIELD_CURSOR_BLINK_RATE_MS = 3501;

public static int TEXT_FIELD_MAX_LENGTH_ERROR_EVENT_ID = 1;

public static int TEXT_FIELD_MAX_LENGTH_ERROR_TYPE = 0;
```

The first field is the default value for the text field's max length. The text field class supports drawing a background image scaled to the specified dimensions. To accomplish this, the text field class uses an Mmg9Slice object. The second field listed is the value to use for the Mmg9Slice's offset field. This controls how the background image is sliced. The next field, TEXT_FIELD_CURSOR, controls what character is used as the text field's cursor. The blink rate of the cursor is controlled by the blink rate static field. The last two entries are an event ID and type to use when the class fires a max length error event.

Class Fields

The MmgTextField class has a few class fields for us to review. The first set of fields is listed in the following. These are fields used to control how the text field is displayed and what event to fire when a max length error occurs.

Listing 6-2. MmgTextField Class Fields 1

```
private Mmg9Slice bground;
private MmgBmp bgroundSrc;
private boolean cursorBlinkOn;
private long cursorBlinkStart;
private int displayChars;
private MmgEvent errorMaxLength = new MmgEvent(null, "error_max_length",
MmgTextField.TEXT_FIELD_MAX_LENGTH_ERROR_EVENT_ID, MmgTextField.TEXT_FIELD_
MAX_LENGTH_ERROR_TYPE, null, null);
```

The first class field is an Mmg9Slice object to use as the background border of the text field. The subsequent entry, bgroundSrc, is the image used as the source MmgBmp for the Mmg9Slice object. In other words, the bgroundSrc image is the image that will get sliced and resized to the desired text field dimensions.

The next two fields control the cursor blink. The first field, cursorBlinkOn, determines if the cursor blinks at all, while the next entry, cursorBlinkStart, is used by the class to time the cursor blink rate. The displayChars entry determines how many characters the text field can display at one time. Lastly, we have the max length error template, errorMaxLength, already prepared and just about ready to use.

Listing 6-3. MmgTextField Class Fields 2

```
private MmgFont font;
private int fontHeight;
private boolean isDirty;
private int maxLength;
private boolean maxLengthOn;
private int padding;
private String textFieldString = "";
```

The second set of class fields for us to review is listed in the preceding. The font field is used to render the text in the text field. You can specify the font size, type, and color using the MmgFont's class fields. The fontHeight field is used in the text's vertical centering calculations. The text is attempted to be centered within the background image's height.

The isDirty flag is a Boolean that controls if the class runs certain update code on the next game frame. We don't want the class working unnecessarily during the update calls, so we control the amount of work we do using this Boolean flag. Now with this capability, the class will only run its update calculations when the cursor blinks or other events cause a change that requires it to be updated.

The next two fields control if the max length error is on and how many characters can be entered into the text field before the error event is triggered. The padding field is used to fine-tune the font's position in the text field's background image. The textFieldString class is used to hold the actual string value the text field represents, not just the text visible in the text field's display.

Support Method Details

The MmgTextField class has support methods that fall into three general groups. There are background image methods, text field font-rendering methods, and text field text methods. As the classes we review become more complex, they tend to have more support methods to allow access to their fields. I'll try to organize the methods for you when they start becoming too numerous.

Listing 6-4. MmgTextField Support Method Details 1

```
//Background image methods
public MmgBmp GetBgroundSrc() { ... }
public void SetBgroundSrc(MmgBmp bg) { ... }
public void SetBground(Mmg9Slice bg) { ... }
Public Mmg9Slice GetBground() { ... }

//Text field font rendering methods
public MmgFont GetFont() { ... }
public void SetFont(MmgFont f) { ... }
public int GetFontHeight() { ... }
public void SetFontHeight(int i) { ... }
public boolean GetIsDirty() { ... }
public void SetIsDirty(boolean b) { ... }
public int GetPadding() { ... }
public void SetPadding(int i) { ... }

//Text field text methods
public int GetDisplayChars() { ... }
public void SetDisplayChars(int i) { ... }
public String GetTextFieldString() { ... }
public void SetTextFieldString(String str) { ... }
public boolean GetMaxLengthOn() { ... }
public void SetMaxLengthOn(boolean b) { ... }
public int GetMaxLength() { ... }
public void SetMaxLength(int i) { ... }
public MmgEvent GetErrorMaxLength() { ... }
public void SetErrorMaxLength(MmgEvent e) { ... }
```

The first group of methods for us to review are the class' background image methods. These are get and set methods that allow you to access the background's source image as well as the prepared `Mmg9Slice` instance that holds the resized background source.

The second group of support methods allows you to access the class fields that control the way the text field's font is rendered. These are get and set methods for the font, the font height, and the padding used to fine-tune the font's position. The only set of methods I'd like to talk about with regard to this group are the get and set methods for the `isDirty` field. In general, you should let the class manage its dirty flag by itself, but if you want to force the class to update itself before the next call to `MmgDraw`, then set the `isDirty` field to true.

The third group of methods listed in the preceding allow you to interact with the widget's text. The first two methods, `GetDisplayChars` and `SetDisplayChars`, allow you to set the number of characters that the text field can display at one time. The actual text stored by the class can be accessed via the `GetTextFieldString` and `SetTextFieldString` methods. The next three sets of get and set methods are all designed to allow you to turn on max length detection. You can turn on the feature, set the maximum allowed string length for the text field, and set the event that is fired when the max length condition is triggered and all from these six support methods.

Main Method Details

The `MmgTextField` class has four groups of main methods for us to review.

Listing 6-5. MmgTextField Main Method Details 1

```
//Class constructors
public MmgTextField(MmgBmp BgroundSrc, MmgFont Font, int Width, int Height,
int Padding, int DisplayChars) { ... }

public MmgTextField(MmgTextField obj) { ... }


//Cloning methods
public MmgObj Clone() { ... }
public MmgTextField CloneTyped() { ... }
```

```
//Text field management methods
public boolean ProcessKeyClick(char c, int code) { ... }

public void DeleteChar() { ... }
public void Prep() { ... }

//Standard main methods
public boolean ApiEquals(MmgTextField obj) { ... }
public boolean MmgUpdate(int updateTick, long currentTimeMs, long
msSinceLastFrame) { ... }

public void MmgDraw(MmgPen p) { ... }
```

The first group of main methods to review consists of two constructors. The first constructor takes arguments for the background image, font, width, height, padding, and display character length. The arguments are used to set class fields. Even though this constructor does not set a text value for the class, the Prep method is called to configure the text field and position the child objects.

The next constructor listed is a specialized class constructor we've seen before. This constructor takes an MmgTextField as an argument and uses it to create a new, unique copy of the object. This constructor supports the class' cloning functionality. The Clone and CloneTyped methods are used to create new, unique copies of this class. The methods use the specialized constructor, as we've seen previously, and return either a cast MmgObj instance or an MmgTextField instance, respectively.

The third group of methods, text field management methods, starts with the input handler, the ProcessKeyClick method. This method updates the textFieldString field and checks to see if the max length constraint is on and if it has been triggered. If so, the max length event will be fired. The DeleteChar method will remove a character from the end of the text field's string. Note that the ProcessKeyClick and DeleteChar methods both set the isDirty flag to true before they exit. The last method in this group is the Prep method. The Prep method is responsible for setting up the nine-slice background image, the font, and the cursor timing. It prepares the class for use.

The last group of methods are standard main methods that we won't go over again here. You've seen these methods a number of times by now: standard game engine drawing routine update and draw methods, MmgUpdate and MmgDraw, respectively, and an API-level comparison method ApiEquals, for determining object equality. I should mention that the update method is responsible for powering the text field's cursor.

If you use the text field in a more manual way, outside the game screen's list of drawable objects, you'll need to explicitly call the class' MmgUpdate method in the screen's update method if you want the cursor to blink.

Demonstration: MmgTextField Class

The following demonstration code is from the LoadResources method of the ScreenTestMmgTextField class from the MmgTestSpace library. The two methods that follow the initial code snippet are from the same class. These methods show the keyboard input processing and the API event handling. Let's jump into some code!

Listing 6-6. MmgTextField Class Demonstration 1

```
//ScreenTestMmgTextField.LoadResources
01 int width = MmgHelper.ScaleValue(256);
02 int height = MmgHelper.ScaleValue(64);

...

03 bground = MmgHelper.GetBasicCachedBmp("popup_window_base.png");
04 txtField = new MmgTextField(bground, MmgFontData.
   CreateDefaultMmgFontLg(), width, height, 12, 15);
05 MmgHelper.CenterHorAndVert(txtField);
06 txtField.SetMaxLengthOn(true);
07 txtField.SetEventHandler(this);
08 txtField.SetY(txtField.GetY() - MmgHelper.ScaleValue(30));
09 AddObj(txtField);

//ScreenTestMmgTextField.ProcessKeyClick
01 public boolean ProcessKeyClick(char c, int code) {
02     if(Character.isLetterOrDigit(c)) {
03         txtField.ProcessKeyClick(c, code);
04     } else if(code == 8) {
05         txtField.DeleteChar();
06     }
```

```
07    txtFieldText.SetText("Text Field Text: " + txtField.
      GetTextFieldString());
08    MmgHelper.CenterHor(txtFieldText);
09    return true;
10 }
```

```
//ScreenTestMmgTextField.MmgHandleEvent
01 public void MmgHandleEvent(MmgEvent e) {
02    MmgHelper.wr("ScreenTestMsgTextField.HandleMmgEvent: Msg: " +
      e.GetMessage() + " Id: " + e.GetEventId());
03    if(e.GetMessage() != null && e.GetMessage().equals("error_max_
      length") == true) {
04        txtFieldMaxLenError.SetText("Max Len Error Current Time MS: " +
          System.currentTimeMillis());
05        MmgHelper.CenterHor(txtFieldMaxLenError);
06    }
07 }
```

The preceding snippet starts off with the code needed to prepare a new text field for display. The desired dimensions are calculated on lines 1 and 2. The background source image, used in the creation of an Mmg9Slice object, is loaded on line 3 with a call to the MmgHelper class' GetBasicCachedBmp method. Lines 4–9 handle creating and configuring the MmgTextField class.

The constructor is called on line 4 with the background image, width, height, and other arguments being passed in to set the class fields. The text field object is centered on line 5, and on lines 6 and 7, the max length error detection is turned on and an event is registered to be handled by the MmgTextField class. The new object is added to the game screen's list of drawable objects on line 9.

The ScreenTestMmgTextField class has input events mapped from the application's core code to event handler methods in the MmgCore package's GamePanel class, or namespace if you're following along in C#. The GamePanel class forwards the events onto the current game screen. In this case, the ScreenTestMmgTextField class receives them and after some internal logic calls the MmgTextField class' ProcessKeyClick or DeleteChar method depending on what key was pressed.

If the pressed key is an alphanumeric character, then it's sent to the text field object's ProcessKeyClick method. If the pressed key is the Backspace key, then the object's DeleteChar method is called. In the next snippet of code, the MmgHandleEvent method is listed. This method responds to events coming from the text field we created in the first code snippet. In this case, since we have only one event, we don't check for the event ID and type. We simply check the event's message and make a note of the event by displaying it on the game screen.

Widget Classes: MmgTextBlock

The MmgTextBlock class is used to display larger blocks of text like paragraphs of a story or parts of a dialog. The MmgTextBlock class will parse a string of text and break it up into a series of strings that display correctly in the dimensions of the MmgTextBlock object. This class is used to break a large amount of text into multiple pages of properly formatted text.

I would like to take a moment to point out that up until, roughly this chapter, most classes required very small amounts of configuration. Some classes would implement a preparation method internally and automatically call it when certain fields changed, some would call the preparation method at the end of the constructor, and others would require you to call the proper method at the proper time. This class is the latter type of class.

The last thing I should mention is that the MmgTextBlock class extends the MmgObj class, so it's a part of the set of drawable objects. Think about this for a minute. So were the text field and the label-value pair and the MmgBmp image and the MmgFont-based text class. The game engine really doesn't care which class it's processing. They all look like MmgObj classes to the engine's drawing routine.

Static Class Members

There are only two static class members for us to review. I'll list them here.

Listing 6-7. MmgTextBlock Static Class Members 1

```
public static String NEW_LINE = "[b]";
public static boolean SHOW_CONTROL_BGROUND_STORY_BOUNDING_BOX = false;
```

The first field is the NEW_LINE string. This field holds the string encoding used to mark a new line in the class' source text. The second static class field is a Boolean flag that indicates if a bounding box should be drawn around the MmgTextBlock object. Using this Boolean can really help when positioning your text block.

Class Fields

The first set of fields to review are listed in the following. These fields control aspects of the text rendering.

Listing 6-8. MmgTextBlock Class Fields 1

```
private int STARTING_LINE_COUNT = 20;
private int STARTING_TXT_COUNT = 100;
private MmgColor cl;
private int height;
private int lineHeight;
```

The first two fields are private and are used to initialize the arrays used to store lines of words, as well as for storing the words themselves. The MmgColor field, cl, is used to color the text in the text block. The next two fields track the text block's height and the line height for the current MmgFont.

Listing 6-9. MmgTextBlock Class Fields 2

```
private ArrayList<MmgFont> lines;
private int paddingY;
private int paddingX;
private int pages;
private Font paint;
private ArrayList<MmgFont> txt;
private int width;
private int words;
```

The second set of class fields to review are listed in the preceding group. The first is an ArrayList, or a List if you're following along in C#. The lines represented are the available preformatted lines of text that fit in the current text block. Think of these as a pool of lines that can be displayed. Each page in a series has the same available lines to fill with text. The next two class fields, paddingX and paddingY, are for fine-tuning the positioning. The pages field holds the number of pages it takes to display the parsed text.

The Font object paint is used in rendering text in the text block. The next class field is also an ArrayList of type MmgFont objects. This data structure is filled up with available lines of text from the lines class field. Lastly, we have the width of the text block and the number of words that were found when parsing the provided text.

Support Method Details

The MmgTextBlock class has a laundry list of support methods. I've listed them in the following set. I've broken down the methods into four groups. Take a look at each group before we move on to talk about each method.

Listing 6-10. MmgTextBlock Support Method Details 1

```
//Font control methods
public MmgColor GetColor() { ... }
public void SetColor(MmgColor Cl) { ... }
public Font GetSpriteFont() { ... }
public void SetSpriteFont(Font p) { ... }
public int GetLineHeight() { ... }
public void SetLineHeight(int l) { ... }

//Text block drawing methods
public int GetHeight() { ... }
public void SetHeight(int h) { ... }
public int GetWidth() { ... }
public void SetWidth(int w) { ... }
public int GetPaddingX() { ... }
public void SetPaddingX(int p) { ... }
public int GetPaddingY() { ... }
public void SetPaddingY(int p) { ... }

//Text block statistics methods
public int GetLineCount() { ... }
public int GetPageCount() { ... }
public int GetUsedLineCount() { ... }
```

```
public int GetLinesInBox() { ... }
public int GetPages() { ... }
public void SetPages(int p) { ... }
public int GetWordCount() { ... }
public void SetWordCount(int i) { ... }

//Text block data methods
public ArrayList<MmgFont> GetLines() { ... }
public void SetLines(ArrayList<MmgFont> a) { ... }
public ArrayList<MmgFont> GetTxt() { ... }
public void SetTxt(ArrayList<MmgFont> a) { ... }
public MmgFont GetText(int i) { ... }
public void SetText(int i, MmgFont f) { ... }
```

The first group of methods let you control how the font is drawn in the text block. You can access the color and the framework font class used to create the MmgFont objects the class uses to draw the text. The last two methods let you control the line height. This field is used to space out the lines in the text block.

The second group of methods control how the text block is drawn: the position of the objects, the dimensions it uses to format the text, and the padding values used to fine-tune how the text is displayed inside the text block. The third group of methods provide statistics about the text that was parsed and the way the text is formatted inside the text block.

The GetLineCount method returns the number of lines that fit inside the text block. The GetPageCount method returns the number of pages the text takes up when displayed using the current text block dimensions and calculated number of lines. The GetUsedLineCount method returns the number of lines used to display text on the current page. The GetLinesInBox method may seem redundant, but it's the lower-level method used to calculate the number of lines in the box.

The next two methods give you access to the pages field, and the final two methods give you access to the number of words parsed from the provided text. The last group of methods lets you get and set the data that is generated by the class. These methods are self-explanatory and seldom used, so I won't go into great detail over them here. Read through them and make sure you understand them.

Listing 6-11. MmgTextBlock Main Method Details 1

```
//Constructors
public MmgTextBlock() { ... }
public MmgTextBlock(MmgTextBlock obj) { ... }

//Cloning methods
public MmgObj Clone() { ... }
public MmgTextBlock CloneTyped() { ... }

//Text preparation methods
public void PrepLinesInBox(int len) { ... }
public void PrepLinesInBox() { ... }
public void PrepPage(int page) { ... }
public void PrepTextSplit(String text, Font typeFace, int fontSize, int
width, FontType fontType) { ... }

//Data reset method
public void Reset() { ... }

//Drawing and comparison methods
public void MmgDraw(MmgPen p) { ... }
public boolean ApiEquals(MmgTextBlock obj) { ... }
```

The first group of main methods we'll look at are the class' constructors. The first constructor takes no arguments and puts the class in a state that is ready to be configured but not quite ready to be drawn to the screen. Due to the complexity of this class, you'll have to run some preparation methods by hand. The second constructor is the specialized constructor we know and love. It powers the class' cloning functionality.

The second group of main methods are the cloning methods. We've covered these enough times that I think we can safely move past them. Read over them on your own and make sure you understand them. Third, the text preparation methods are by far the most important in the class. They prepare the provided text for display and control what page of text is displayed in the case of a multi-page text block.

The PrepLinesInBox methods will reset the entries in the txt data structure. Remember that data structure is used to hold the available lines of text that can be displayed. The PrepPage method loads up the txt data structure with the next set of available preformatted lines. This is what constitutes a page in terms of the text block. If there are more lines to display, then the next page can be loaded into view.

The Reset method clears the class' data structures, and the remaining methods are game engine methods that we've seen before, so I won't go over them again here.

Demonstration: MmgTextBlock Class

The demonstration code for this class is from the LoadResources method of the ScreenTestMmgTextBlock class in the MmgTestSpace package. Be sure to run the example application and view this game screen so you can see the class in action.

Listing 6-12. MmgTextBlock Class Demonstration 1

```
01 txt = "Lorem ipsum dolor sit ...";
02
03 MmgTextBlock.SHOW_CONTROL_BGROUND_STORY_BOUNDING_BOX = true;
04 txtBlock = new MmgTextBlock();
05 txtBlock.SetLineHeight(MmgFontData.GetTargetPixelHeightScaled() +
   MmgHelper.ScaleValue(5));
06 txtBlock.SetHeight(MmgHelper.ScaleValue(300));
07 txtBlock.SetWidth(MmgHelper.ScaleValue(400));
08 txtBlock.SetPaddingX(MmgHelper.ScaleValue(txtBlock.GetPaddingX()));
09 txtBlock.SetPaddingY(MmgHelper.ScaleValue(txtBlock.GetPaddingY()));
10 txtBlock.PrepLinesInBox(txtBlock.GetLinesInBox());
11 txtBlock.PrepTextSplit(txt, MmgFontData.GetFontNorm(), MmgFontData.
   GetFontSize(), MmgHelper.ScaleValue(375), FontType.NORMAL);
12 txtBlock.SetColor(MmgColor.GetWhite());
13
14 MmgHelper.CenterHorAndVert(txtBlock);
15 txtBlock.PrepPage(0);
16
17 //Must be done after the text split to set the position of each line of text.
18 txtBlock.SetPosition(txtBlock.GetPosition());
19 AddObj(txtBlock);
```

The code snippet is fairly direct. The string to be parsed and displayed is initialized on line 1. It's actually very long, so I cut it down here. We set the show bounding box flag to true so we can see the dimensions of the text block object. A default `MmgTextBlock` is created on line 4. The line height is set to the default font size's height plus a padding factor, line 5.

On lines 6–9, we have a series of calls that are made just to ensure the values have been properly scaled. The placeholders for lines of text inside the text block are initialized on line 10. The bulk of the work is done on line 11 with a call to the `PrepTextSplit` method. This call creates the entries for the preformatted lines of text. On line 12, the color of each placeholder line is set to the color white with a call to the `SetColor` method.

The last two lines of code in the preceding snippet are very important. You must call the `SetPosition` method at least once to position the object, which forces the repositioning of all child objects including the placeholder lines of text that are displayed on the game screen. Lastly, you have to add the object to the game engine's drawing routine with a call to the `AddObj` method.

It should stand out to you how we are just passing in a very complex object and it will get rendered along with everything else. That is the power of the general game engine we've built. It's very easy to add new and interesting classes into the drawable set of objects. I hope you'll add some of your own.

Widget Classes: Scroll Pane Classes

The next class review will apply to a group of classes known as the scroll pane classes. These are the `MmgScrollHor`, `MmgScrollVert`, and `MmgScrollHorVert` classes of the MmgBase API. They all function very similarly, so I won't cover each one individually. We'll review the `MmgScrollHor` class, and you can take what you've learned about it and apply it to the other two scroll pane classes.

Static Class Members

There are a couple of static class fields for us to review. Take a look at the following listing before we review them.

Listing 6-13. MmgScrollHor Static Class Members 1

```
public static boolean SHOW_CONTROL_BOUNDING_BOX = false;

public static int SCROLL_HOR_CLICK_EVENT_TYPE = 0;
public static int SCROLL_HOR_CLICK_EVENT_ID = 3;
public static int SCROLL_HOR_SCROLL_LEFT_EVENT_ID = 4;

public static int SCROLL_HOR_SCROLL_RIGHT_EVENT_ID = 5;
```

The first entry controls the display of a bounding box that marks the dimensions of the scroll pane. This field controls all horizontal scroll panes, not just the one you're working with. The next four fields are event ID and type entries used to describe the different events supported by the scroll pane. The MmgScrollHor scroll pane supports left and right scroll events and scroll pane click events.

Class Fields

The MmgScrollHor class is on the complex side, and as such it has a number of fields that allow you to control all sorts of different aspects of the class and its functionality. All that is well and good; but with a class this complex, you really want to start at a baseline, the demonstration code, and work from there making small changes until you understand exactly how the class functions. I've broken down the class fields into groups and listed them as follows.

Listing 6-14. MmgScrollHor Class Fields 1

```
//Viewport and scrollpane fields
private MmgBmp viewPort;
private MmgRect viewPortRect;
private int viewPortWidth;
private MmgBmp scrollPane;
private MmgRect scrollPaneRect;
private int scrollPaneWidth;

//Scroll bar button display fields
private int scrollBarLeftRightButtonWidth;
private MmgBmp scrollBarLeftButton;
private MmgRect scrollBarLeftButtonRect;
```

```
private MmgBmp scrollBarRightButton;
private MmgRect scrollBarRightButtonRect;
private MmgBmp scrollBarCenterButton;
private MmgRect scrollBarCenterButtonRect;
private MmgColor scrollBarCenterButtonColor;
private int scrollBarCenterButtonWidth;

//Scroll bar display fields
private boolean scrollBarVisible = false;
private MmgColor scrollBarColor;
private int scrollBarHeight;
private int intervalX;
private double intervalPrctX;
private int offsetXScrollBarCenterButton;
private int offsetXScrollPane;
private boolean isDirty;

//Event fields
private MmgEvent clickScreen = new MmgEvent(null, "hor_click_screen",
MmgScrollHor.SCROLL_HOR_CLICK_EVENT_ID, MmgScrollHor.SCROLL_HOR_CLICK_
EVENT_TYPE, null, null);

private MmgEvent clickLeft = new MmgEvent(null, "hor_click_left",
MmgScrollHor.SCROLL_HOR_SCROLL_LEFT_EVENT_ID, MmgScrollHor.SCROLL_HOR_
CLICK_EVENT_TYPE, null, null);

private MmgEvent clickRight = new MmgEvent(null, "hor_click_right",
MmgScrollHor.SCROLL_HOR_SCROLL_RIGHT_EVENT_ID, MmgScrollHor.SCROLL_HOR_
CLICK_EVENT_TYPE, null, null);
```

The first group of fields describe the view port or the static portion of the scroll pane that presents scroll bars and a panel where the scroll pane is visible. These are fields describing its position and dimension using an MmgRect object and the viewPortWidth and scrollPaneWidth fields that describe the width of each object. It's important to note that some class fields are merely descriptive and do not alter the object in any way. You'll pick up on how things work with more experience; for now, we'll focus on going over the basics.

The second group of fields describe the scroll pane's scroll bar buttons. In a horizontal scroll pane, there is one scroll bar that sits underneath the scroll pane's window. That scroll bar has two side buttons and a center button. The left and right buttons are functional but the center slider is not as mouse drag support has not been implemented in the scroll pane classes. There is one field to describe both the left and right scroll bar buttons' widths, `scrollBarLeftRightButtonWidth`, and one to describe the center button's width, `scrollBarCenterButtonWidth`. You can alter the color of the center button using the `scrollBarCenterButtonColor` field, and there are `MmgBmp` button and `MmgRect` entries for all three buttons.

I should also mention that this class uses a few default resources. These are resources that are considered part of the game engine's runtime and load up as part of the auto load directories. This should give you a solid guide on how to customize the scroll pane resources for your own games.

The third group of fields for us to look over are the scroll bar display fields. These fields help control how the scroll bar is displayed. The only two worth mentioning directly are the `intervalX` field and the `isDirty` field. The `intervalX` class field controls the amount the scroll bar moves on one button click. The `isDirty` class field prevents the class from doing too much work by restricting the update method to only run if the class is marked dirty. Keep your eye on how you use this field; if your scroll pane isn't updating, you may need to mark the object as dirty.

The final group of fields are class events. The event objects are already prepared; they just need to have a target event handler set and they are ready to go. That wraps up the review of the class fields. Next, we'll take a look at the class' support methods.

Support Method Details

The `MmgScrollHor` class has a long list of support methods. We won't cover all of them in detail here because they are just get and set methods. I've listed the methods as follows in the same groups as the corresponding class fields.

Listing 6-15. MmgScrollHor Support Method Details 1

```
//ViewPort and ScrollPane methods
public MmgBmp GetViewPort() { ... }
public void SetViewPort(MmgBmp ViewPort) { ... }
public MmgRect GetViewPortRect() { ... }
```

```
public void SetViewPortRect(MmgRect r) { ... }
public MmgBmp GetScrollPane() { ... }
public void SetScrollPane(MmgBmp ScrollPane) { ... }
public MmgRect GetScrollPaneRect() { ... }
public void SetScrollPaneRect(MmgRect r) { ... }

//Scroll bar button display fields
public int GetScrollBarLeftRightButtonWidth() { ... }
public void SetScrollBarLeftRightButtonWidth(int w) { ... }

public MmgBmp GetScrollBarLeftButton() { ... }
public void SetScrollBarLeftButton(MmgBmp b) { ... }
public MmgRect GetScrollBarLeftButtonRect() { ... }
public void SetScrollBarLeftButtonRect(MmgRect r) { ... }

public MmgBmp GetScrollBarRightButton() { ... }
public void SetScrollBarRightButton(MmgBmp b) { ... }
public MmgRect GetScrollBarRightButtonRect() { ... }
public void SetScrollBarRightButtonRect(MmgRect r) { ... }

public MmgBmp GetScrollBarCenterButton() { ... }
public void SetScrollBarCenterButton(MmgBmp b) { ... }

public MmgRect GetScrollBarCenterButtonRect() { ... }
public void SetScrollBarCenterButtonRect(MmgRect r) { ... }

public MmgColor GetScrollBarCenterButtonColor() { ... }

public void SetScrollBarCenterButtonColor(MmgColor c) { ... }

public int GetScrollBarCenterButtonWidth() { ... }
public void SetScrollBarCenterButtonWidth(int w) { ... }

//Scroll bar display methods
public boolean GetScrollBarVisible() { ... }
public void SetScrollBarVisible(boolean b) { ... }
public MmgColor GetScrollBarColor() { ... }
public void SetScrollBarColor(MmgColor c) { ... }
public int GetScrollBarHeight() { ... }
```

151

```
public void SetScrollBarHeight(int h) { ... }
public int GetOffsetX() { ... }
public void SetOffsetX(int OffsetX) { ... }
public int GetIntervalX() { ... }
public void SetIntervalX(int IntervalX) { ... }
public boolean GetIsDirty() { ... }
public void SetIsDirty(boolean IsDirty) { ... }

//Event methods
public MmgEvent GetClickScreen() { ... }
public void SetClickScreen(MmgEvent e) { ... }
public MmgEvent GetClickLeft() { ... }
public void SetClickLeft(MmgEvent e) { ... }
public MmgEvent GetClickRight() { ... }
public void SetClickRight(MmgEvent e) { ... }
public MmgEventHandler GetEventHandler() { ... }
public void SetEventHandler(MmgEventHandler e) { ... }
```

There is one set of methods I want to mention: the GetEventHandler and SetEventHandler methods. The SetEventHandler method actually sets the target event handler for all three class events. The GetEventHandler method only returns the target event handler from the click screen event. Keep this in mind when working with this class' events. Be sure to look over the support methods listed in the preceding and get an understanding of how they work. Again, they are simple get and set methods in most cases.

Main Method Details

The first set of main methods listed in the following contains constructors and cloning methods. Take a look at them, and then we'll talk about them next.

Listing 6-16. MmgScrollHor Main Method Details 1

```
public MmgScrollHor(MmgBmp ViewPort, MmgBmp ScrollPane, MmgColor
ScrollBarColor, MmgColor ScrollBarCenterButtonColor, int IntervalX) { ... }

public MmgScrollHor(MmgScrollHor obj) { ... }
public MmgObj Clone() { ... }
public MmgScrollHor CloneTyped() { ... }
```

The first constructor listed is your standard scroll pane constructor. You'll need to have prepared the view port and scroll pane MmgBmp objects. The second constructor is a specialized constructor that takes an MmgScrollHor object as an argument and uses it to create a new, unique copy of that object. The last two methods listed are cloning methods. They use the specialized constructor to create a clone of the current object and cast it to the necessary object type before returning it.

Listing 6-17. MmgScrollHor Main Method Details 2

```
public void MmgDraw(MmgPen p) { ... }
public boolean MmgUpdate(int updateTick, long currentTimeMs, long
msSinceLastFrame) { ... }

public boolean ApiEquals(MmgScrollHor obj) { ... }
public void PrepDimensions() { ... }
public void PrepScrollPane() { ... }
public boolean ProcessDpadRelease(int dir) { ... }
public boolean ProcessScreenClick(int x, int y) { ... }
```

The second set of main methods starts with the standard game engine drawing routine methods, MmgDraw and MmgUpdate. They are followed by an API-level comparison method that is used to test two MmgScrollHor objects for equality. The next two methods are used to prepare the scroll pane. The process is as such: The constructor calls the PrepDimensions method, which prepares all the different objects by positioning them correctly. Then the PrepScrollPane method is called, which is responsible for resetting the scroll interval and the drawing surface used to draw the scroll pane onto the view port display rectangle.

The last two methods listed are input event handlers. The scroll panes, by default, are configured to scroll left, right, up, and down, depending on which one you're working with, using the directional keys. You can also click the buttons to move the scroll pane. And of course, you can click the scroll pane and trigger a screen click event.

Demonstration: MmgScrollHor Class

The example code listed in the following code block is from the LoadResources method of the ScreenTestMmgScrollHor class in the MmgTestSpace library. Be sure to run the example application and view this test screen to see the class in action.

Listing 6-18. MmgScrollHor Class Demonstration 1

```
01 dBmpSetScrollPane = MmgHelper.CreateDrawableBmpSet(hund4, hund2, false,
MmgColor.GetBlack());
02 dBmpSetScrollPane.graphics.setColor(Color.RED);
03 dBmpSetScrollPane.graphics.fillRect(0, 0, hund4 / 4, hund2);
04 dBmpSetScrollPane.graphics.setColor(Color.BLUE);
05 dBmpSetScrollPane.graphics.fillRect(hund4 / 4, 0, hund4 / 4, hund2);
06 dBmpSetScrollPane.graphics.setColor(Color.GREEN);
07 dBmpSetScrollPane.graphics.fillRect(hund4 / 2, 0, hund4 / 4, hund2);
08
09 dBmpSetViewPort = MmgHelper.CreateDrawableBmpSet(hund2, hund2, false,
   MmgColor.GetBlack());
10 dBmpSetViewPort.graphics.setColor(Color.LIGHT_GRAY);
11 dBmpSetViewPort.graphics.fillRect(0, 0, hund2, hund2);
12
13 vPort = dBmpSetViewPort.img;
14 sPane = dBmpSetScrollPane.img;
15
16 sBarColor = MmgColor.GetLightGray();
17 sBarSldrColor = MmgColor.GetGray();
18 sBarWidth = MmgHelper.ScaleValue(15);
19 sBarSldrHeight = MmgHelper.ScaleValue(30);
20 interval = 10;
21
22 scrollHor = new MmgScrollHor(vPort, sPane, sBarColor, sBarSldrColor,
sBarWidth, sBarSldrHeight, interval);
23 scrollHor.SetIsVisible(true);
24 scrollHor.SetWidth(sWidth);
25 scrollHor.SetHeight(sHeight + scrollHor.GetScrollBarHeight());
26 scrollHor.SetEventHandler(this);
27 MmgScrollHor.SHOW_CONTROL_BOUNDING_BOX = true;
28 MmgHelper.CenterHorAndVert(scrollHor);
29 AddObj(scrollHor);
```

The preceding snippet of code is from the LoadResources method of the ScreenTestMmgScrollHor class. Let's take a look at some code! The first few lines of code, 1–7, are there to create a scroll pane MmgBmp object that is the same height as the view port but is much wider. The scroll pane image is filled with different color rectangles so we can easily see that the pane is moving.

Similarly, the view port MmgBmp is created on line 9 and filled with a light gray color, on lines 10 and 11. That takes care of prepping the scroll pane and view port objects to be used with the MmgScrollHor instance. On lines 13 and 14, we make a local variable point to the MmgBmp image portion of the MmgDrawableBmpSet we used to create the view port and scroll pane. The remaining colors and dimensions for constructing the scroll view are initialized on lines 16–20. The MmgScrollHor object is initialized on line 22, and its visibility is set on line 23. The dimensions are set on lines 24 and 25.

Take a moment to notice that the scroll view height includes the scroll bar height. On line 26, the event handler is set to the game screen. Finally, on lines 27–29, the bounding box display flag is set to true. The scroll view is centered horizontally and vertically, and it's added to the game screen's set of drawable objects via a call to the AddObj method on line 29.

Listing 6-19. MmgScrollHor Class Demonstration 2

```
01 public boolean ProcessDpadRelease(int dir) {
02     MmgHelper.wr("ScreenTestMmgScrollHor.ProcessDpadRelease: " + dir);
03     scrollHor.ProcessDpadRelease(dir);
04     isDirty = true;
05     return true;
06 }
```

```
01 public boolean ProcessMouseClick(int x, int y) {
02     MmgHelper.wr("ScreenTestMmgScrollHor.ProcessScreenClick");
03     scrollHor.ProcessScreenClick(x, y);
04     isDirty = true;
05     return true;
06 }
```

```
01 public boolean MmgUpdate(int updateTick, long currentTimeMs, long
   msSinceLastFrame) {
02      lret = false;
03
04      if (pause == false && isVisible == true) {
05          if (isDirty == true) {
06              super.GetObjects().SetIsDirty(true);
07
08              if (super.MmgUpdate(updateTick, currentTimeMs,
                  msSinceLastFrame) == true) {
09                  lret = true;
10              }
11          }
12      }
13
14      return lret;
15 }
```

We know that the scroll view widget gets updated by input from the directional keys and mouse, so we should expect to see the MmgUpdate method of the ScreenTestMmgScrollHor support calling the update method of its child objects. The first method in the preceding snippet is the ProcessDpadRelease method. It passes input from the game screen to the scroll pane and marks the screen as dirty to force an update call. The next method to review, ProcessMouseClick, works in the same way as the directional keys method. It sends mouse click events to the scroll pane for processing.

The last method in the snippet of code is the ScreenTestMmgScrollHor class' MmgUpdate method. At first glance, we don't see any update calls being made on the scroll view object. If the screen is not paused and is visible, we then check to see if the local isDirty flag is set to true. If so, we call a super class method, GetObjects, which returns all the game screen's child objects.

The call to SetIsDirty with a true argument sets all child objects to have an isDirty flag set to true. Then, on line 8, the MmgUpdate method of the super class is called. This will ensure that all child objects get their update methods called including the MmgScrollHor object.

Widget Classes: MmgMenuContainer

The MmgMenuContainer class is a widget class that works in conjunction with the MmgGameScreen and MmgMenuItem classes. It's not exactly like previous widgets we've reviewed. Those widgets were very much self-contained, UI-based widgets. The MmgMenuContainer is designed to share some responsibility with the game screen that's displaying the menu and the MmgMenuItem instances.

Class Fields

The MmgMenuContainer class has only one class field we need to worry about.

Listing 6-20. MmgMenuContainer Class Fields 1

```
private ArrayList<MmgMenuItem> container;
```

The container field holds all the menu items displayed by this container object.

Support Method Details

The MmgMenuContainer class comes equipped with a set of support methods that let you interact with the data it contains. I've listed the methods in the following grouping. Take a look at them before we review them.

Listing 6-21. MmgMenuContainer Support Method Details 1

```
//Data control methods
public void Add(MmgMenuItem obj) { ... }
public void Remove(MmgMenuItem obj) { ... }
public void Clear() { ... }
public int GetCount() { ... }

//Data access methods
public MmgMenuItem[] GetArray() { ... }
public ArrayList<MmgMenuItem> GetContainer() { ... }
public void SetContainer(ArrayList<MmgMenuItem> aTmp) { ... }
```

The class methods are outlined in the preceding in two groups. The first group gives you control of the class' data. You can add and remove items to and from the container and clear the container using these methods. The GetCount method returns a count of the number of children in the container. The second group of methods gives you access to the container's data. You can get an array representation of the child objects using the GetArray method, or you can interact with the container field using the two get and set methods listed.

Main Method Details

The class' main methods fall into three groups: constructors, cloning methods, and general main methods.

Listing 6-22. MmgMenuContainer Main Method Details 1

```
//Constructors
public MmgMenuContainer() { ... }
public MmgMenuContainer(ArrayList<MmgMenuItem> objects) { ... }

public MmgMenuContainer(MmgMenuContainer obj) { ... }


//Cloning methods
public MmgObj Clone() { ... }
public MmgMenuContainer CloneTyped() { ... }

//General main methods
public void MmgDraw(MmgPen p) { ... }
public boolean ApiEquals(MmgMenuContainer obj) { ... }
```

The first constructor listed in the preceding takes no arguments and creates an empty but ready-to-use menu container. The second constructor listed takes an ArrayList of menu items as an argument and uses it to initialize the container's child objects. The final constructor listed is a specialized constructor that takes an MmgMenuContainer as an argument and uses it to make a new, unique copy of the object.

The next group of methods listed are cloning methods, and they are used to create unique copies of the current object. The MmgDraw method is used by the game engine drawing routine, and the ApiEquals method provides API-level comparison functionality. That wraps up the main method review. Next, let's take a look at the class in action.

Demonstration: MmgMenuContainer Class

The following snippet of example code demonstrates preparing the menu item MmgBmp objects for use.

Listing 6-23. MmgMenuContainer Class Demonstration 1

```
//ScreenTestMmgMainMenu.LoadResources
01 key = "bmpMenuItemStartGame1p";
02 imgId = MmgHelper.ContainsKeyString(key, "start_game_1p.png",
   classConfig);
03 lval = MmgHelper.GetBasicCachedBmp(imgId);
04 menuStartGame1P = lval;
05 if (menuStartGame1P != null) {
06     MmgHelper.CenterHor(menuStartGame1P);
07     menuStartGame1P.GetPosition().SetY(menuSubTitle.GetY() +
       menuSubTitle.GetHeight() + MmgHelper.ScaleValue(10));
08     menuStartGame1P = MmgHelper.ContainsKeyMmgBmpScaleAndPosition
       ("menuStartGame1p", menuStartGame1P, classConfig, GetPosition());
09 }
10
11 key = "bmpMenuItemStartGame2p";
12 imgId = MmgHelper.ContainsKeyString(key, "start_game_2p.png",
   classConfig);
13 lval = MmgHelper.GetBasicCachedBmp(imgId);
14 menuStartGame2P = lval;
15 if (menuStartGame2P != null) {
16     MmgHelper.CenterHor(menuStartGame2P);
17     menuStartGame2P.GetPosition().SetY(menuStartGame1P.GetY() +
       menuStartGame1P.GetHeight() + MmgHelper.ScaleValue(10));
18     menuStartGame2P = MmgHelper.ContainsKeyMmgBmpScaleAndPosition
       ("menuStartGame2p", menuStartGame2P, classConfig, GetPosition());
19 }
20
21 key = "bmpMenuItemExitGame";
22 imgId = MmgHelper.ContainsKeyString(key, "exit_game.png", classConfig);
```

159

```
23 lval = MmgHelper.GetBasicCachedBmp(imgId);
24 menuExitGame = lval;
25 if (menuExitGame != null) {
26     MmgHelper.CenterHor(menuExitGame);
27     menuExitGame.GetPosition().SetY(menuStartGame2P.GetY() +
        menuStartGame2P.GetHeight() + MmgHelper.ScaleValue(10));
28     menuExitGame = MmgHelper.ContainsKeyMmgBmpScaleAndPosition(
        "menuExitGame", menuExitGame, classConfig, GetPosition());
29 }
```

Each code block in the preceding is similar, just designed to work with a different menu item. Take a look at the code and make sure you understand it. Take notice of how the class config file is used to customize the example menu screen.

Listing 6-24. MmgMenuContainer Class Demonstration 2

```
//ScreenTestMmgMainMenu.DrawScreen
01 pause = true;
02 if(menu == null) {
03     menu = new MmgMenuContainer();
04     menu.SetMmgColor(null);
05     MmgMenuItem mItm = null;
06
07     if (menuStartGame1P != null) {
08         mItm = MmgHelper.GetBasicMenuItem(handleMenuEvent, "Main
           Menu Start Game 1P", HandleMainMenuEvent.MAIN_MENU_EVENT_
           START_GAME_1P, HandleMainMenuEvent.MAIN_MENU_EVENT_TYPE,
           menuStartGame1P);
09         mItm.SetSound(menuSound);
10         menu.Add(mItm);
11     }
12
13     if (menuStartGame2P != null) {
14         mItm = MmgHelper.GetBasicMenuItem(handleMenuEvent, "Main
           Menu Start Game 2P", HandleMainMenuEvent.MAIN_MENU_EVENT_
           START_GAME_2P, HandleMainMenuEvent.MAIN_MENU_EVENT_TYPE,
           menuStartGame2P);
```

```
15        mItm.SetSound(menuSound);
16        menu.Add(mItm);
17    }
18
19    if (menuExitGame != null) {
20        mItm = MmgHelper.GetBasicMenuItem(handleMenuEvent, "Main Menu
          Exit Game", HandleMainMenuEvent.MAIN_MENU_EVENT_EXIT_GAME,
          HandleMainMenuEvent.MAIN_MENU_EVENT_TYPE, menuExitGame);
21        mItm.SetSound(menuSound);
22        menu.Add(mItm);
23    }
24
25    SetMenuStart(0);
26    SetMenuStop(menu.GetCount() - 1);
27    SetMenu(menu);
28    SetMenuOn(true);
29 }
30 isDirty = false;
31 pause = false;
```

The snippet of code listed in the preceding is from the ScreenTestMmgMainMenu's
DrawScreen method. This method is used to initialize the game screen's menu system.
Notice that on line 1 the screen is paused. This is to prevent rendering artifacts caused
by an incomplete configuration. On line 2, we check to see if the menu is null or if it
has already been configured. On line 3, we set up the menu container and set the color
to null. We'll start loading up the menu items now. The items are protected to prevent
loading if the image required is null.

Take a look at lines 7–11. This is the basic process used to load up a new menu item.
Notice that we use the MmgHelper method GetBasicMenuItem to create a new menu item.
On line 9, we set the sound that will play when the menu item is selected; and on line
10, we add the new item to the menu. The next two menu items follow the same process.
Take a look at the code on lines 13–17 and 19–23. Make sure you understand the code
and follow what's going on.

The code on lines 25 and 26 sets the menu's start and stop indexes. In this case, the
menu uses the full set of child objects we've loaded up. An important method call takes
place on line 27. This is where the menu is activated as the screen's menu system. Lastly,

on line 28, the menu is turned on. Before the method exits, we set the pause field to false. That concludes our review of the MmgMenuContainer class. The next class we'll look at is the MmgMenuItem class.

Widget Classes: MmgMenuItem

The MmgMenuItem class is used by the MmgMenuContainer class as the menu items that are displayed by the container. The MmgMenuItem class has support for different states, normal, selected, and inactive. The class also has support for playing a sound when the menu item is the currently selected item.

Static Class Members

The MmgMenuItem class has a few static class fields that define the different states the item can be in. It also has support for displaying a bounding box as we've seen in other widget classes.

Listing 6-25. MmgMenuItem Static Class Members 1

```
public static int STATE_NONE = -1;
public static int STATE_NORMAL = 0;
public static int STATE_SELECTED = 1;
public static int STATE_INACTIVE = 2;
public static boolean SHOW_MENU_ITEM_BOUNDING_BOX = false;
```

The class fields listed in the preceding start with four entries that are used to indicate different menu item states. The last entry enables the display of a bounding box so you can see the dimensions of the menu items.

Class Fields

The MmgMenuItem class has a few fields. I've listed them in the following group. They mainly deal with the display of the menu item and the management of its state.

Listing 6-26. MmgMenuItem Class Fields 1

```
private MmgEvent eventPress;
private MmgObj normal;
private MmgObj selected;
private MmgObj inactive;
private MmgObj current;
private MmgSound sound;
private int state;
```

The eventPress field is the event for the menu item. If the menu item is clicked, the event fires and is sent to the registered event handler. This is how you would react to menu item events. The next four class fields are all MmgObj instances and are all used to display the menu item in a different state. The sound field holds the sound that should be played if the menu item is selected. The last entry in the list is the state field, and it tracks the current state of the menu item. The state determines if the menu item is normal, selected, inactive, or current.

Support Method Details

The class' support methods are listed in the following group. Take a moment to look over them. They are all basically just field access methods.

Listing 6-27. MmgMenuitem Support Method Details 1

```
public MmgEvent GetEventPress() { ... }
public void SetEventPress(MmgEvent e) { ... }
public MmgObj GetNormal() { ... }
public void SetNormal(MmgObj m) { ... }
public MmgObj GetSelected() { ... }
public void SetSelected(MmgObj m) { ... }
public MmgObj GetInactive() { ... }
public void SetInactive(MmgObj m) { ... }
public MmgSound GetSound() { ... }
public void SetSound(MmgSound Sound) { ... }
public void SetState(int i) { ... }
public int GetState() { ... }
```

I've listed the support methods in the same order as their corresponding class fields we've reviewed earlier. They are just straightforward get and set methods, so I won't go into any detail over them here. I should mention that the SetState method is a bit more complex than you might think. It checks the state that is being set and determines if a sound needs to be played. It updates some internal class fields and also resets the dimensions of the menu item to match the new state.

Main Method Details

The MmgMenuItem class' main methods are listed in the following in three groups. Take a moment to look over the methods before we review them.

Listing 6-28. MmgMenuItem Main Method Details 1

```
//Constructors
public MmgMenuItem() { ... }
public MmgMenuItem(MmgEvent me, MmgObj Normal, MmgObj Selected, MmgObj
Inactive, int State){ ... }
public MmgMenuItem(MmgMenuItem obj){ ... }

//Cloning methods
public MmgObj Clone(){ ... }
public MmgMenuItem CloneTyped(){ ... }

//General main methods
public void MmgDraw(MmgPen p){ ... }
public boolean ApiEquals(MmgMenuItem obj) { ... }
```

The first constructor listed creates an empty class instance that is not suitable for use. This constructor expects you to further configure the class before using it. The second constructor is a full constructor that takes an argument for every major class field. The third constructor is a specialized class constructor that takes an MmgMenuItem object as an instance and uses it to create a new, unique copy of the object.

The cloning methods use the specialized constructor to create a copy of the class and cast it to the specified type before returning it. The last group of methods are just standard main methods. The MmgDraw method is part of the game engine's drawing routine, and the ApiEquals method is an API-level comparison method.

Demonstration: MmgMenuItem Class

The demonstration code posted in the following is from the MmgHelper class from the MmgBase library. Take a moment to look over the method before we review it.

Listing 6-29. MmgMenuItem Class Demonstration

```
01 public static MmgMenuItem GetBasicMenuItem(MmgEventHandler handler,
String name, int eventId, int eventType, MmgBmp img) {
02      MmgMenuItem itm;
03      itm = new MmgMenuItem();
04      itm.SetNormal(img);
05      itm.SetSelected(img);
06      itm.SetInactive(img);
07      itm.SetPosition(img.GetPosition());
08      itm.SetState(MmgMenuItem.STATE_NORMAL);
09      itm.SetEventPress(new MmgEvent(handler, name, eventId, eventType,
        handler, null));
10      itm.SetMmgColor(null);
11      return itm;
12 }
```

The GetBasicMenuItem method is a convenient easy-access method and creates a simple menu item for use with an MmgMenuContainer object. The method is simplified because it uses the same MmgBmp object for all menu item states. Notice that the menu item's event handler is prepped by the method. This example shows you how to instantiate a new menu item object, but I would just use the helper method.

Chapter Conclusion

In this chapter, we completed a review of the MmgBase API's widget classes. The classes we've covered have complex implementations and advanced functionality. Notice that no matter how complex the class gets, as long as it extends the MmgObj class, we can still just plug it into the game screen and it works. This is the power of the game engine starting to show itself. Let's take a look at a summary of the classes we've just reviewed:

- MmgTextField: An API class for representing a text field a user can input text into.

- MmgTextBlock: An API class for representing a multipage text block.

- MmgScrollHor/MmgScrollVert/MmgScrollHorVert: A set of API classes for representing scrollable panes.

- MmgMenuContainer: An API class for representing a menu system. This class plugs into the MmgGameScreen class as part of its menu system.

- MmgMenuItem: The menu item class used by the MmgMenuContainer class.

The power of our tool chest is increasing exponentially. Now we've just added a slew of UI widgets that you can use in your game's menu system or the game HUD. We haven't defined a complex graphics API, but we've defined a series of drawable objects that act like self-contained UI widgets. There's enough here to create solid menus, game settings screens, and more. I hope you see the flexibility and power in the design we're working with. Keep these classes in mind when you're building your next game.

CHAPTER 7

Animation Classes

In this chapter, we'll review a set of animation classes that can be used to provide basic animation support for certain elements of your next game. The `MmgPositionTween` class in particular is an advanced implementation that takes into account child objects, timing, drawing, and positioning. This class needs to be plugged into the game engine's drawing routine and receive update calls to maintain the correct timing during the animation:

- MmgPulse
- MmgPositionTween/MmgSizeTween

Animation Classes: MmgPulse

The `MmgPulse` class provides support for simple animations. It's specifically designed for animations that pulse or return back to the start of the animation and repeat. A good example of a pulse animation would be a torch that flickers from dim to bright light and back again.

I should mention that this class doesn't extend the `MmgObj` class, so it's not in the set of drawable objects. This class is not drawn to the screen. Instead, the `MmgPulse` class updates an `MmgVector2` object that can be a reference to an active object's position, or it can be used to drive attributes of an object.

Class Fields

The first set of class fields listed in the following group are used to control the start and stop limits, the direction, and the rate of change of the pulse. Take a look at the fields listed. We'll review them in just a bit.

© Victor G Brusca 2021
V. G. Brusca, *Introduction to Video Game Engine Development*, https://doi.org/10.1007/978-1-4842-7039-4_7

Listing 7-1. MmgPulse Class Fields 1

```
private MmgVector2 adjScaling;
private MmgVector2 baseLineScaling;
private double change;
private double changePerMs;
private int direction; //growing or shrinking, 1 or -1
```

The first field listed, adjScaling, represents the apex of the pulse or the point at which the pulse starts returning to its starting point. The second field, baseLineScaling, represents the starting point of the pulse. The change field represents the total change that must occur. It's easiest to think of the pulse as a distance from a start point and the change as the total distance that must be covered by the pulse. That makes the changePerMs field the rate of change for the pulse and the direction field, you guessed it, the direction of the pulse.

Listing 7-2. MmgPulse Class Fields 2

```
private long timeDiff;
private long timeFlip;
private long timeStart;
private long timeTotal;
```

The second set of class fields has four entries for us to review. These fields deal mostly with the timing involved in the pulse animation. The first entry, timeDiff, tracks the time difference in milliseconds between the current time and the value held by the timeStart class field. The next entry, timeFlip, tracks how much time into the animation it takes for the direction of the pulse to change. The timeStart class field marks the starting time, in milliseconds, that the pulse animation began. The timeTotal class field holds the total amount of time the animation takes, also in milliseconds.

Support Method Details

The MmgPulse class has support methods that allow access to most of the class' fields. The only field we reviewed that doesn't have get and set methods is the timeDiff field because it is calculated on the fly as part of the object's update method calls. I've ordered the support methods to match the order of the class fields we just reviewed.

Listing 7-3. MmgPulse Support Method Details 1

```
public MmgVector2 GetAdjScaling() { ... }
public void SetAdjScaling(MmgVector2 v) { ... }
public MmgVector2 GetBaseLineScaling() { ... }
public void SetBaseLineScaling(MmgVector2 v) { ... }
public double GetChange() { ... }
public void SetChange(double c) { ... }
public double GetChangePerMs() { ... }
public void SetChangePerMs(double d) { ... }

public long GetTimeFlip() { ... }
public void SetTimeFlip(long l) { ... }
public long GetTimeStart() { ... }
public void SetTimeStart(long l) { ... }
public long GetTimeTotal() { ... }
public void SetTimeTotal(long l) { ... }
```

Because these are just simple get and set methods, I won't go into any detail reviewing them. As with any class, it may not be clear just exactly how to use the methods properly. The best approach is to start from the demonstration code, establish a baseline of functionality, and then experiment until you understand how the class' fields and methods should be used.

Main Method Details

The main methods we have to review for the MmgPulse class are listed in the following. They are very straightforward. These are standard main methods we've seen before during the API review.

Listing 7-4. MmgPulse Main Method Details 1

```
public MmgPulse(int startDir, long totalMs, double chng, MmgVector2 blS)
{ ... }

public MmgPulse(MmgPulse obj) { ... }
public MmgPulse Clone() { ... }
public String ApiToString() { ... }
public boolean ApiEquals(MmgPulse obj) { ... }
```

The first two methods listed in the preceding are class constructors as you might expect. The first constructor takes arguments for all the major class fields. Each argument is used to initialize its associated field. This constructor creates a new MmgPulse object that is ready to use given the current arguments. You should make sure you understand how the pulse class works before experimenting with more exotic pulse parameters.

The second constructor listed is a specialized constructor that is used to create a new, unique copy of an existing MmgPulse object. This method powers the class' cloning functionality, the Clone method. Last but not least, there are two API-level methods for representing the class as a string and comparing two MmgPulse objects. These methods are also very direct, so I won't go into any detail about them here. Make sure to look over the main methods and understand how they work.

Demonstration: MmgPulse Class

In this demonstration section, we'll take a look at the MmgPulse class in use. The code we'll look at here is from the LoadResources and MmgUpdate methods of the ScreenTestMmgContainer class from the MmgTestSpace package, or namespace in C#.

Listing 7-5. MmgPulse Class Demonstration 1

```
01 frame1 = MmgHelper.GetBasicCachedBmp("soldier_frame_1.png");
02 frame1 = MmgBmpScaler.ScaleMmgBmp(frame1, 2.0f, true);
03 MmgHelper.CenterHorAndVert(frame1);
04 frame1.SetY(frame1.GetY() - MmgHelper.ScaleValue(80));
05 frame1.SetX(frame1.GetX() - MmgHelper.ScaleValue(110));
06 AddObj(frame1);
07
08 frame2 = MmgHelper.GetBasicCachedBmp("soldier_frame_2.png");
09 frame2 = MmgBmpScaler.ScaleMmgBmp(frame2, 2.0f, true);
10 MmgHelper.CenterHorAndVert(frame2);
11 frame2.SetY(frame2.GetY() - 0);
12
13 frame3 = MmgHelper.GetBasicCachedBmp("soldier_frame_3.png");
14 frame3 = MmgBmpScaler.ScaleMmgBmp(frame3, 2.0f, true);
```

```
15 MmgHelper.CenterHorAndVert(frame3);
16 frame3.SetY(frame2.GetY() + MmgHelper.ScaleValue(80));
17
18 holder = new MmgContainer();
19 holder.Add(frame2);
20 holder.Add(frame3);
21 holder.SetWidth(frame1.GetWidth());
22 holder.SetHeight(MmgHelper.ScaleValue(160));
23 MmgHelper.CenterHorAndVert(holder);
24 AddObj(holder);
25
26 posTmp = frame1.GetPosition().Clone();
27 pulse = new MmgPulse(1, 2000l, 0.75d, frame1.GetPosition().Clone());
```

The snippet of code listed in the preceding shows the loading of an image resource that will be used by an MmgPulse animation. You can check out this test screen by opening the example application and navigating to the "Screen Test Mmg Container and Mmg Pulse" example game screen. On lines 2 and 3, the image is scaled up 100% and positioned at the center of the screen. The position is finalized on lines 4 and 5, and the MmgBmp object is added to the game screen's list of drawable objects on line 6.

The next two blocks of code are very similar to the lines we just reviewed, lines 8–11 and 12–16. In these blocks of code, two more images are loaded up and positioned, but they aren't added to the game screen's list of objects; they are added to an MmgContainer instance instead. The container has two image frames added to it on lines 19 and 20, and its dimensions are set on lines 21 and 22. Lastly, it's positioned at the center of the screen, line 23, and added to the screen's list of drawable objects on line 24.

A clone of the first image's position is made on line 26 so we can access the position without worrying about actually changing it. On line 27, a new MmgPulse object is initialized with default values for the starting direction, the total animation time, the position scaling amount, and the starting position. Notice that the pulse object doesn't use any drawable objects as part of its animation routine. The reason is that this class doesn't animate the objects; it animates a value, like a position vector, that can be used to power different drawable classes like MmgBmp images and MmgSprite animations.

Listing 7-6. MmgPulse Class Demonstration 2

```
01 lret = false;
02
03 if (pause == false && isVisible == true) {
04     //always run this update
05     prevDir = pulse.GetDirection();
06     pulse.Update(posTmp);
07     frame1.SetX(posTmp.GetX());
08
09     if(prevDir != pulse.GetDirection()) {
10         holder.SetIsVisible(!holder.GetIsVisible());
11     }
12 }
13
14 return lret;
```

The snippet of code listed in the preceding is from the MmgUpdate method of the ScreenTestMmgContainer class from the MmgTestSpace library. These lines of code show us how the game screen is configured to handle the MmgUpdate method call. Take a look at line 6; this is where the MmgPulse class is updated based on the current position of the pulse.

On line 7, the new position, updated by the MmgPulse object, is used to set the location of the frame1 MmgBmp object we reviewed earlier. In this way, the pulse animation controls the position of the image and moves it back and forth from the starting position to the ending position repeating the process over and over again.

Animation Classes: MmgPositionTween/ MmgSizeTween

The MmgPositionTween class is another animation class that works a bit differently than the MmgPulse class we've just reviewed. The MmgPulse class really only updates an MmgVector2 object via a call to the class' update method. In this way, the class doesn't act like many of the drawable classes we've reviewed thus far.

The MmgPulse class acts more like a generator, generating the next vector in the animation for use as you see fit. The MmgPositionTween class, on the other hand, extends the MmgObj class and is a member of the drawable set of objects. The MmgPositionTween class is designed to move an object from a starting position to an ending position in a specified amount of time.

The MmgSizeTween class is very similar to the position tween class except that instead of adjusting an object's position, it alters the object's size. These classes are very similar and have almost the exact same structure, fields, and methods, save that the MmgSizeTween class uses a slightly different naming convention for its methods.

Make sure you check out the size tween example screen, ScreenTestMmgSizeTween class in the MmgTestSpace library. You'll find the code to be very familiar just slightly adjusted to handle resizing as opposed to repositioning.

Static Class Members

The MmgPositionTween class has four static class members listed in the following. These fields are used to describe the class' event IDs and types.

Listing 7-7. MmgPositionTween Static Class Members 1

```
public static int MMG_POSITION_TWEEN_REACH_FINISH = 0;

public static int MMG_POSITION_TWEEN_REACH_START = 1;
public static int MMG_POSITION_TWEEN_REACH_FINISH_TYPE = 0;

public static int MMG_POSITION_TWEEN_REACH_START_TYPE = 1;
```

The preceding field listings are event ID and type values for the class' reach start and reach finish events. The MmgPositionTween class supports firing an event when the object is at the start and end of the animation.

Class Fields

Let's take a look at the MmgPositionTween class' fields. I've listed the first set of fields for us to review in the following section.

Listing 7-8. MmgPositionTween Class Fields 1

```
private boolean atFinish;
private boolean atStart;
private boolean dirStartToFinish;
private MmgVector2 finishPosition;
private MmgVector2 startPosition;
private boolean moving;
private long msStartMove;
private float msTimeToMove;
```

The first set of class fields for us to review starts with the atFinish field. This field is a Boolean flag indicating if the animation has reached the finish position. Similarly, the atStart field indicates if the animation is at the starting position. The next field, dirStartToFinish, is another Boolean flag that is true when the animation is running forward, from start to finish, and false when the animation is running in reverse.

The finish and start position fields are just what they seem. The moving Boolean flag is set to true when the animation is active and the object is moving. The msStartMove field holds the animation's starting time, and the msTimeToMove field holds the total amount of time the animation has to complete.

Listing 7-9. MmgPositionTween Class Fields 2

```
private MmgEventHandler onReachFinish;
private MmgEventHandler onReachStart;
private MmgVector2 pixelDistToMove;
private float pixelsPerMsToMoveX;
private float pixelsPerMsToMoveY;
private MmgObj subj;

private MmgEvent reachFinish = new MmgEvent(null, "reach_finish",
MmgPositionTween.MMG_POSITION_TWEEN_REACH_FINISH, MmgPositionTween.MMG_
POSITION_TWEEN_REACH_FINISH_TYPE, null, null);

private MmgEvent reachStart = new MmgEvent(null, "reach_start",
MmgPositionTween.MMG_POSITION_TWEEN_REACH_START, MmgPositionTween.MMG_
POSITION_TWEEN_REACH_START_TYPE, null, null);
```

The second set of class fields for us to review is listed in the preceding. The first two fields are event handlers. The class supports onReachFinish and onReachStart event handlers. The next entry, pixelDistToMove, is a vector representing the difference between the finish and the start positions. This vector represents the pixel distance that the subject has to move during the animation.

We break down this info further and determine the pixelsPerMsToMoveX and pixelsPerMsToMoveY. These two fields track the distance that must be moved on each axis. The subject of the class you'll notice is an MmgObj instance. This means that the position tween will work with any of the drawable objects in the MmgBase API. Now that's pretty powerful stuff.

Templates for the reachFinish and reachStart events are the last two class fields. These events are just about ready to go except they need to have a target event handler set.

Support Method Details

The MmgPositionTween class' support methods are just get and set methods for the class' fields. Nothing crazy going on here. I've taken the time to list the methods in the same order as the class fields we just reviewed.

Listing 7-10. MmgPositionTween Support Method Details 1

```
public boolean GetAtFinish() { ... }
public void SetAtFinish(boolean b) { ... }
public boolean GetAtStart() { ... }
public void SetAtStart(boolean b) { ... }
public boolean GetDirStartToFinish() { ... }
public void SetDirStartToFinish(boolean b) { ... }

public MmgVector2 GetFinishPosition() { ... }
public void SetFinishPosition(MmgVector2 v) { ... }
public MmgVector2 GetStartPosition() { ... }
public void SetStartPosition(MmgVector2 v) { ... }
public boolean GetMoving() { ... }
public void SetMoving(boolean b) { ... }

public long GetMsStartMove() { ... }
public void SetMsStartMove(long l) { ... }
```

```
public float GetMsTimeToMove() { ... }
public void SetMsTimeToMove(float i) { ... }

public MmgEventHandler GetOnReachFinish() { ... }
public void SetOnReachFinish(MmgEventHandler o) { ... }

public MmgEventHandler GetOnReachStart() { ... }
public void SetOnReachStart(MmgEventHandler o) { ... }

public MmgVector2 GetPixelDistToMove() { ... }
public void SetPixelDistToMove(MmgVector2 v) { ... }
public float GetPixelsPerMsToMoveX() { ... }
public void SetPixelsPerMsToMoveX(float i) { ... }
public float GetPixelsPerMsToMoveY() { ... }
public void SetPixelsPerMsToMoveY(float i) { ... }

public int GetFinishEventId() { ... }
public void SetFinishEventId(int i) { ... }
public int GetStartEventId() { ... }
public void SetStartEventId(int i) { ... }
public MmgObj GetSubj() { ... }
public void SetSubj(MmgObj b) { ... }
```

Again, these are basic get and set methods. Notice that you don't have direct access to the class' events. You can however set their target event handler and event IDs. There are a lot of methods here. Don't feel pressured to understand how all of them work in the context of using the class. Focus on just getting a feel for what the class offers. You'll get the details down later on after some practice with the code.

Main Method Details

The class' main methods are listed as follows. We have a pretty standard set of constructors and cloning, comparison, and drawing routine methods. These should all look familiar to you by now. You should have a solid idea of how each method is used just based on its type and name.

Listing 7-11. MmgPositionTween Main Method Details 1

```
public MmgPositionTween(MmgObj subj, float msTimeToMove, MmgVector2
startPos, MmgVector2 finishPos) { ... }

public MmgPositionTween(MmgPositionTween obj) { ... }
public MmgObj Clone() { ... }
public MmgPositionTween CloneTyped() { ... }
public void MmgDraw(MmgPen p) { ... }
public boolean MmgUpdate(int updateTick, long currentTimeMs, long
msSinceLastFrame) { ... }

public boolean ApiEquals(MmgPositionTween obj) { ... }
```

The first entry is the class' default constructor. You can use this to create a new instance of the class configured and ready to use. The second constructor is the specialized constructor we've come to know and love. This constructor takes an MmgPositionTween instance as an argument and uses it to create a new, unique copy of the object. The cloning methods create a new, unique copy of the class using the specialized constructor.

The MmgUpdate and MmgDraw methods take responsibility for updating and drawing the animation. The MmgDraw method is very simple; it just draws the subject on the screen at its specified position. The MmgUpdate method is a bit more complicated and needs to be called each frame in order for the animation to work properly. This method updates the position of the subject based on the number of pixels that the object needs to move each frame on the X and Y axes. The ApiEquals method provides API-level comparison between two MmgPositionTween objects.

Demonstration: MmgPositionTween Class

The demonstration code for this class is from the LoadResources method of the ScreenTestMmgPositionTween class in the MmgTestSpace library. I'll cover loading and initializing the resources used by the class, as well as the event handler and the drawing methods.

Listing 7-12. MmgPositionTween Class Demonstration 1

```
01 frame1 = MmgHelper.GetBasicCachedBmp("soldier_frame_1.png");
02 frame1 = MmgBmpScaler.ScaleMmgBmp(frame1, 2.0f, true);
03 MmgHelper.CenterHorAndVert(frame1);
04
05 frame2 = MmgHelper.GetBasicCachedBmp("soldier_frame_2.png");
06 frame2 = MmgBmpScaler.ScaleMmgBmp(frame2, 2.0f, true);
07 MmgHelper.CenterHorAndVert(frame2);
08
09 frame3 = MmgHelper.GetBasicCachedBmp("soldier_frame_3.png");
10 frame3 = MmgBmpScaler.ScaleMmgBmp(frame3, 2.0f, true);
11 MmgHelper.CenterHorAndVert(frame3);
12
13 frames = new MmgBmp[4];
14 frames[0] = frame1;
15 frames[1] = frame2;
16 frames[2] = frame3;
17 frames[3] = frame2;
18
19 MmgVector2 tmpPos = frame1.GetPosition().Clone();
20 tmpPos.SetY(tmpPos.GetY() + MmgHelper.ScaleValue(15));
21 sprite = new MmgSprite(frames, tmpPos);
22 sprite.SetFrameTime(200l);
23 AddObj(sprite);
24
25 posTweenLabel = MmgFontData.CreateDefaultBoldMmgFontLg();
26 posTweenLabel.SetText("MmgSprite Example with 4 Frames Attached to an
   MmgPositionTween");
27 MmgHelper.CenterHorAndVert(posTweenLabel);
28 posTweenLabel.SetY(GetY() + MmgHelper.ScaleValue(70));
29 AddObj(posTweenLabel);
30
```

```
31 MmgVector2 start = new MmgVector2(MmgHelper.ScaleValue(100), GetY() +
   (GetHeight() - frame1.GetHeight()) / 2);
32 MmgVector2 stop = new MmgVector2(GetWidth() - MmgHelper.ScaleValue(100),
   GetY() + (GetHeight() - frame1.GetHeight()) / 2);
33
34 posTween = new MmgPositionTween(sprite, 10000, start, stop);
35 posTween.SetOnReachStart(this);
36 posTween.SetOnReachFinish(this);
37 posTween.SetMsStartMove(System.currentTimeMillis());
38 posTween.SetMoving(true);
```

The snippet of code listed in the preceding shows you how to load and set up the MmgSprite class that we'll use as the subject of the MmgPositionTween. On lines 1–11, in three similar blocks of code, the image resources are loaded, scaled up 100%, and positioned at the center of the screen. An array with four images is created and initialized on lines 13–17.

Now that we have the resource loaded, we need the start and stop positions for the position tween, lines 31 and 32. The position tween is initialized with the MmgSprite object as the subject. Think about why we can do this. A ten-second animation time and the start and stop vectors are used as constructor arguments. The class' event handlers are set on lines 35 and 36; both are set to the current game screen. The start time is set on line 37, and the position tween is marked as moving on line 38. This will start the animation.

Listing 7-13. MmgPositionTween Class Demonstration 2

```
01 public void MmgDraw(MmgPen p) {
02     if (pause == false && isVisible == true) {
03         super.MmgDraw(p);
04     }
05 }
```

```
01 public boolean MmgUpdate(int updateTick, long currentTimeMs, long
   msSinceLastFrame) {
02     lret = false;
03
```

```
04    if (pause == false && isVisible == true) {
05        //always run this update
06        posTween.MmgUpdate(updateTick, currentTimeMs, msSinceLastFrame);
07        sprite.MmgUpdate(updateTick, currentTimeMs, msSinceLastFrame);
08    }
09
10    return lret;
11 }
```

```
01 public void MmgHandleEvent(MmgEvent e) {
02    MmgHelper.wr("ScreenTestMmgPositionTween.HandleMmgEvent: Msg: " +
      e.GetMessage() + " Id: " + e.GetEventId());
03    eventLabel.SetText("Event: " + e.GetMessage() + " Id: " +
      e.GetEventId() + " Type: " + e.GetEventType());
04    MmgHelper.CenterHor(eventLabel);
05    if(e.GetEventId() == MmgPositionTween.MMG_POSITION_TWEEN_REACH_
      FINISH) {
06        posTween.SetDirStartToFinish(false);
07        posTween.SetMsStartMove(System.currentTimeMillis());
08        posTween.SetMoving(true);
09
10    } else {
11        posTween.SetDirStartToFinish(true);
12        posTween.SetMsStartMove(System.currentTimeMillis());
13        posTween.SetMoving(true);
14
15    }
16 }
```

The next snippet of demonstration code for us to review are the
ScreenTestMmgPositionTween class' MmgDraw, MmgUpdate, and MmgHandleEvent
methods. Notice how simple the MmgDraw method is. All the objects that are drawn to
the screen are part of the screen's list of drawable objects, so all the drawing is done for
us, for free. The MmgUpdate method has a little more meat to it. Notice that we force the
sprite and the position tween to update every frame by calling their update methods
directly. This ensures that the animation updates happen on every frame.

The last method in the snippet listed in the preceding is the `MmgHandleEvent` method. This method is configured to receive both start and finish events from the position tween class. Notice that when it receives a finish event, it restarts the position tween animation in reverse from the finish position to the start position, lines 6–8. Similarly, when the start event is received, the method will reset the position tween again, lines 11–13. This ensures the position tween keeps running indefinitely. It's also a nice little example of the class' events.

Chapter Conclusion

In this chapter, we completed a review of the MmgBase API's animation classes. The classes we've covered demonstrate two different types of class-based animation. The `MmgPulse` class exemplified a hands-off approach in which the class was responsible only for animating numeric values that would then be applied to an on-screen object.

The `MmgPositionTween` and `MmgSizeTween` classes are examples of a hands-on approach to object animation. These classes are part of the drawable set of objects and handle all their own drawing and updating logic.

- MmgPulse: An API class for animating a numeric value by changing it over time. The resulting series of values can be used to drive object position animations among others.

- MmgPositionTween/MmgSizeTween: An API class for animating an object over time by either adjusting its position, in the case of the MmgPositionTween class, or its size, in the case of the MmgSizeTween class.

The animation classes we've reviewed demonstrate how high-level complex classes can interact to create new and exciting functionality. For instance, in the example code for the `MmgPositionTween` class, we used an `MmgSprite` object as the subject for the position tween; and as such we ended up with an animation, the position tween, animating another animation, the sprite object.

Stop and think about why we're able to do this. The game engine is designed such that classes can work together easily. We also saw how simple it was to use these new, complex, animation classes. All we had to do was add them to the current screen's list of drawable objects and make sure their update method is called each frame if need be. It's that easy.

CHAPTER 8

Game Screen Classes

In this chapter, we'll review the MmgBase API's game screen classes. These are the base classes for more advanced and concrete game screen implementations. There are three classes, one for a splash screen, one for a loading screen, and one for a general screen that supports a menu system.

These classes are very important because they are the connection point at which the MmgBase API interacts with the MmgCore API. The game panel class is responsible for sending the current game screen update and draw method calls as well as input method calls. The current game screen is an instance of the MmgGameScreen class:

- MmgSplashScreen

- MmgLoadingScreen

- MmgGameScreen

Game Screen Classes: MmgSplashScreen

The MmgSplashScreen class provides a foundation for creating game splash screens. The screen is designed to display for a few seconds; then it fires an event that should be caught by the game panel class, which should respond by changing states to the loading screen.

I should mention that this class extends the MmgGameScreen class and implements the MmgUpdateHandler so that the class can receive update events from the splash screen timer. The MmgGameScreen class extends the MmgObj class, so even at this level, the game screen is part of the set of drawable objects and is specially configured to plug into the game panel class to facilitate drawing the current game screen at the desired frame rate.

© Victor G Brusca 2021
V. G. Brusca, *Introduction to Video Game Engine Development*, https://doi.org/10.1007/978-1-4842-7039-4_8

Static Class Members

The class has only one static class field listed as follows.

Listing 8-1. MmgSplashScreen Static Class Members 1

```
public static int DEFAULT_DISPLAY_TIME_MS = 3000;
```

This field controls the amount of time, in milliseconds, that the splash screen will display.

Class Fields

The MmgSplashScreen class has two class fields for us to review.

Listing 8-2. MmgSplashScreen Class Fields 1

```
private int displayTime;
private MmgUpdateHandler update;
```

The first field listed, displayTime, holds the number of milliseconds to display the splash screen before firing an event indicating the display period is over. The second class field, update, is the handler designed to receive and process update events.

Support Method Details

The MmgSplashScreen support methods are very simple and direct. There are two sets of get and set methods I've listed in the following group in the same order as their corresponding class fields.

Listing 8-3. MmgSplashScreen Support Method Details 1

```
public int GetDisplayTime() { ... }
public void SetDisplayTime(int i) { ... }
public MmgUpdateHandler GetUpdateHandler() { ... }
public void SetUpdateHandler(MmgUpdateHandler Update) { ... }
```

These methods are very direct, so I won't cover them in any detail here. Let's move on to the class' main methods.

Main Method Details

The main methods we have to review for the MmgSplashScreen class are listed in the following grouping. These are standard main methods we've seen before during the API review. One method that stands out, however, is the MmgHandleUpdate method. This method is designed to receive an event from the timer thread and pass it onto the game panel so that the next game screen can be displayed.

Listing 8-4. MmgSplashScreen Main Method Details 1

```
//Constructors
public MmgSplashScreen() { ... }
public MmgSplashScreen(int DisplayTime) { ... }
public MmgSplashScreen(MmgSplashScreen obj) { ... }

//Cloning methods
public MmgObj Clone() { ... }
public MmgSplashScreen CloneTyped() { ... }

//Event handler method
public void MmgHandleUpdate(Object obj) { ... }

//General main methods
public void MmgDraw(MmgPen p) { ... }
public boolean ApiEquals(MmgSplashScreen obj) { ... }
```

The first two constructors use the default display time and a user-specified display time, respectively. They will create a bare-bones class that displays default images and is ready for use. The third constructor is a specialized constructor that takes an MmgSplashScreen object as an argument and uses it to create a new, unique copy of the class.

The cloning methods follow the standard pattern of providing a basic clone method and a clone method that returns an MmgSplashScreen type. The MmgHandleUpdate method receives an event from the splash screen timing class and then fires an event that gets sent to the game panel class where it should trigger a game screen change from the splash screen to the loading screen.

The last two methods listed in the preceding are standard main methods MmgDraw and ApiEquals. The draw method is called as part of the game engine's default drawing routine. The ApiEquals method is an API-level comparison method that compares two MmgSplashScreen objects for equality.

Demonstration: MmgSplashScreen Class

For the MmgSplashScreen class' demonstration section, we'll take a look at the MmgCore API's implementation of the ScreenSplash class that extends the MmgBase API's MmgSplashScreen class. This should give us a good example of the class in use.

This is the first time we'll do a class review as part of a demonstration section. Just to be clear, the following subsections are for the ScreenSplash class of the MmgCore API.

Demo Review: Static Class Members

The MmgCore API's ScreenSplash class has one static class field listed in the following.

Listing 8-5. Demo Review: ScreenSplash Static Class Members 1

```
public static int EVENT_DISPLAY_COMPLETE = 0;
```

The EVENT_DISPLAY_COMPLETE field is used to mark an event to indicate the splash screen is done displaying.

Demo Review: Class Fields

The ScreenSplash's fields are listed in the following. There are four fields for us to review. Remember, this class extends the MmgGameScreen class, so it picks up a lot of functionality from that class for free.

Listing 8-6. Demo Review: ScreenSplash Class Fields 1

```
public GameStates state;
public GenericEventHandler handler;
public GamePanel owner;
public Hashtable<String, MmgCfgFileEntry> classConfig;
```

The first field listed holds the game state associated with the splash screen. Because the ScreenSplash implementation is more concrete, it's actually used in an application; it has fields that help associate the game screen with an identifying value. The second class field is an event handler that is used to process MmgBase API's generic events. This event handler will receive an event indicating the splash screen is done displaying.

The third field, owner, is an instance of the GamePanel class and is meant to indicate the game panel that holds the game screen. The game panel class is part of the MmgCore API; it's not a class we've reviewed thus far. The final entry in the preceding list is the classConfig field, which is used to store any class config data available. The config file is loaded as part of the class' load resources method. The values found, if any, are used to adjust how the game screen is displayed.

Demo Review: Support Method Details

The ScreenSplash class' support methods are listed in the following group. There are only three methods for us to review.

Listing 8-7. Demo Review: ScreenSplash Support Method Details 1

```
public void SetGenericEventHandler(GenericEventHandler Handler) { ... }

public GenericEventHandler GetGenericEventHandler() { ... }

public GameStates GetGameState() { ... }
```

The first two methods listed are basic get and set methods that give you access to the class' handler field. This field is used to send events to the specified handler when the display time for the game screen is up. The final support method listed simply returns the gameState associated with the screen.

Demo Review: Main Method Details

The class' main methods are listed in the following. These methods should look similar to some of the methods we've encountered during the demonstration sections of the MmgBase API review.

Listing 8-8. Demo Review: ScreenSplash Main Method Details 1

```
public ScreenSplash(GameStates State, GamePanel Owner) { ... }

public void LoadResources() { ... }
public void UnloadResources() { ... }
public void MmgHandleUpdate(Object obj) { ... }
public void MmgDraw(MmgPen p) { ... }
```

The class constructor defines the screen's game state and the game panel that the screen belongs to. The LoadResources method is used to prepare the resources used by the game screen before it's drawn. The UnloadResources method is used to clear the class' loaded resources.

The MmgHandleUpdate class is used to handle update events from the splash screen's timer. Lastly, the MmgDraw method is used to draw the game screen. I should mention that the MmgGameScreen class extends the MmgObj class. So even at this level, the MmgObj class is driving the underlying functionality.

This class demonstrates extending a general MmgBase API class and customizing it for use in an application or game. During the customization, the class becomes more concrete and less general as it plugs into the existing application infrastructure.

Game Screen Classes: MmgLoadingScreen

The MmgLoadingScreen class is another high-level class in the MmgBase API. The class is used to run the game engine's default resource loading process. Much like the MmgSplashScreen class that extends the MmgGameScreen class and provides a loose implementation of a splash screen, the MmgLoadingScreen class also extends the MmgGameScreen class and provides a loose implementation of a loading screen.

I describe the implementation as loose only because the class hasn't been plugged into a runtime environment, so it's left somewhat open as to how the class can be used. When we cover an implementation example of this class in the demonstration section, you'll see a more concrete implementation of the screen that is designed to plug into the game engine's default runtime.

Class Fields

The MmgLoadingScreen class has two fields for use to review.

Listing 8-9. MmgLoadingScreen Class Fields 1

```
private MmgLoadingBar loadingBar;
private float loadingBarOffsetBottom = 0.10f;
```

The first field is a loading bar class instance that will be used to indicate the progress of the game's resource load. The second field listed is used to adjust the position of the loading bar by a percentage of the loading screen's height.

Support Method Details

The MmgLoadingScreen's support methods provide access to the class' fields. You can get and set the loading bar and get access to the loading bar offset value.

Listing 8-10. MmgLoadingScreen Support Method Details 1

```
public MmgLoadingBar GetLoadingBar() { ... }
public void SetLoadingBar(MmgLoadingBar lb, float lBarOff) { ... }

public float GetLoadingBarOffsetBottom() { ... }
```

The support methods are very simple and direct, so I won't go into any more detail about them here. Make sure to look them over and understand how they're used.

Main Method Details

The class' main methods comprise a standard assortment of constructors, cloning methods, and general main methods. Many of these methods should look familiar from the previous class reviews we have done.

Listing 8-11. MmgLoadingScreen Main Method Details 1

```
//Constructors
public MmgLoadingScreen() { ... }
public MmgLoadingScreen(MmgLoadingBar LoadingBar, float lBarOff) { ... }
```

```
public MmgLoadingScreen(MmgLoadingScreen obj) { ... }

//Cloning methods
public MmgObj Clone() { ... }
public MmgLoadingScreen CloneTyped() { ... }

//General main methods
public void MmgDraw(MmgPen p) { ... }
public boolean ApiEquals(MmgLoadingScreen obj) { ... }
```

The first constructor takes no arguments and creates a new instance of the class that is not ready for use. Some further customizations regarding the loading bar are required. Fortunately, there is a second constructor option that takes a loading bar and a positioning offset as arguments. This constructor creates a new class instance that is ready to use.

The third constructor listed is a specialized constructor that takes an MmgLoadingScreen object as an argument and uses it to create a new, unique copy of the object. The next two methods, cloning methods, provide class cloning functionality. These methods use the specialized constructor to create a copy of the current class and then return that copy cast to the specified type.

Last but not least are the draw method, MmgDraw, and the comparison method, ApiEquals. The draw method is called as part of the game engine's default drawing routine, as we've seen before. The ApiEquals method is an API-level comparison method used to check for equality between two MmgLoadingScreen instances.

Demonstration: MmgLoadingScreen Class

For the MmgLoadingScreen class' demonstration section, we'll take a look at the MmgCore API's implementation of the ScreenLoading class that extends the MmgBase API's MmgLoadingScreen class. This will give us a great example of the class in use. Just to be clear, the following subsections are for the review of the ScreenLoading class from the MmgCore API.

Demo Review: Static Class Members

Similarly to the ScreenSplash class, the MmgCore API's ScreenLoading class has one static field for us to cover.

Listing 8-12. Demo Review: ScreenLoading Static Class Members 1

```
public static int EVENT_LOAD_COMPLETE = 0;
```

The EVENT_LOAD_COMPLETE field is used to indicate in an event that the resource load has finished. The event is meant to be processed by the game panel class causing it to change the current screen from the loading screen to the main menu screen.

Demo Review: Class Fields

The ScreenLoading class has a few class fields that it uses to extend the functionality of the super class, the MmgLoadingScreen class, to perform an actual resource load.

Listing 8-13. Demo Review: ScreenLoading Class Fields 1

```
public GameStates state;
public GamePanel owner;
public long slowDown;
public RunResourceLoad datLoad;
public GenericEventHandler handler;
public Hashtable<String, MmgCfgFileEntry> classConfig;
```

The state and owner fields are set by the class constructor and are used to create the association between the game screen and the game panel class. The slowDown field is used to add a delay, in milliseconds, to the resource loading process. This can be helpful when you're only loading a few resources but want to see the loading progress.

The datLoad field is an instance of the RunResourceLoad class, and it's used to run the resource load on its own thread. The handler field is a generic event handler, and it's used to send a resource load complete event to the game panel class so that it can respond by changing game screens to the main menu. The ScreenLoading class implements the LoadResourceUpdateHandler interface.

This means that the class receives updates on the progress of the resource load and uses that data to set the loading bar's value. The last entry listed in the preceding is the classConfig field. This is a private class field used to hold config file data if any is found. The data is used to customize the display of the game screen.

Demo Review: Support Method Details

The first set of support methods I'd like to discuss are related to the resource load process. Take a moment to look over the following methods.

Listing 8-14. Demo Review: ScreenLoading Support Method Details 1

```
public RunResourceLoad GetLoader() { ... }
public void SetLoader(RunResourceLoad DatLoad) { ... }

public long GetSlowDown() { ... }
public void SetSlowDown(long l) { ... }
public boolean GetLoadResult() { ... }
public boolean GetLoadComplete() { ... }
```

The preceding first two entries give you access to the resource loader. This class is meant to be run in a separate thread. The following two methods are the access methods for the slowDown field. The last two methods are used to return information about the loading process. The GetLoadResult method returns a Boolean indicator regarding the last read operation's result. The GetLoadComplete method returns true if the resource loading process has completed.

Listing 8-15. Demo Review: ScreenLoading Support Method Details 2

```
public GameStates GetGameState() { ... }
public GenericEventHandler GetGenericEventHandler() { ... }

public void SetGenericEventHandler(GenericEventHandler Handler) { ... }
```

The next support method to discuss is the GetGameState method. This method returns the game state that the game screen is associated with. The game panel class uses the game state values to track the different game screens in a game or application.

Demo Review: Main Method Details

The ScreenLoading class has the following main methods.

Listing 8-16. Demo Review: ScreenLoading Main Method Details 1

```
//Constructors
public ScreenLoading(MmgLoadingBar LoadingBar, float lBarOff, GameStates
State, GamePanel Owner) { ... }

public ScreenLoading(GameStates State, GamePanel Owner) { ... }

//Class prep/clean methods
public void LoadResources() { ... }
public void UnloadResources() { ... }

//Resource loading methods
public boolean GetResourceFileData() { ... }
public void StartDatLoad() { ... }
public void StopDatLoad() { ... }

//General main methods
public void HandleUpdate(LoadResourceUpdateMessage obj) { ... }

public void MmgDraw(MmgPen p) { ... }
```

The first constructor listed takes a full set of arguments and uses them to initialize pertinent class fields. This constructor will create a new ScreenLoading class that is ready to use. The second constructor listed takes fewer arguments and only sets the gameState and owner fields.

The class has the same preparation method as every game screen class we've reviewed thus far, the LoadResources method. This method is used to prepare the screen for use. The UnloadResources method should be the reverse of the LoadResources method and clean out any resources that were loaded.

The next group of main methods listed in the preceding are the loading methods. These methods are involved with the resource loading process. The GetResourceFileData method returns true if there are some resources to load. The StartDatLoad method begins the resource loading process by starting the threaded loading class, datLoad. Similarly, the StopDatLoad method stops the resource loading process.

The last two methods to review are the HandleUpdate method and the MmgDraw method. The HandleUpdate method is configured to receive update events from the resource loading process. When the method detects that the resource load has completed, it will send a generic event to the registered generic event handler.

This should be the game panel class. The final entry in the preceding set is the MmgDraw method. This is a standard method implementation that just calls the super class, base class in C#, to ensure default drawing functionality is used. That concludes the class' main method review. Up next, we'll take a look at the MmgGameScreen class.

Game Screen Classes: MmgGameScreen

The MmgGameScreen class is the super class of the MmgSplashScreen and the MmgLoadingScreen. Much like the splash and loading screens, the MmgGameScreen class is a loose implementation of a game screen offering a lot of features but requiring few to be implemented. This gives you the best setup with regard to flexibility.

The MmgGameScreen class is a subclass of the MmgObj class. In this way, all of the game screen classes in the MmgBase API are also MmgObj instances. They are all part of the set of drawable objects. The screen classes represent the apex level of class functionality in the MmgBase API. These classes are at the top of the rendering chain in this API. But take a moment to think about them and how we use them. They are really just like any other MmgObj-based class we've worked with.

Class Fields

The MmgGameScreen class is the core game screen class of the MmgBase API. The class has a number of fields listed in the following in groups.

Listing 8-17. MmgGameScreen Class Fields 1

```
//Render control fields
public boolean pause;
public boolean ready;

//Screen feature fields
private MmgContainer objects;
private MmgObj background;
```

```
private MmgObj foreground;
private MmgObj header;
private MmgObj footer;
private MmgObj message;

//Menu fields
private MmgMenuContainer menu;
private MmgObj leftCursor;
private MmgObj rightCursor;
private int menuIdx;
private int menuStart;
private int menuStop;
private int menuCursorLeftOffsetX;
private int menuCursorLeftOffsetY;
private int menuCursorRightOffsetX;
private int menuCursorRightOffsetY;
private boolean menuOn;

//Event field
private MmgUpdateHandler updateHandler;
```

Because there are such a large number of fields, we are going to have a large number
of support methods to review. I'll try and shorten the review of the class fields and
support methods when possible. The first group of fields are for controlling the rendering
of the class. Screens that are paused or not ready won't be rendered or updated unless
coded to specifically do so.

The second group of fields contains all of the drawable features of the screen that
aren't directly associated with the menu. As you can see, there are placeholders for a
number of different features of the game screen. You can choose not to use any of these
and set them to null.

The third group of fields are the menu fields. The first entry is the menu container,
menu. The next two entries can be used to set a left- and right-hand-side menu cursor.
You can choose to implement just one side if you want. You should implement at least
one of them though so the user can easily see where they are in the menu system.

The menuIdx, menuStart, and menuStop fields are used to control which menu items
are active in the current menu. The next four entries are for fine-tuning the positioning
of the menu cursors, and lastly a Boolean flag controls if the menu is on or off. If you

aren't implementing a menu, set this Boolean to false and make sure the menu field is null. The last field in the list is an update event handler for processing update events like those from the splash or loading screen. The class' update method is used to send events to the handler specified by this field.

Support Method Details

The MmgGameScreen class has a laundry list of support methods. I've listed them in the following grouping and in the same order as their corresponding class fields. New methods that don't associate to a class field have been inserted where appropriate. Take a look at the methods in the following listing and make sure you understand them.

Listing 8-18. MmgGameScreen Support Method Details 1

```
//Render control methods
public boolean IsReady() { ... }
public void SetReady(boolean b) { ... }
public void Pause() { ... }
public void UnPause() { ... }
public boolean IsPaused() { ... }

//Screen feature methods
public MmgContainer GetObjects() { ... }
public void SetObjects(MmgContainer c) { ... }
public void AddObj(MmgObj obj) { ... }
public void RemoveObj(MmgObj obj) { ... }
public void ClearObjs() { ... }
public MmgObj GetBackground() { ... }
public void SetBackground(MmgObj b) { ... }
public void SetCenteredBackground(MmgObj b) { ... }
public void CenterObjects() { ... }
public MmgObj GetForeground() { ... }
public void SetForeground(MmgObj b) { ... }
public MmgObj GetHeader() { ... }
public void SetHeader(MmgObj m) { ... }
public MmgObj GetFooter() { ... }
```

```
public void SetFooter(MmgObj m) { ... }
public MmgObj GetMessage() {
public void SetMessage(MmgObj m) { ... }

//Menu methods
public MmgMenuContainer GetMenu() { ... }
public void SetMenu(MmgMenuContainer m) { ... }
public MmgObj GetLeftCursor() { ... }
public void SetLeftCursor(MmgObj m) { ... }
public MmgObj GetRightCursor() { ... }
public void SetRightCursor(MmgObj m) { ... }
public int GetMenuIdx() { ... }
public void SetMenuIdx(int i) { ... }
public int GetMenuStart() { ... }
public void SetMenuStart(int i) { ... }
public int GetMenuStop() { ... }
public void SetMenuStop(int i) { ... }
public int GetMenuCursorLeftOffsetX() { ... }
public void SetMenuCursorLeftOffsetX(int i) { ... }
public int GetMenuCursorLeftOffsetY() { ... }
public void SetMenuCursorLeftOffsetY(int i) { ... }
public int GetMenuCursorRightOffsetX() { ... }
public void SetMenuCursorRightOffsetX(int i) { ... }
public int GetMenuCursorRightOffsetY() { ... }
public void SetMenuCursorRightOffsetY(int i) { ... }
public boolean GetMenuOn() { ... }
public void SetMenuOn(boolean m) { ... }

//Event methods
public void SetMmgUpdateHandler(MmgUpdateHandler u) { ... }

public MmgUpdateHandler GetMmgUpdateHandler() { ... }
```

We won't review all these support methods in detail here. They are simple get and set methods for the most part. However, there are a few entries I'd like to quickly discuss. The AddObj, RemoveObj, and ClearObjs methods give you more granular control over the child objects without having to use the GetObjects method. We've seen the AddObj method time and time again. This is the underlying class method that was actually being called the entire time.

The SetCenteredBackground and CenterObjects methods are support methods that provide a quick way to center the class' features. This is a common task, so these methods help speed things up. The SetCenteredBackground method sets the background and centers it. Similarly, the CenterObjects method centers all of the class features except for the menu.

All of the remaining methods are basic get and set methods that line up directly with their associated class fields, so we'll move on to the class' input methods.

Input Method Details

We've never had to create a section like this before, but there are so many input handling methods that I decided to give them a section of their own. They are self-explanatory, so I won't talk about them in any detail. As you read through them, think about using them in your next game.

Listing 8-19. MmgGameScreen Input Method Details 1

```
//Mouse move methods
public boolean ProcessMouseMove(int x, int y) { ... }
public boolean ProcessMouseMove(MmgVector2 v) { ... }

//Mouse button methods
public boolean ProcessMousePress(MmgVector2 v) { ... }

public boolean ProcessMousePress(MmgVector2 v, int btnIndex) { ... }

public boolean ProcessMousePress(int x, int y) { ... }

public boolean ProcessMousePress(int x, int y, int btnIndex) { ... }

public boolean ProcessMouseRelease(MmgVector2 v) { ... }

public boolean ProcessMouseRelease(MmgVector2 v, int btnIndex) { ... }

public boolean ProcessMouseRelease(int x, int y) { ... }

public boolean ProcessMouseRelease(int x, int y, int btnIndex) { ... }
```

```
public boolean ProcessMouseClick(MmgVector2 v) { ... }

public boolean ProcessMouseClick(MmgVector2 v, int btnIndex) { ... }

public boolean ProcessMouseClick(int x, int y) { ... }

public boolean ProcessMouseClick(int x, int y, int btnIndex) { ... }

//A button methods
public boolean ProcessAPress(int src) { ... }
public boolean ProcessARelease(int src) { ... }
public boolean ProcessAClick(int src) { ... }
public boolean ProcessBPress(int src) { ... }
public boolean ProcessBRelease(int src) { ... }
public boolean ProcessBClick(int src) { ... }

//Keyboard key methods
public boolean ProcessKeyPress(char c, int code) { ... }

public boolean ProcessKeyRelease(char c, int code) { ... }

public boolean ProcessKeyClick(char c, int code) { ... }

//D-Pad button methods
public boolean ProcessDpadPress(int dir) { ... }
public boolean ProcessDpadRelease(int dir) { ... }
public boolean ProcessDpadClick(int dir) { ... }

//Debug method
public void ProcessDebugClick() { ... }
```

The only method I'd like to talk about is the ProcessDebugClick method. This method is mapped to the keyboard's "D" key by default, and if pressed it will call the game screen's ProcessDebugClick method. This is a great place to enter in some debugging code that prints information to standard output.

Main Method Details

The MmgGameScreen class' main methods are grouped and listed as follows.

Listing 8-20. MmgGameScreen Main Method Details 1

```
//Constructors
public MmgGameScreen() { ... }
public MmgGameScreen(MmgGameScreen obj) { ... }

//Cloning Methods
public MmgObj Clone() { ... }
public MmgGameScreen CloneTyped() { ... }

//Event Methods
public void EventHandler(MmgEvent e) { ... }

//General Main Methods
public boolean ApiEquals(MmgGameScreen obj) { ... }
public void Update(Object data) { ... }
public void MmgDraw(MmgPen p) { ... }
public boolean MmgUpdate(int updateTick, long currentTimeMs, long
msSinceLastFrame) { ... }

//Menu Methods
public void MoveMenuSelUp() { ... }
public void MoveMenuSelDown() { ... }
private void DrawMenu(MmgPen p) { ... }
public void ProcessMenuItemSel(MmgMenuItem item) { ... }
```

The first constructor takes no arguments and creates a clean new game screen ready for you to use. It won't do much, but it's ready to go. The second entry is a specialized constructor that takes an MmgGameScreen object as an argument and uses it to make a new, unique copy of the object. This constructor supports the cloning methods in the next group. These cloning methods use the specialized constructor and cast the resulting object to the specified type before returning.

The next method lets you set the game screen's event handler. This is wired by default to handle using the menu if enabled. The ApiEquals method is an API-level comparison method that determines if two MmgGameScreen objects are equal. The MmgDraw and MmgUpdate methods are part of the game engine's drawing routine and are responsible for updating the object and rendering it. The update method is configured to fire the updateHandler with the given event data.

The last group of main methods are responsible for processing menu input, menu up and down events, drawing the menu, and selecting a menu item. That wraps up the class' main method review.

Demonstration: MmgGameScreen Class

Because the MmgGameScreen class is the super class, base class in C#, of all MmgBase API screen classes and all MmgCore screen classes, I recommend going over the MmgSplashScreen, MmgLoadingScreen, and their respective demonstration sections as a solid example of the MmgGameScreen class in use.

Chapter Conclusion

In this chapter, we completed a review of the MmgBase API's game screen classes. These classes represent the apex of functionality in the MmgBase API. The classes also represent the point of functionality in the MmgBase API that interacts directly with the MmgCore API via the game panel class.

Keep in mind that these classes, like many of the classes in the MmgBase API, are loosely defined. This means you'll most likely have to extend their functionality and adjust the class so that it works with your design goals. In this case, we saw the MmgCore API's ScreenSplash and ScreenLoading classes as examples of a concrete implementation of the game screens. Let's take a look at a summary of the classes we've reviewed:

- MmgSplashScreen: An API class for representing a game's splash screen. This class is designed to display a logo for a few seconds before firing a finishing event.

- MmgLoadingScreen: An API class for representing a game's loading screen. This class is loosely defined and doesn't enforce a resource loading structure.

- MmgGameScreen: An API class for representing a game screen as you would see on any 2D video game. This class has a number of features that can be turned off to simplify its rendering.

You should start to see the structure of the game engine now that we've finished reviewing all the major classes in the engine's MmgBase API. These classes constitute a set of tools designed to work around the MmgObj class facilitating the advanced interaction of the API's set of drawable classes. We've seen how easy it is to add new functionality to the API while still maintaining the ability to plug directly into the game engine's drawing routine.

I should mention that you will want to be careful when implementing a new game screen for the first time. Be sure to understand how your game screen's underlying class handles update and draw calls. Some screen classes may be designed to only update when the isDirty field is set to true. Some objects and screens require the class to update on every frame, so be aware of this, or you'll end up scratching your head wondering why your objects aren't animating.

PART 2

CHAPTER 9

MmgCore API Introduction

Part 2 of this book contains a comprehensive review of the game engine's runtime code. This code exists in both Java and C# and is included in the main project under the MmgCore package, or namespace if you're following along in C#. The MmgCore API is responsible for handling command-line arguments, processing game engine config files, creating the game's window, routing input, managing game screens, and much, much more.

In many game engine implementations, there is a "player" designed to run the compiled game code. In our implementation, the runtime code is included as part of the compiled game. This is done by including all of the core functionality of the game engine in the MmgCore API. Thus, any game created will include all of the runtime code, and that allows you to control it and customize it as needed. In the end, I think it was the better decision to make the runtime code more available and part of the game.

Runtime API Overview

Before we get into a detailed code review, let's talk a little bit about the MmgCore API. This API has the most differences between the C#/MonoGame and the Java/Swing implementations. Although both APIs are functionally equivalent, there are a few major differences between the two implementations I'd like to discuss.

One major difference between the two implementations is that the `MainFrame` class doesn't exist in the C# implementation. This is because the Java implementation uses Swing to drive the windowing for the game and there is a concept of a frame to hold the game panel. In the C# implementation, there is no main frame, and that functionality has been moved into a hybrid game panel class.

© Victor G Brusca 2021
V. G. Brusca, *Introduction to Video Game Engine Development*, https://doi.org/10.1007/978-1-4842-7039-4_9

You'll find that equivalent methods exist for both implementations and that the same code exists just in a slightly different location. In any case, it should still be very easy to follow along in C#. Another difference between the implementations I should mention is that in the C# version certain actions cannot be performed on a thread. This is because the actions require access to the graphics context, which is not thread-safe. In the C# version, a set of classes, designed to move the work from the child thread to the main thread, are used to overcome this limitation.

The next difference I'd like to mention is that the unit tests also need access to the graphics context. To overcome this limitation, the unit tests are executed from the main game thread via a command-line argument. The test output is dumped to standard output.

There is potential for having different keyboard codes between different operating systems and certainly between the C# and Java implementations. To overcome this limitation, there is a global flag that enables a key code conversion method to be called. You can use this method to create a uniform set of keyboard codes. The setting can be found in the GameSettings class, specifically the INPUT_NORMALIZE_KEY_CODE field.

Similarly, the system fonts render a little bit differently across operating systems and between the C# and Java versions of the game engine. For the most part, you should be using images for your text and not MmgFont objects; but in any case, there is a global flag to turn on a font position adjustment method. This method will allow you to normalize font positioning between platforms. The flag can be found in the MmgPen class of the MmgBase API, specifically the FONT_NORMALIZE_POSITION field.

The last major difference I should mention are the fonts. In Java, fonts can be resized on the fly, and you can create different sized fonts as you see fit. In the C# version, the fonts have to be prepared ahead of time. To overcome this difference in the C# implementation, we load up default fonts from size 1 to size 50 and set a maximum font size of 50 for the game engine.

We can mimic the Java version's ability to create a new font instantly by preloading all the fonts that can be used. In this way, we overcome the technological differences between the two implementations. In this book, we'll mainly follow the Java code, but you should be able to follow along in C# without too much trouble. The following is a summary of the classes we'll cover in this part of the book.

Game Engine Settings

- DatConstantsEntry
- DatExternalStrings
- GameSettings
- GameSettingsImporter

Game Resource Loading Classes

- RunResourceLoad
- GenericEventHandler
- GenericEventMessage
- LoadResourceUpdateHandler
- LoadResourceUpdateMessage

Game Screens/Worker Threads

- RunFrameRate
- Screen
- ScreenMainMenu
- ScreenSplash
- ScreenLoading
- HandleMainMenuEvent

Static Entry Point/Windowing Classes

- MmgApiGame
- MainFrame
- GamePanel

Completing this part of the game engine review will give you the full picture. You'll be able to see in the code exactly where the MmgCore API hands off the work to the MmgBase API. You'll gain experience understanding how to customize the game engine and configure the resource directories to support multiple projects. Once you're done with this part of the text, you'll be ready to build some games!

CHAPTER 10

Static Main Entry Point

Now that you've reviewed the lower-level MmgBase API and you're adept at how the different classes work together to support aspects of game development, you're ready to take a look at the runtime API. The runtime API, MmgCore, is responsible for setting up the game's environment and resources. During this chapter, we'll review the following classes and topics:

- MmgApiGame

- MainFrame

- GamePanel

- Topic: Launching a Game

Static Main Entry Point: MmgApiGame

The MmgApiGame class is the entry point into your game. This is the code that is executed when your game is launched. This class, included in the MmgCore API, is an example of a game's fully configured static main entry point. This placeholder class won't run an actual game, but it will perform all the resource and configuration loading steps that an actual game would.

This class is designed to receive command-line arguments, set up the game's panel and window, and process game engine config files. A lot of work is done in this part of the game's code. We can use this class as a template for a game's static main entry point. Let's take a look at some code!

© Victor G Brusca 2021
V. G. Brusca, *Introduction to Video Game Engine Development*, https://doi.org/10.1007/978-1-4842-7039-4_10

Static Class Members

The MmgApiGame class has some important static class fields I've listed in the following grouping. As I've mentioned before, everything in this class is static, which makes sense because it's the static entry point. Take a look at the following fields before we get into the review process.

Listing 10-1. MmgApiGame Static Class Members 1

```
//Windowing fields
public static MainFrame mf;
public static GamePanel pnlGame;

//Frame rate fields
public static RunFrameRate fr;
public static Thread t;
public static long FPS = 16l;

//Window dimensions
public static int WIN_WIDTH = 858;
public static int WIN_HEIGHT = 600;
public static int PANEL_WIDTH = 854;
public static int PANEL_HEIGHT = 596;
public static int GAME_WIDTH = 854;
public static int GAME_HEIGHT = 416;

//Arguments and config
public static String[] ARGS = null;
public static String ENGINE_CONFIG_FILE = "../cfg/engine_config.xml";
```

The first group of fields are the windowing fields. They contain a MainFrame object and a GamePanel object. If you are following along with the C# code, you'll notice there is only a GamePanel field. The C#/MonoGame implementation of the game engine does not have an equivalent MainFrame class. That functionality has been merged into the GamePanel class. The next group of fields are used to control the game's frame rate.

In the Java version of the game, a worker thread is responsible for running a game frame every few milliseconds, depending on the frames per second you have set. That is what the fr, RunFrameRate, field is used for. The C# version of the game engine runs on top of MonoGame, which is much more suited for building games than Java Swing, so the frame rate is controlled internally by the MonoGame library. We only have to set the desired rate, and the rest is taken care of for us.

The Thread instance, t, is used in the Java implementation to run the frame rate worker in its own thread. The FPS field holds the current, desired frame rate. The game engine will attempt to achieve this frame rate, but it's not possible in all cases. It will depend heavily on the version of the game engine you're working with and the type of game you're making and its requirements. You don't want to set the frame rate so high that you cause issues with the system. So don't put in a frame rate of 1000!

When working in windowed mode and while an IDE is running, you'll want to use a conservative frame rate. It will generate fewer logs, take fewer resources, and still give you enough to accurately test and debug your game. That being said, if you have some exceptional frame rate requirements, you should test your game with the maximum number of objects and see how fast it runs.

The Java version of the engine should really only be used at around 30 frames or fewer. I develop with 18–24 FPS. For many of the games I make, I don't need 60 FPS at all. It's just not that kind of game. The C#/MonoGame version of the engine should be able to reach 60 FPS easily. You'll see even more improvement if you alter your game to run in full-screen mode. I don't think that the Java version has an equivalence to full-screen mode that also gives you the efficiency benefit of being the only program that is active. This is because in Java you can only pretend to be in full-screen mode when in actuality you have just maximized the view port.

The next group of fields define the dimensions. These fields describe the dimensions of each aspect of the game's windowing. The window dimensions describe the outer, OS-driven window the game runs in. The panel dimensions control the size of the window's contents. In most cases, the panel and the window should be the same size. Finally, the game has its own set of dimensions. These should fit inside the panel and window, but if they don't, the engine will try to scale the game dimensions so they do.

This can come in handy for testing a game with different screen sizes to get a feel for how it looks and runs, but you should have your dimensions configured such that the game does not need to be scaled. The last two fields have to do with game engine customization. The command-line arguments provided to the game are stored in the ARGS field. You can use the CLI arguments to alter the game's dimensions among other things.

The last entry is the game engine config file to process for configuration settings. This can be altered by a CLI argument so you can drive the game engine settings from the game's launch command. This lets you run custom game settings in a data-driven, dynamic fashion. Next, let's take a look at the static class methods.

Listing 10-2. MmgApiGame Static Class Members 2

```
//Entry Point
public static final void main(String[] args) { ... }

//Config Methods
public static String ArrayHasEntryLike(String v, String[] s) { ... }

public static void SetField(DatConstantsEntry ent, Field f) throws
Exception { ... }

//OS Support Methods
public static void RunOsSpecificCode() { ... }
public static void LoadNativeLibraries() { ... }
public static boolean isWindows(String OS) { ... }
public static boolean isMac(String OS) { ... }
public static boolean isUnix(String OS) { ... }
public static boolean isSolaris(String OS) { ... }
```

The first method listed is the static main entry point. It runs the following sequence of steps as the start of the runtime process:

1. Run OS-specific code – if enabled.

2. Load native libraries – if enabled.

3. Process command-line arguments.

4. Process the engine config file.

5. Initialize the main frame.

6. Initialize the game panel.

7. Start the frame rate worker thread.

The C# implementation runs the following sequence of steps that are just a little bit different:

1. Run OS-specific code – if enabled.

2. Load native libraries – if enabled.

3. Process command-line arguments.

4. Process the engine config file.

5. Initialize the game panel.

The `ArrayHasEntryLike` method is used to find entries in the list of command-line arguments. The engine supports the following CLI-driven properties out of the box:

- WIN_WIDTH

- WIN_HEIGHT

- PANEL_WIDTH

- PANEL_HEIGHT

- FPS

- ENGINE_CONFIG_FILE

You can easily add your own entries for your game's specific needs. The `SetField` method is used in game engine config file processing. As the file is processed, it will set the specified static field values in the specified class. The game engine supports the `GameSettings`, `MmgHelper`, and `MmgApiGame` classes out of the box. Again, you can add support for any game-specific classes you need.

The last group of methods are the OS support methods. These are used to determine which operating system the game is running on and to either run OS-specific code or to load the OS-specific libraries for gamepad support. The C# implementation does not require native library support because it has built-in gamepad support.

In Depth: MmgApiGame

The MmgCore API is a higher-level API than the MmgBase API we reviewed in Part 1. As such, the classes in this library are so specialized that they are often only used once. Sometimes it's difficult to show a demonstration of a class in use when it's only used in one place.

Instead of the usual demonstration section, we'll do an "in depth" section where we'll cover an aspect of the class we're reviewing in depth. The following snippet of code is from the end of the MainApiGame class' main method.

Listing 10-3. MmgApiGame in Depth 1

```
01 mf = new MainFrame(WIN_WIDTH, WIN_HEIGHT, PANEL_WIDTH, PANEL_HEIGHT,
   GAME_WIDTH, GAME_HEIGHT);
02 pnlGame = new GamePanel(mf, PANEL_WIDTH, PANEL_HEIGHT, (WIN_WIDTH -
   PANEL_WIDTH) / 2, (WIN_HEIGHT - PANEL_HEIGHT) / 2, GAME_WIDTH, GAME_
   HEIGHT);
03 mf.SetGamePanel(pnlGame);
04 mf.InitComponents();
05 fr = new RunFrameRate(mf, FPS);
06
07 mf.setSize(WIN_WIDTH, WIN_HEIGHT);
08 mf.setResizable(false);
09 mf.setVisible(true);
10 mf.setName(GameSettings.NAME);
11
12 if (GameSettings.DEVELOPMENT_MODE_ON == false) {
13     mf.setTitle(GameSettings.TITLE);
14 } else {
15     mf.setTitle(GameSettings.TITLE + " - " + GameSettings.DEVELOPER_
       COMPANY + " (" + GameSettings.VERSION + ")");
16 }
17
18 mf.setDefaultCloseOperation(JFrame.EXIT_ON_CLOSE);
19 mf.GetGamePanel().PrepBuffers();
20 t = new Thread(fr);
21 t.start();
```

The first two lines of code show the initialization of the MainFrame and the GamePanel classes. On lines 3-4, the main frame sets the game panel and initializes its components. The RunFrameRate field, fr, is initialized on line 5. The window's dimensions and certain class properties are set on lines 7–10. If the development mode flag is set to true, then the title is configured to have a little bit more information about the game than usual.

The MainFrame is responsible for handling the close of the game, and to do so, we set the type of exit operation the window should use. The code on line 18 configures the main frame to exit if the window is closed. The game panel's drawing surfaces, buffers, are prepared on line 19; and the frame rate thread is started on lines 20 and 21. At this point, the game is up and running, and the first game screen is rendering.

Static Main Entry Point: MainFrame

The MainFrame class extends the Java framework's JPanel class and is responsible for creating the window that the game runs in. The MainFrame class handles the game close event. You might need to add code to this class to handle special closing tasks for your game. The closing event is registered in the InitComponents method. This class is also responsible for adding the canvas created by the GamePanel class to the window to be actively rendered.

Class Fields

The MainFrame class has a number of fields listed in the following grouping. The fields roughly fall into the groups they are listed under.

Listing 10-4. MainFrame Class Fields 1

```
//Dimensions
public final int winWidth;
public final int winHeight;
public final int panelWidth;
public final int panelHeight;
public final int gameWidth;
public final int gameHeight;

//Offsets
public final int myX;
public final int myY;

//Game panel
public GamePanel pnlGame;
```

The first group of fields are dimensions passed in from the static main class. These fields hold copies of the values configured when the game starts up. Two new fields are listed in the Offsets group. The myX and myY fields are used to track the offset of the game panel inside the window.

The last field, pnlGame, is an instance of the GamePanel class and is responsible for presenting a canvas that is drawn in the MainFrame. If you're following along in C#, then you won't see the same structure. You'll only see the GamePanel class handling the same responsibilities that the MainFrame and GamePanel classes from the Java implementation do.

Support Method Details

The class' support methods are direct get methods for the most part. You also have methods that open up access to the pnlGame field and force the game panel to redraw itself. It is very rare that you would interact with this class in any way. Its main job is just to get a window up and running with the proper dimensions and then hand things off. It still makes sense for us to review the methods though, so let's get to it!

Listing 10-5. MainFrame Support Method Details 1

```
//Dimension methods
public int GetWindowWidth() { ... }
public int GetWindowHeight() { ... }
public int GetGamePanelWidth() { ... }
public int GetGamePanelHeight() { ... }
public int GetGameWidth() { ... }
public int GetGameHeight() { ... }

//Offset methods
public int GetOffsetX() { ... }
public int GetOffsetY() { ... }

//Game panel methods
public void SetGamePanel(GamePanel gp) { ... }
public GamePanel GetGamePanel() { ... }

//Redraw method
public void Redraw() { ... }
```

The support methods listed in the preceding follow the same order and grouping as their associated class fields we reviewed earlier. There is nothing really to cover here. These methods just provide access to the different class fields. There is one new method, the Redraw method. This method can be used to force the game panel to redraw itself.

Main Method Details

The MainFrame class has a modest set of main methods. Even though the class is important in the game's startup process, it's really just connecting the game panel's canvas to the window frame. Due to this, there aren't any very complex main methods. Let's take a look at the ones we have listed in the following set.

Listing 10-6. MainFrame Main Method Details 1

```
//Constructors
public MainFrame(int WinWidth, int WinHeight) { ... }

public MainFrame(int WinWidth, int WinHeight, int PanWidth, int PanHeight,
int GameWidth, int GameHeight) { ... }

//Main methods
public void SetFrameRate(long fr, long rfr) { ... }
public void InitComponents() { ... }
```

The first two entries listed in the preceding are class constructors. The first constructor seems a bit underpowered, but it actually comes in handy when you're working with a game that's not in development and you can set the game panel and window to the same dimensions. The second constructor is probably the one you'll use most often as it gives you more granular control over the game panel and window sizes.

The next method has a very misleading name. This method doesn't actually set the frame rate. It sets the frame rate debugging text in the development header that is displayed if the MmgHelper field, LOGGING_ON, is set to true. The last entry is the InitComponents method. We saw this method get called from the static main class. It's responsible for reinforcing the window settings and registering the on-close event handler. That concludes our review of the MainFrame class. Up next, we'll take an in-depth look at a particular block of code from this class.

In Depth: MainFrame

The in-depth code review for the MainFrame class comes from the class' InitComponents method. Let's take a look at some code!

Listing 10-7. MainFrame in Depth 1

```
01 add(pnlGame.GetCanvas());
02
03 pnlGame.GetCanvas().setFocusable(true);
04 pnlGame.GetCanvas().requestFocus();
05 pnlGame.GetCanvas().requestFocusInWindow();
06
07 setDefaultCloseOperation(JFrame.EXIT_ON_CLOSE);
08 addWindowListener(new WindowListener() {
09     public void windowClosing(WindowEvent e) {
10         try {
11             MmgHelper.wr("MainFrame: WindowClosing");
12             GamePanel.PAUSE = true;
13             GamePanel.EXIT = true;
14             RunFrameRate.PAUSE = true;
15             RunFrameRate.RUNNING = false;
16         } catch (Exception ex) {
17             MmgHelper.wrErr(ex);
18         }
19         dispose();
20     }
21
22     ...
23
24 });
```

The first line of code is very important. This is where the canvas, the surface the game is drawn on, is set as the current window's active canvas. On lines 3–5, the window properties are reinforced. The on-close event type is set on line 7. This tells the window class that it should exit the game when the window is closed. The on-close event handler is registered on line 8.

The handler is defined in-line as an anonymous class. You'll notice that the windowClosing method is defined, and this is where we'll put any game closing code. Take a look at the functional equivalent of the on-close event handler from the C# version of the engine listed in the following code snippet.

Listing 10-8. MainFrame in Depth 2

```
01 try
02 {
03     MmgHelper.wr("GamePanel: WindowClosing");
04     GamePanel.PAUSE = true;
05     GamePanel.EXIT = true;
06     Dispose();
07     Environment.Exit(0);
08 }
09 catch (Exception ex)
10 {
11     MmgHelper.wrErr(ex);
12 }
```

This snippet of code is from the C# project's GamePanel class in the MmgCore namespace, specifically the windowClosing method. We created and named that method to match the naming found in the Java version. This method is registered as the program's exit handler. Notice that the same code exists, almost line for line, in the C# version as in the Java version. Also, note that all of the MmgBase API code is exactly the same.

Static Main Entry Point: GamePanel

The GamePanel class is the last of the static main classes for us to review. This class is very important. It's the connection point between the input and game screens. It's the connection point between the MmgCore API and the MmgBase API, and it provides the game engine drawing routines that power all the example screens we looked at in Part 1 of this text.

Static Class Members

The class' static members are listed in the following loosely grouped by the comment header.

Listing 10-9. GamePanel Static Class Members 1

```
//Game controls
public static boolean EXIT = false;
public static boolean PAUSE = false;

//Game dimensions
public static int GAME_HEIGHT = 416;
public static int GAME_WIDTH = 854;

//Development HUD
public static String FPS = "Drawing FPS: 0000 Actual FPS: 00";
public static String VAR1 = "** EMPTY **";
public static String VAR2 = "** EMPTY **";

//General fields
public static GameType GAME_TYPE = GameType.GAME_NEW;
public static Hashtable<String, Object> VARS = new Hashtable<String,
Object>();
```

The EXIT and PAUSE fields are used to control the game's execution. The EXIT field doesn't cause the game to exit; it indicates the game is exiting. The game dimensions are stored in static fields. These are used in creating the game's drawing surface. The next set of static fields only come into play if the MmgHelper class' LOGGING_ON flag is set to true. If so, then there is a header drawn at the top of the game window.

Note, you must set the window dimensions to include space for the development header if you plan to use it. The header will draw every frame and give you information about the current frame rate. There are also two variables that are displayed. You can use these variables to display debugging information during game play.

The last two fields are general fields. The GAME_TYPE field is used to indicate the type of game that is running. The VARS static field can be used to hold global data that can be easily accessed from anywhere in your game.

Enumerations

Next up, you guessed it, enumerations. There are two very important enumerations for us to review listed in the following code block.

Listing 10-10. GamePanel Enumerations 1

```
01 public enum GameStates {
02      LOADING,
03      BLANK,
04      SPLASH,
05      MAIN_MENU,
06      ABOUT,
07      HELP_MENU,
08      HELP_PROLOGUE,
09      HELP_ITEM_DESC,
10
11      ...
12
13      GAME_SCREEN_39,
14      GAME_SCREEN_40
15 }

01 public enum GameType {
02      GAME_NEW,
03      GAME_CONTINUE,
04      GAME_ONE_PLAYER,
05      GAME_TWO_PLAYER,
06      GAME_NETWORK_TWO_PLAYER,
07      GAME_NETWORK_TWO_PLAYER_P1,
08      GAME_NETWORK_TWO_PLAYER_P2,
09      GAME_NETWORK_TWO_PLAYER_LEFT,
10      GAME_NETWORK_TWO_PLAYER_RIGHT
11 }
```

Now the GamePanel class has a number of responsibilities. It really is the heart of the game engine. One of those responsibilities is to manage the game screens. There should be one game screen class for each screen in your game, roughly speaking. The class is designed to associate game screens with a GameState value. To facilitate its use, there are a number of default game states in the first enumeration and up to 40 generic game states that can be used for anything.

Feel free to expand the entries in this enumeration to accommodate your next game. The second enumeration is of equal importance. It describes the type of game that's running. There are a few default values to indicate single player, two players, and different network games. If you're just making a simple single-player game, try to still use this enumeration. You never know when you might want to go back and add network support someday.

Class Fields

As one might expect, a class of this importance is going to have a decent number of class fields and usually a long list of support methods. The GamePanel class is no exception. Take a look at the first block of class fields for us to review listed in the following grouping.

Listing 10-11. GamePanel Class Fields 1

```
//Game positioning
public MainFrame mf;
public int winWidth;
public int winHeight;
public int myX;
public int myY;

//Scaled game positioning
public double scale = 1.0;
public int sWinWidth;
public int sWinHeight;
public int sMyX;
public int sMyY;

//Game state management
public Hashtable<GameStates, MmgGameScreen> gameScreens;
```

```
public MmgGameScreen currentScreen;
public GameStates prevGameState;
public GameStates gameState;

//Game drawing
public MmgPen p;
public Canvas canvas;
public BufferStrategy strategy;
public BufferedImage background;
public Graphics2D backgroundGraphics;
public Graphics2D graphics;
public int updateTick = 0;
```

The first group of fields contains a reference to the main frame. You can consider the main frame to be like a parent class to the game panel class. The next four entries are used to track the game's dimensions and the game panel's offset. The following group of fields are very similar, but these are applied when the game panel needs to be scaled to fit inside the window's frame.

The next group of fields are very important. This group contains game state management functionality. The first field in the group provides you with a data structure that you can use to track the game screens you're using. You can choose not to use this data structure, but it's there for you to use if you see fit. The currentScreen field represents the active game screen and receives all input the game panel receives and is plugged into the game engine's update and draw calls.

The next two fields, gameState and prevGameState, are used to track the current and previous game states of the game panel class. The reason for this is so that the previous game screen can be cleaned up, resources released, before the next game screen takes over. The last group of class fields are part of the class' drawing routine. The MmgPen instance, p, is used to draw on the background image via the backgroundGraphics framework drawing class.

The canvas field is used to hold a framework-level class that represents the window's drawable area. The strategy field is used to configure the framework's drawing process to include double buffering the canvas. This means that internally the canvas will support two drawing surfaces. One surface is being displayed, while the other, representing the next game frame, is being drawn.

When the second frame is ready, the two surfaces are flipped, and the process is repeated. As I mentioned in the preceding, the background and backgroundGraphics are used to draw the game onto a surface, and the graphics field is then used to draw that game frame onto the window's canvas. Last but not least, the updateTick field is used as part of the update call. It keeps track of how many times the update call has been made. This corresponds with the number of frames the game has displayed. We're not out of the woods yet. There is another set of class fields for us to look at. Take a look at the fields listed in the following grouping before we delve into their review.

Listing 10-12. GamePanel Class Fields 2

```
//Development header drawing
public Font debugFont;
public Color debugColor = Color.WHITE;
private MmgFont mmgDebugFont = null;

//Other
public int lastX;
public int lastY;
public long lastKeyPressEvent = -1;
public int mouseOffsetX = 0;
public int mouseOffsetY = 0;
public static GameType GAME_TYPE = GameType.GAME_NEW;

//Game screens
public ScreenSplash screenSplash;
public ScreenLoading screenLoading;
public ScreenMainMenu screenMainMenu;

//Game engine context data
public MmgScreenData screenData;
public MmgFontData fontData;

//Gamepad support
public GamePadHub gamePadHub;
public GamePadHubRunner gamePadRunner;
public Thread gpadTr;
```

```
public GpioHub gpioHub;
public GpioHubRunner gpioRunner;
public Thread gpioTr;
```

When the logging on flag in the `MmgHelper` class is set to true, the engine will add a special debugging header above the game panel. The `debugFont`, `mmgDebugFont`, and `debugColor` class fields are used to draw the debugging text in the development header. The `lastX` and `lastY` fields are used to track the mouse's last recorded X and Y coordinates.

This information can be used to determine mouse drag-and-drop operations among other things. The `lastKeyPressEvent` field records the last time a keyboard key was pressed. The mouse offset fields give you the ability to fine-tune the mouse cursor by adding an X or Y offset to its positioning. The `GAME_TYPE` field holds a value indicating what type of game is running: one player, two players, networked, local, and so on.

The game screens are coming up next. We decided not to use the data structure for storing the game screens and just made a class field for the screens that this implementation supports. The splash, loading, and main menu screens are displayed by this example game runtime. The `MmgScreenData` and `MmgFontData` instances, `screenData` and `fontData`, should be familiar to you from their review in Part 1 of this text. These fields are useful for accessing the engine's screen and font runtime data.

The last group of fields have to do with gamepad support. The game engine supports two types of gamepads. A traditional USB gamepad is supported in the Java version via jInput libraries and in the C# version natively in MonoGame. Another type of gamepad is supported on the Linux operating system only. This implementation allows you to use GPIO pins on a single-board computer to create a gamepad using a breadboard, some buttons, and some jumper cables. You can then control your game using the GPIO gamepad. I won't cover gamepad or GPIO support in any detail in the text but I encourage you to experiment with the classes.

The gamepad hub is used to read the gamepad state and convert the input to button information. This data is then processed by the gamepad hub runner, which polls the gamepad for data at an interval. The thread `gpadTr` is used to run the gamepad processing code in a separate thread as opposed to the main game thread. The last three fields in the block are exactly the same as the gamepad fields we just discussed except these are designed to work with the Linux file system and the GPIO interface.

Support Method Details

Because the GamePanel class has such a large number of support methods, I've decided to break out the input processing methods into their own section. Let's begin the review by covering the support methods listed in the following set.

Listing 10-13. GamePanel Support Method Details 1

```
//Support methods
public Hashtable<GameStates, MmgGameScreen> GetGameScreens() { ... }

public void SetGameScreens(Hashtable<GameStates, MmgGameScreen>
GameScreens) { ... }

public MmgGameScreen GetCurrentScreen() { ... }
public void SetCurrentScreen(MmgGameScreen CurrentScreen) { ... }

public int GetWinWidth() { ... }
public int GetWinHeight() { ... }
public int GetX() { ... }
public int GetY() { ... }
```

The first four entries are get and set methods for the gameScreens and currentScreen fields, respectively. The next two methods provide access to the window's dimensions, while the GetX and GetY methods provide access to the game panel's X and Y offsets.

Input Method Details

There are so many input handling methods that I decided to, once again, give them a section of their own. They are self-explanatory, so I won't talk about them in any detail. As you read through them, think about using them in your next game.

Listing 10-14. GamePanel Input Method Details 1

```
//Mouse move methods
public void ProcessMouseMove(int x, int y) { ... }

//Mouse button methods
public void ProcessMousePress(int x, int y, int btnIndex) { ... }
```

```
public void ProcessMouseRelease(int x, int y, int btnIndex) { ... }

public void ProcessMouseClick(int x, int y, int btnIndex) { ... }

//A button methods
public void ProcessAPress(int src) { ... }
public void ProcessARelease(int src) { ... }
public void ProcessAClick(int src) { ... }

//B button methods
public void ProcessBPress(int src) { ... }
public void ProcessBRelease(int src) { ... }
public void ProcessBClick(int src) { ... }

//Keyboard key methods
public void ProcessKeyPress(char c, int code) { ... }

public void ProcessKeyRelease(char c, int code) { ... }

public void ProcessKeyClick(char c, int code) { ... }

//D-Pad input
public void ProcessDpadPress(int dir) { ... }
public void ProcessDpadRelease(int dir) { ... }
public void ProcessDpadClick(int dir) { ... }

//Debug method
public void ProcessDebugClick() { ... }
```

The only method I'd like to talk about is the ProcessDebugClick method. This method is mapped to the keyboard's "D" key by default, and if pressed it will call the game screen's ProcessDebugClick method. This is a great place to enter in some debugging code that prints information to standard output.

Main Method Details

The GamePanel class has a few main methods, listed in the following grouping, that we should discuss.

Listing 10-15. GamePanel Main Method Details 1

```
//Rendering methods
public void PrepBuffers() { ... }
public BufferedImage create(int width, int height, boolean alpha) { ... }

public Canvas GetCanvas() { ... }
public Graphics2D GetBuffer() { ... }
public boolean UpdateScreen() { ... }
public void UpdateGame() { ... }
public void RenderGame() { ... }

//Assorted main methods
public GamePanel(MainFrame Mf, int WinWidth, int WinHeight, int X, int Y,
int GameWidth, int GameHeight) { ... }

public void SwitchGameState(GameStates g) { ... }
public void HandleGenericEvent(GenericEventMessage obj) { ... }
```

The PrepBuffers method sets the canvas buffer strategy to use two buffers, hence double buffering. The method also prepares the background and backgroundGraphics fields used in drawing the game panel. The GetCanvas method returns the GamePanel's canvas field, and the GetBuffer method gets the next active buffer from the canvas.

The UpdateScreen method causes the canvas' double buffer to flip and a new buffer to be created. The UpdateGame method runs the update call of the game engine's drawing routine. This results in the current game screen's MmgUpdate method being called each game frame. Last but not least, the RenderGame method is responsible for getting the game frame built and drawing it on the canvas. This results in the current screen's MmgDraw method being called each frame.

The next method up for review is the class constructor. There is only one constructor, so you'll have to live with it. It's designed to plug into the static main class and be called after the MainFrame is initialized. It takes a reference to the main frame and some dimension and offset information as arguments. This constructor will create a new class instance that is ready to use.

The SwitchGameState method is the default method for changing game states and subsequently game screens in the GamePanel class. This method is responsible for cleaning up the previous game state. This results in the previous game screen's

UnloadResources method being called. Once that's done, the next game screen is prepped with a call to its LoadResources method. It then becomes the current screen and is actively drawn to the game's window.

The last method for us to review is the HandleGenericEvent method. This method handles generic events from the splash screen and loading screen classes. The splash screen class sends an event when its display time is up. The loading screen class sends an event when the loading process is complete. The game panel class reacts to these events by changing game states to the next state in the game loading sequence. The main menu is the last state in the startup process.

In Depth: GamePanel

For this class' in-depth review section, we'll be taking a look at a snippet of code from the RenderGame method. Take a look at the following listing.

Listing 10-16. GamePanel in Depth 1

```
01      p.SetGraphics(g);
02      p.SetAdvRenderHints();
03      currentScreen.MmgDraw(p);
04
05      if (MmgHelper.LOGGING == true) {
06          tmpF = g.getFont();
07          g.setFont(debugFont);
08          g.setColor(debugColor);
09          g.drawString(GamePanel.FPS, 15, 15);
10          g.drawString("Var1: " + GamePanel.VAR1, 15, 35);
11          g.drawString("Var2: " + GamePanel.VAR2, 15, 55);
12          g.setFont(tmpF);
13      }
14 }
15
16 //draws a scaled version of the state of the background buffer to the
   screen buffer if scaling is enabled
17 if (scale != 1.0) {
18      bg.drawImage(background, sMyX, sMyY, sWinWidth, sWinHeight, 0, 0,
        winWidth, winHeight, null);
```

```
19 } else {
20     bg.drawImage(background, myX, myY, null);
21 }
```

This little piece of innocuous code is actually the core of the game engine's drawing routine. The first two lines of code set up the MmgPen field, p, to draw on a target surface, g. Remember g is the surface that will hold one game frame and is rendered by the current game screen. Advanced render hints are set, and the screen is drawn on line 3. The block of code from lines 5 to 13 is the debugging header that is drawn if the game has logging turned on. This header displays the game's frame rate as well as two variables for debugging purposes.

In this example, the graphics object g is set to draw on the background image. This is the surface that will hold the game's next frame. Notice that on lines 17–21, the image is drawn to the canvas, using the framework's pen class, bg. Notice that because we're drawing on an internal surface, the background image, we have implemented a triple buffering system for the game's rendering engine. The game frame rendered by the current screen is then passed on to the canvas' internal double buffer.

Topic: Launching a Game

This is the third new review section we've encountered in this part of the book. We've seen the "Input Method Details" and "In Depth" sections in this and previous chapters. The new review section I'd like to introduce here is the "Topic" review section. In this type of review section, we won't be reviewing a class or a class' use. Instead, we'll be reviewing a larger overarching concept. In this case, that concept is "Launching a Game."

Launching a Game: Java

First, we'll take a look at the Java game engine implementation and the different ways we can start a game. Navigate to the project folder you've been using for the NetBeans IDE. Find the MmgGameApiJava project and open that folder. There should be a **dist** folder in the main project folder.

If not, open the IDE and right-click the project. Select the Clean and Build option and answer the following dialog such that the build is forced. You should now have a **dist** folder if your project is properly configured. If you still don't see a folder, go back to Chapter 1 and go over the Java setup process again.

Inside the **dist** folder is where the compiled version of the game is created. In order to start a game, we need to know how to run some command-line interface, console, commands. In Windows, you should use the command program, **cmd.exe**. You can find this program on the Start menu or search for **cmd** in the run bar.

For other platforms, you'll just need to open up a terminal. If you don't know how to do this, simply search the Internet for some instructions on how to open up a terminal window for your particular operating system. Once you have a terminal window open, we'll want to verify the Java runtime environment is set up correctly. Run the following command in the console window:

```
java -version
```

If you get a message indicating that the Java program could not be found, then we'll have to make sure that Java is on the system's path environment variable. In Windows, you will see the following message if Java cannot be found. You will see a similar message on Mac OSX and Linux:

```
'java' is not recognized as an internal or external command, operable
program or batch file.
```

If this is the case, you'll want to visit the following link or search the Internet for "add java to your path" and look at one of the top results:

```
https://docs.oracle.com/javase/tutorial/essential/environment/paths.html
```

If everything is up and running properly, then you'll see a message similar to the one listed in the following instead of an error message:

```
java version "12.0.1" 2019-04-16 Java(TM) SE Runtime Environment (build
12.0.1+12) Java HotSpot(TM) 64-Bit Server VM (build 12.0.1+12, mixed mode,
sharing)
```

The Java implementation supports multiple static main entry points in a single jar file. The default static main is the MmgTestScreens class from the MmgTestSpace library. This static main adds the ability to specify which test to launch. You'll see the added command-line argument in the following examples.

Execute the Default Static Main

```
java -jar MmgGameApiJava.jar
```

Execute the Default Static Main with Arguments

```
java -jar MmgGameApiJava.jar FPS=30 TEST=1
```

Execute the Default Static Main with Native Lib Path and Arguments

```
java -Djava.library.path= C:\netbeans_projects\MmgGameApiJava\lib\jinput-
platform\native-libs -jar MmgGameApiJava.jar FPS=30 TEST=1
```

In the next two examples, we are specifying the static main class to run from the command line. Notice that in the second example, we are running the MmgApiGame static main through the MmgCentralMain. The reason for this is that the C# framework doesn't allow there to be more than one static main entry point. To keep the two projects functionally equivalent, I've created an entry point that can be configured to run many different main classes.

Execute Target Static Main with Arguments

```
java -cp MmgGameApiJava.jar net.middlemind.MmgGameApiJava.MmgCore.
MmgApiGame FPS=30
```

Execute Central Main with Target Main and Args

```
java -cp MmgGameApiJava.jar net.middlemind.MmgGameApiJava.MmgCore.
MmgCentralMain mmgapigame FPS=15
```

All MmgCentralMain Execution Commands

```
//Executes the example application
java MmgGameApiJava.jar mmgtestspace
//Executes the bare bones static main
java MmgGameApiJava.jar mmgapigame
//Executes the PongClone Chapter 16 project
java MmgGameApiJava.jar chapter16
//Executes the PongClone Chapter 17 project
```

```
java MmgGameApiJava.jar chapter17
//Executes the PongClone Chapter 18 project
java MmgGameApiJava.jar chapter18
//Executes the DungeonTrap Chapter 20 project
java MmgGameApiJava.jar chapter20
//Executes the DungeonTrap Chapter 21 project
java MmgGameApiJava.jar chapter21
//Executes the DungeonTrap Chapter 22 project
java MmgGameApiJava.jar chapter22
//Executes the DungeonTrap Chapter 23 project
java MmgGameApiJava.jar chapter23
//Executes the DungeonTrap Chapter 23 demo project
java MmgGameApiJava.jar chapter23_demoscreen
//Executes the DungeonTrap Chapter 24 project phase 1
java MmgGameApiJava.jar chapter24_phase1
//Executes the DungeonTrap Chapter 24 project phase 2
java MmgGameApiJava.jar chapter24_phase2
//Executes the DungeonTrap Chapter 24 project phase 3
java MmgGameApiJava.jar chapter24_phase3
```

That concludes the review of how to launch a Java version of your game. Next up, we'll take a look at how to launch your game using the C# version of the engine. I should mention that the compiled games look for the resource directory to be one directory up from where they are executed. So if we are running the game in the **dist** folder, the resources will be located in the **../cfg** directory.

Launching a Game: C#

Let's take a look at the C# game engine implementation and the different ways we can start a game. Navigate to the project folder you've been using for the Visual Studio IDE. Find the MmgGameApiCs solution folder and the project folder with the same name; open that folder. You should see the following folder structure in that directory: **bin\Debug\netcoreapp3.1**.

If not, open the IDE and right-click the project. Select the Rebuild option. You should now have the correct **bin** folder in your project's main directory. If you still don't see a folder, go back to the Chapter 1 and go over the C# setup process again.

Inside the **bin\Debug\netcoreapp3.1** folder is where the compiled version of the game is created. In order to start a game, we need to know how to run some command-line interface, console, commands. In Windows, you should use the command program, **cmd.exe**. You can find this program on the Start menu or search for **cmd** in the run bar.

For other platforms, you'll just need to open up a terminal. If you don't know how to do this, simply search the Internet for some instructions on how to open up a terminal window for your particular operating system. Once you have a terminal window open, we'll want to verify the C# runtime environment is set up correctly. Run the following command in the console window:

```
dotnet --version
```

If you get a message indicating that the DotNet program could not be found, then we'll have to make sure that DotNet is on the system's path environment variable. In Windows, you will see the following message if DotNet cannot be found. You will see a similar message on Mac OSX and Linux:

```
'dotnet' is not recognized as an internal or external command, operable
program or batch file.
```

If this is the case, you'll want to visit the following link or search the Internet for "add dotnet to your path" and look at one of the top results:

```
https://docs.microsoft.com/en-us/dotnet/core/tools/troubleshoot-usage-issues
```

If everything is up and running properly, then you'll see a rather unceremonious message similar to the one listed in the following instead of an error message:

```
5.0.101
```

The C# implementation does not support multiple static main entry points in a single library file. The default static main is the MmgCentralMain class from the MmgCore library. This static main adds the ability to specify which other main class to launch. You'll see the added command-line argument in the following command examples.

Execute the Default Static Main

```
dotnet MmgGameApiCs.dll default
```

Execute the Default Static Main with Arguments

```
dotnet MmgGameApiCs.dll default FPS=30 TEST=1
```

In the next two examples, we are specifying the static main class to run from the command line. The examples demonstrate running the template application, MmgApiGame, and the example application, MmgTestScreens.

Execute Central Main with MmgTestScreens and Args

```
dotnet MmgGameApiCs.dll mmgtestspace TEST=20
```

Execute Central Main with MmgApiGame and Args

```
dotnet MmgGameApiCs.dll mmgapigame FPS=15
```

All MmgCentralMain Execution Commands

```
//Executes the example application
dotnet MmgGameApiCs.dll mmgtestspace
//Executes the bare bones static main
dotnet MmgGameApiCs.dll mmgapigame
//Executes the PongClone Chapter 16 project
dotnet MmgGameApiCs.dll chapter16
//Executes the PongClone Chapter 17 project
dotnet MmgGameApiCs.dll chapter17
//Executes the PongClone Chapter 18 project
dotnet MmgGameApiCs.dll chapter18
//Executes the DungeonTrap Chapter 20 project
dotnet MmgGameApiCs.dll chapter20
//Executes the DungeonTrap Chapter 21 project
dotnet MmgGameApiCs.dll chapter21
//Executes the DungeonTrap Chapter 22 project
dotnet MmgGameApiCs.dll chapter22
//Executes the DungeonTrap Chapter 23 project
dotnet MmgGameApiCs.dll chapter23
```

```
//Executes the DungeonTrap Chapter 23 demo project
dotnet MmgGameApiCs.dll chapter23_demoscreen
//Executes the DungeonTrap Chapter 24 project phase 1
dotnet MmgGameApiCs.dll chapter24_phase1
//Executes the DungeonTrap Chapter 24 project phase 2
dotnet MmgGameApiCs.dll chapter24_phase2
//Executes the DungeonTrap Chapter 24 project phase 3
dotnet MmgGameApiCs.dll chapter24_phase3
```

That concludes the review of how to launch a C# version of your game. I should mention that the compiled games look for the resource directory to be three directories up from where they are executed. So if we are running the game in the **netcoreapp3.1** folder, the resources will be located in the **../../../cfg** directory. You can adjust this configuration in the GameSettings class.

Chapter Conclusion

In this chapter, we completed a review of the MmgCore API's runtime classes. These classes represent the "execution code" so to speak, the code that prepares and executes your game. Again, we chose to include the runtime code, from source, as part of your game project's setup. This gives you complete control over the game's launch process.

We saw how the static main entry point prepared a game window using the MainFrame class – in the C# version, the GamePanel class handles this responsibility – and attached the GamePanel class to the window's drawable space. We reviewed the heart of the game engine, the GamePanel class, which connects the MmgCore API to the MmgBase API and manages all game screens. Let's take a look at a summary of the chapter's main points:

- MmgApiGame: An MmgCore API class that runs a template, bare-bones, game. This game will run through the startup process showing a splash screen and displaying a loading screen before concluding on a main menu.

- MainFrame: An MmgCore API class that is responsible for creating the window frame for the game in the Java implementation of the game engine.

- GamePanel: An MmgCore API class that is the heart of the game engine. This class is responsible for routing input to the current game screen, managing game screens, and much more. This is the point in the MmgCore API where we connect to the MmgBase API via the different game screens.

- Topic: Launching a Game: In this topic section, we learned exactly how to launch our games from the command-line interface using a console. We covered the different, default, applications you can run and how to run them for both the Java and C# implementations.

At this point in time, you should see the big picture. The structure of the MmgBase API and the main aspects of the MmgCore API have been detailed to you. Take some time to think about the libraries and their structure – how the lower-level API has lots of support for cloning, comparison, and interoperability of classes, while the mid-level API, MmgCore, has mainly single, highly specialized classes that run a specific aspect of the game engine. Pay special attention to the GamePanel class and its drawing and update routines. Make sure you understand how the two APIs are connected. Here's a hint: explore the currentScreen class field.

CHAPTER 11

Dynamic Settings

We've covered a fair amount of the game engine's code up to this point in the text. Most of the classes have been tied closely to the engine's models or runtime code. The next set of classes we'll review show us how the game engine can pull in data from different sources to customize settings and game play.

In the upcoming sections, we'll review the structure and syntax of a game engine config file and detail the settings loading process so that you have complete control over how your game loads and processes dynamic data. The classes we'll review in this chapter are as follows:

- DatConstantsEntry

- GameSettingsImporter

- DatExternalStrings

- GameSettings

Dynamic Settings: DatConstantsEntry

The game engine has the ability to load values from an XML file into the static fields of certain classes. Can you think of a reason why we might want to limit this to static class fields? Using static fields requires less initialization because the field being updated can be accessed statically with no class initialization.

This allows us to data drive the setup of the game engine and the game, through the use of settings and config files. We can create multiple config files for one game or many config files for many games. It's really up to you. The `DatConstantsEntry` class is designed to hold a single row of data from a game engine config file.

© Victor G Brusca 2021
V. G. Brusca, *Introduction to Video Game Engine Development*, https://doi.org/10.1007/978-1-4842-7039-4_11

The engine also lets you specify a config file as one of the default command-line arguments. If you add the text `ENGINE_CONFIG_FILE=` followed by a valid config file to the end of your game's launch command, you can dynamically set the config file the engine uses at runtime. If the game's launch commands seem unfamiliar, feel free to flip back to Chapter 10 for a refresher.

The ability to dynamically alter game settings is a very powerful tool, but be careful. When you override settings via a config file, you may not be aware of this when looking at, or even testing, the code. This can leave you wondering why your code driven values aren't being applied. Remember to check all the different ways a value can be set, including config files.

Class Fields

The `DatConstantsEntry` class' fields are used to describe a value that is to be stored in a target static field. Let's take a look!

Listing 11-1. DatConstantsEntry Class Fields 1

```
public String key;

public String val;
public String type;
public String from;
```

The key field is not only the key by which the data entry is stored, but it's also the exact name of the destination field that will hold the data. You must make sure that the field type and the data you're attempting to store in it match up. The `val` field is a string representation of the value that will be stored in the target field. The string will be converted accordingly as part of the process used to set the target field's value.

The `type` field is used to describe the data held in the `val` field. The `type` field can be set to `int`, `float`, `double`, `short`, `string`, or `bool`. Again, make sure that the target field and the type of data being stored are compatible. The last entry in the list is the `from` field. This field should be set to the target class that the static field, the name of which is stored in the key field, belongs to.

Main Method Details

The class' main methods are all constructors. There are three, listed in the following. Make sure to take a look at them before we review them.

Listing 11-2. DatConstantsEntry Main Method Details 1

```
public DatConstantsEntry(String k, String v) { ... }
public DatConstantsEntry(String k, String v, String t) { ... }

public DatConstantsEntry(String k, String v, String t, String f) { ... }
```

I've arranged the constructors in order of increasing complexity. I should mention that the class defaults the type field to int and the from field to the GameSettings class when there are no arguments to use for values. With that in mind, the first two constructors are just quicker ways to initialize a GameSettings config file entry. The last constructor listed is probably the one you'll use the most. This entry lets you specify each field directly using constructor arguments.

That concludes the DatConstantsEntry class review. Next, we'll take a look at the class in detail. I would normally segue into a demonstration section here, but we'll come across the DatConstantsEntry class again as part of the config file import process, so instead we're going to do an in-depth review of the config file's format.

In Depth: DatConstantsEntry

First, let's review where the game engine config files are normally stored. Of course, you can specify your own path to these files as part of the game's launch arguments. There are a few default game engine config files included in the game engine project for you to take a look at.

The normal structure of a game project's setup should include a config folder, **cfg**, on the root of the project. The following is a simple diagram showing the setup of the **cfg** folder.

Listing 11-3. DatConstantsEntry in Depth 1

```
MmgGameApiJava
|-> cfg (Resource and Configuration Directory)
    |-> class_config (Class Config Files)
    |-> playable (Audio Resources)
        |-> auto_load (Global Audio Resources)
            |-> sound1.wav
        |-> MmgTestSpace (Project Specific Audio Resources)
            |-> jump2.wav

    |-> drawable (Image Resources)
        |-> auto_load (Global Image Resources)
            |-> a_btn.png
        |-> MmgTestSpace (Project Specific Image Resources)
            |-> b_btn.png

    |-> engine_config.xml (Direct Path Game Engine Config)
    |-> engine_config_mmg_test_space.xml
    |-> engine_config_mmg_dungeon_trap.xml
```

The default game engine config file to load is specified in the static main class'
ENGINE_CONFIG_FILE field. This defaults to the file **engine_config.xml**. You can open the
config file in your IDE for viewing, but I'll print a short example of one here.

Listing 11-4. DatConstantsEntry in Depth 2

```
01 <?xml version="1.0" encoding="UTF-8"?>
02 <engineconfig version="1.0">
03     <entry key="LOGGING" val="true" type="bool" from="MmgHelper" />
04     <entry key="BMP_CACHE_ON" val="true" type="bool" from="GameSettings" />
05     <entry key="BMP_PREFIX" val="images_" type="string"
       from="GameSettings" />
06     <entry key="BMP_PREFIX_CONSOLE" val="console_images_" type="string"
       from="GameSettings" />
07 </engineconfig>
```

You can use this XML file, **engine_config.xml**, as a template for starting a new file for your next game. The first line in the file is a standard XML header. The second entry defines the main tag used, the engineconfig tag. You must specify a version number as an attribute to this tag.

Can you think of a reason why this would be a good idea? Using this attribute, you can specify a version number allowing you to create new XML config file formats in the future. As long as you have a unique version number, you can use that information to change the code that parses the XML file. With this setup, you can future-proof your game configurations.

Lines 3–6 hold the actual configuration information. The XML tags match up perfectly with the DatConstantsEntry class' fields, and you can see that part of the loading process involves simply converting the XML entries to a list of DatConstantsEntry objects.

Dynamic Settings: GameSettingsImporter

The GameSettingsImporter class is responsible for parsing a game engine config file and generating an array of DatConstantsEntry objects based on the config file's entry tags. Let's review some code!

Class Fields

This class has only two fields, listed in the following group, for us to worry about.

Listing 11-5. GameSettingsImporter Class Fields 1

```
public Hashtable<String, DatConstantsEntry> values;
public String version;
```

The first field is a data structure used to hold the config file entries. Notice that the data structure is a key-value pair structure. The key in this case will be the key field of the associated DatConstantsEntry object. In the C# version, this field would be a Dictionary object instead of a Hashtable. The next field is the config file version. We've encountered this value earlier when we covered the config file's engineconfig tag.

Support Method Details

The GameSettingsImporter class has two sets of get and set methods listed in the following group.

Listing 11-6. GameSettingsImporter Support Method Details 1

```
public Hashtable<String, DatConstantsEntry> GetValues() { ... }

public void SetValues(Hashtable<String, DatConstantsEntry> v) { ... }

public String GetVersion() { ... }
public void SetVersion(String v) { ... }
```

The first set of support methods gives you access to the values that have been loaded up. The second set of methods gives you access to the version number of the engine config file.

Main Method Details

We only have two main methods to discuss with regard to the GameSettingsImporter class. Short and sweet.

Listing 11-7. GameSettingsImporter Main Method Details 1

```
public void RunImportGameSettings(String xmlFile) throws
ParserConfigurationException, SAXException, IOException, Exception { ... }

public boolean ImportGameSettings(String xmlFile) { ... }
```

The first method listed is the actual engine config processing method. This method will parse the XML file if the version matches the value in the TARGET_GAME_SETTINGS_ XML_VERSION of the GameSettings class from the MmgCore API. If anything goes wrong, the method will throw an exception. The next method listed is a safe wrapper for the RunImportGameSettings method. It will run the method, catch any exceptions, and return a Boolean value representing the success of the operation.

Demonstration: GameSettingsImporter Class

The demonstration code that we'll look at next is from the MmgApiGame class of the MmgCore API. Remember, this is a template static main class. In the main method, there is a section for loading engine config files.

Listing 11-8. GameSettingsImporter Demonstration 1

```
01 if (ENGINE_CONFIG_FILE != null && ENGINE_CONFIG_FILE.equals("") ==
   false) {
02     GameSettingsImporter dci = new GameSettingsImporter();
03     boolean r = dci.ImportGameSettings(ENGINE_CONFIG_FILE);
04     MmgHelper.wr("Engine config load result: " + r);
05
06     if(r == true) {
07         int len = dci.GetValues().keySet().size();
08         String[] keys = dci.GetValues().keySet().toArray(new
           String[len]);
09         String key;
10         DatConstantsEntry ent = null;
11         Field f = null;
12
13         for (int i = 0; i < len; i++) {
14             try {
15                 key = keys[i];
16                 ent = dci.GetValues().get(key);
17
18                 if (ent.from != null && ent.from.equals("GameSettings")
                   == true) {
19                     f = GameSettings.class.getField(ent.key);
20                     if (f != null) {
21                         SetField(ent, f);
22                     }
23                 }

               ...
```

```
34              } catch (Exception e) {
35                  MmgHelper.wrErr(e);
36              }
37          }
38      }
39 }
```

If a game engine config file is defined, we initialize a new GameSettingsImporter object on line 2. The XML file is parsed and loaded on line 3 with a call to the ImportGameSettings method. Notice that the result is stored in the local variable r. On line 7, if the config file load was successful, the number of entries to process is stored locally followed by an extraction of the data's keys on line 8. Local variables used in the processing loop are defined on lines 9–11.

Looping over the data items, the key and DatConstantsEntry object for the current item are set on lines 15 and 16. If the entry is properly defined, we compare its from field; remember this is the name of the class that holds the target static field, to a default set of supported classes. In the preceding example code on lines 19–22, the SetField method is used to update the value of the static field of the specified class. That wraps up our review of the GameSettingsImporter class. Up next, we'll take a look at how strings are managed in the game engine.

Dynamic Settings: DatExternalStrings

The DatExternalStrings class is used to hold your game's strings. Instead of hard coding them in-line with your game classes, you can enter them into this class for easy access throughout your game. The class is designed to use static fields and methods. You simply add in an ID for a string and then add the code to load your string to the class' preparation method.

Static Class Members

All of the DatExternalStrings class members are static. Let's take a look at the static fields first.

Listing 11-9. DatExternalStrings Static Class Members 1

```
public static Hashtable<Integer, String> EXT = new Hashtable<Integer,
String>();

public static int EXT_TALK_TREEFOLK_NO_CONVO = 0;
public static int EXT_TALK_TREEFOLK_CONVO = 1;
public static int EXT_TALK_PIGGY_NO_CONVO = 2;
public static String DEFAULT_LANGUAGE = "en";
```

The first field listed in the preceding, EXT, is the data structure that holds all of the class' strings. This field is a default part of the class. The next three fields are examples of added fields that are used as unique string identifiers. To use a string managed by this class, just use the ID field as the key to pull an associated string value.

The last entry listed in the preceding is the default language code. This code can be any value you want really. The main purpose here is to provide a value to drive loading different strings based on the language code provided. Let's move on to the static class methods next.

Listing 11-10. DatExternalStrings Static Class Members 2

```
public static void LOAD_EXT_STRINGS() { ... }
public static void LOAD_EXT_STRINGS(String langCode) { ... }
```

The methods listed in the preceding are used to prep the class for use by loading up a set of strings based on the user-defined IDs and strings. The first entry listed in the preceding, LOAD_EXT_STRINGS, takes no arguments and uses the default language code to load up the configured string data. The second entry performs the same operation except you can provide a language code as a method argument. You can use this system to add multilanguage support to your game.

Demonstration: DatExternalStrings Class

The example code for the DatExternalStrings class comes from the class' LOAD_EXT_STRINGS method.

Listing 11-11. DatExternalStrings Class Demonstration 1

```
1 if (EXT.contains(EXT_TALK_NOBODY_HERE) == false) {
2     EXT.put(EXT_TALK_NOBODY_HERE, "There's nobody here to talk to.");
3 }
```

The code listed in the preceding demonstrates how to load new strings into the external strings class. Note that we check to see if a particular entry exists before adding the ID and string value to the class' list of strings.

Listing 11-12. DatExternalStrings Class Demonstration 2

```
1 DatExternalStrings.EXT.get(DatExternalStrings.STRING_ID);
```

The next short snippet of code listed in the preceding is an example of using the DatExternalStrings class to access a loaded string value. Notice that all we're doing is utilizing static class members to specify which string we want to access.

Dynamic Settings: GameSettings

The GameSettings class is another static value class similar to the DatExternalStrings class we just reviewed. It's mainly used to hold values that configure the game engine and as a place for user-defined fields that control how the game plays. Remember, you can set values for the static fields of this class using the built-in game engine config file support.

Static Class Members

The GameSettings class is essentially a bank of static fields. There are a number of default fields used by the game engine that we'll review next.

Listing 11-13. GameSettings Static Class Members 1

```
//Game engine options
public static boolean INPUT_NORMALIZE_KEY_CODE = false;

public static String TARGET_GAME_SETTINGS_XML_VERSION = "1.0";
```

```
public static boolean LOAD_NATIVE_LIBRARIES = false;
public static boolean RUN_OS_SPECIFIC_CODE = true;
public static boolean DEVELOPMENT_MODE_ON = true;

//Game engine paths
public static String IMAGE_LOAD_DIR = "../cfg/drawable/";

public static String SOUND_LOAD_DIR = "../cfg/playable/";

public static String PROGRAM_IMAGE_LOAD_DIR = "../cfg/drawable/";

public static String PROGRAM_SOUND_LOAD_DIR = "../cfg/playable/";

public static String AUTO_IMAGE_LOAD_DIR = "../cfg/drawable/auto_load/";

public static String AUTO_SOUND_LOAD_DIR = "../cfg/playable/auto_load/";

public static String CLASS_CONFIG_DIR = "../cfg/class_config/";

//Game and developer information
public static String NAME = "Unknown";
public static String VERSION = "0.0.0";
public static String DEVELOPER_COMPANY = "Unknown";
public static String TITLE = "Unknown";
```

Remember, any one of the GameSettings class' static fields can be set at runtime using a game engine config file. The first entry, INPUT_NORMALIZE_KEY_CODE, turns on support for normalizing keyboard input codes. Enabling this will pipe all keyboard input through a normalization method where you can add support to adjust the keyboard input codes. The built-in normalization call is the NormalizeKeyCode method of the MmgHelper class from the MmgBase API.

The next two fields, LOAD_NATIVE_LIBRARIES and RUN_OS_SPECIFIC_CODE, are used in the game's static main class as part of the startup process. If the LOAD_NATIVE_LIBRARIES option is enabled, the engine will attempt to load gamepad drivers for the current operating system.

I should mention that there's no need to load gamepad drivers in the C# version of the engine. The C# implementation has gamepad support built in. Similarly, the RUN_OS_SPECIFIC_CODE field, if enabled, will turn on OS-specific code execution in the static main class. You have to add some code to run of course, but it will now be enabled in the engine. The development mode field is used to turn on developer and version information in the game window's title if enabled.

The next block of fields are the game engine's resource paths. The engine will be configured to look in the default location, based on the version of the engine, for resources. Look over them and make sure you understand what the paths are used for. The last set of fields provides information about the developer and version of the game. Make sure that the NAME field matches the name of the game-specific resource folders. The engine won't be able to find the folders otherwise.

By default, there are a number of input definitions in the GameSettings class. The next set of fields we'll look at define the dpad input IDs for the keyboard. There are also definitions for dpad input for other devices like GPIO and USB gamepads. These are the ID values that are passed along to the game screen when a device's dpad input is activated.

Listing 11-14. GameSettings Static Class Members 2

```
public static int SRC_KEYBOARD = 0;
public static int DOWN_KEYBOARD = 0;
public static int UP_KEYBOARD = 1;
public static int LEFT_KEYBOARD = 2;
public static int RIGHT_KEYBOARD = 3;
```

These fields provide unique identifiers for dpad input coming from the keyboard. Along with the dpad input definitions, there are also default values for processing other GPIO and USB gamepad input. Look over these fields and think about how they might be used. We won't cover gamepad input here, but it's good to have some idea about how it works.

Demonstration: GameSettings Class

The GameSettings class is ubiquitous throughout the MmgCore API. The following snippet of example code is from the GamePanel class' input registration found in the class constructor. Recall that the GamePanel is responsible for managing game screens and input among other things.

Listing 11-15. GameSettings Class Demonstration 1

```
1 if(GameSettings.INPUT_NORMALIZE_KEY_CODE) {
2     ProcessKeyClick(e.getKeyChar(), MmgHelper.NormalizeKeyCode(e.
      getKeyChar(), e.getKeyCode(), e.getExtendedKeyCode(), "java"));
3 } else {
4     ProcessKeyClick(e.getKeyChar(), e.getExtendedKeyCode());
5 }
```

The demonstration code listed in the preceding snippet shows us how the GameSettings class is used throughout the API to enable certain features. In this case, we're looking at the keyboard code normalization feature. If this setting is enabled, the ProcessKeyClick method is called with filtered key codes, line 2. If the option is not enabled, the normal input processing is used, line 4.

Chapter Conclusion

In this chapter, we completed a review of the MmgCore API's dynamic settings capabilities. Let's take a step back for a moment and try to look at the big picture. In the MmgBase API, we encountered very structured classes that were designed for interoperability. They supported features like cloning and comparison.

In the MmgCore API, we're encountering classes of a different nature. These classes are very specialized in nature, and as such there really isn't much use for functionality like cloning and comparison. This is because very often there is only one instance of the class being used. What we're seeing is that the MmgBase API benefits from being a generally defined API without much direct functionality expressed. On the other hand, the MmgCore API benefits from being a specifically defined API with much direct functionality expressed like windowing, resource loading, dynamic settings, and so on.

The functionality we've covered here is the engine's ability to provide settings data to the game. We've seen that you can provide command-line arguments that drive some of the game's settings like dimensions and frame rate. We've seen that you can specify a game engine config file either as a default or a dynamic option provided as a command-line argument. Lastly, we've seen the ability to manage game strings through the use of the `DatExternalStrings` class, and we've looked at the engine's central settings class, `GameSettings`. Let's summarize the classes we've reviewed in this chapter:

- DatConstantsEntry: An API class designed to model one row of data in a game engine config XML file.

- GameSettingsImporter: An API class used to parse and load a game engine config XML file.

- DatExternalStrings: An API class used to load and store strings based on a language code. Provides centralized string management for the API.

- GameSettings: The game engine's central settings class. This is where all the default game settings and options are stored. You can also use this class to store your own game-specific settings.

The ability to data drive aspects of your game is a powerful one. This is a feature that you'll see in other game engines and is integral to game development. Data-driven settings are used all the time to configure input, network connections, game variables, and more. It takes experience to know when certain values in your game should be driven by config files. Don't worry. You'll get that experience and more building games with this engine, and you can take that knowledge and apply it to the next set of tools you'll use in your game development journey.

CHAPTER 12

Event Handlers

In this chapter, we're going to review all of the event handlers that are defined in the MmgCore API. The new event handlers we'll cover are for generic, resource loading, and main menu events. We'll also look at event handlers implemented as an interface and as a class. The classes we'll review in this chapter are listed in the following:

- GenericEventMessage
- GenericEventHandler
- LoadResourceUpdateMessage
- LoadResourceUpdateHandler
- HandleMainMenuEvent

Event Handlers: GenericEventMessage

The GenericEventMessage class is a new event class designed to work with the MmgCore API. Now you might be wondering why we need a new event class when the MmgBase API already has one, the MmgEvent class. There is a good reason for it in this particular case; the GenericEventMessage is designed to work with the classes of the MmgCore API, as you'll see in just a bit.

Class Fields

The GenericEventMessage class is very concise. There are only three class fields for us to review, listed in the following group.

© Victor G Brusca 2021
V. G. Brusca, *Introduction to Video Game Engine Development*, https://doi.org/10.1007/978-1-4842-7039-4_12

Listing 12-1. GenericEventMessage Class Fields 1

```
public int id;
public Object payload;
public GameStates gameState;
```

The first field listed is the id field. This integer is used to identify the type of GenericEventMessage being sent. Note that it's ultimately your responsibility to define events and assign them unique IDs. The second field in the list is the payload. The payload field is an instance of the framework's Object class, or object if you're following along in C#.

The payload field is designed to be general in nature and hold any object you need to include in the event. You can use this field to add data to the event message. The last field listed in the preceding is the gameState field. We've encountered the GameStates enumeration before during the GamePanel class' review.

They are used to track game screens and assign them to a unique game state. The MmgBase API has no real concept of a game state. It has no real concept of a game really. It's just a generalized set of powerful game-building classes. It's not until we reach the MmgCore API that the concepts of a game and a game state are well defined.

It's for this reason that it makes more sense to create a new, MmgCore API, event class that's designed to work with the objects and concepts at this level of the game engine. Next, we'll take a look at the class' support methods.

Support Method Details

The GenericEventMessage class has only a few class fields, so we should expect to see a reasonable number of support methods to review.

Listing 12-2. GenericEventMessage Support Method Details 1

```
public int GetId() { ... }
public Object GetPayload() { ... }
public GameStates GetGameState() { ... }
```

The support methods listed in the preceding are very direct, so I won't go into too much detail about them. Each method listed provides get access to the associated class field.

Main Method Details

There is only one main method for us to look at, the class constructor listed in the following.

Listing 12-3. GenericEventMessage Main Method Details 1

```
public GenericEventMessage(int Id, Object Payload, GameStates GameState) { ... }
```

This is the only main method we have to review. It's a class constructor that sets the class' fields to the associated argument.

Demonstration: GenericEventMessage Class

The snippet of code for this demonstration section is from the GamePanel class' HandleGenericEvent method. First, let's quickly take a look at the class' definition.

Listing 12-4. GenericEventMessage Class Demonstration 1

```
public class GamePanel implements GenericEventHandler, GamePadSimple { ... }
```

Notice that the class implements the GenericEventHandler interface. This means that this class can register as an event handler and receive GenericEventMessage events. Let's take a look at how the same class is defined in the C# version of the game engine.

Listing 12-5. GenericEventMessage Class Demonstration 2

```
public class GamePanel : Game, GenericEventHandler, GamePadSimple { ... }
```

They really do look almost exactly the same. The C# version also implements the GenericEventHandler interface just with slightly different syntax than the Java version. Let's direct our attention to the HandleGenericEvent method of the GamePanel class from the MmgCore API. I've detailed the method in the following.

Listing 12-6. GenericEventMessage Class Demonstration 3

```
01 public void HandleGenericEvent(GenericEventMessage obj) {
02     if (obj != null) {
03         if (obj.GetGameState() == GameStates.LOADING) {
```

```
04              if (obj.GetId() == ScreenLoading.EVENT_LOAD_COMPLETE) {
05                  DatExternalStrings.LOAD_EXT_STRINGS();
06                  SwitchGameState(GameStates.MAIN_MENU);
07              }
08          } else if (obj.GetGameState() == GameStates.SPLASH) {
09              if (obj.GetId() == ScreenSplash.EVENT_DISPLAY_COMPLETE) {
10                  SwitchGameState(GameStates.LOADING);
11              }
12          }
13      }
14 }
```

As a class that implements the GenericEventHandler interface, it must define the HandleGenericEvent method. This method is where the code for handling generic events should be placed. Note that the event handler is set up to process events associated with either the LOADING or SPLASH game state. If the event, the obj argument, is not null, then we begin to process the message by first checking its game state.

Next, we check the event's id field to see exactly what type of event we're handling. If the event is an EVENT_LOAD_COMPLETE event, then we load the game strings by calling the DatExternalStrings class' LOAD_EXT_STRINGS static method, line 5. On the subsequent line of code, the game state is changed to the main menu.

Similarly, the SPLASH game state's EVENT_DISPLAY_COMPLETE event causes a state change to the MAIN_MENU. Remember from the GamePanel class' review that GameStates and game screens are closely connected.

Event Handlers: GenericEventHandler

The GenericEventHandler is implemented as an interface, so we'll review the entire listing in one shot.

Listing 12-7. GenericEventHandler Class Review 1

```
1 public interface GenericEventHandler {
2     public void HandleGenericEvent(GenericEventMessage obj);
3 }
```

The GenericEventHandler interface is very simple. Any class that implements the interface must also declare a class method with the same signature as the HandleGenericEvent method listed. We saw this in the previous class review when we looked at the GamePanel class' HandleGenericEvent method.

Demonstration: GenericEventHandler Class

For the demonstration section of the GenericEventHandler class' review, we're going to take a look at how the GamePanel class is registered as an event handler, and then we'll take a look at from where the events are being fired. The following snippet of code is from the constructor of the GamePanel class from the MmgCore API.

Listing 12-8. GenericEventHandler Class Review 1

```
1 screenSplash.SetGenericEventHandler(this);
2 screenLoading.SetGenericEventHandler(this);
```

Now on lines 1 and 2 in the preceding, the screenSplash and screenLoading fields of the GamePanel class are configured to use the GamePanel as an event handler. This is the method we've just finished reviewing in the previous section. Now when the splash or loading screen fires a GenericEventMessage event, the GamePanel class will receive it. The next few lines of code show us how the ScreenSplash class fires an event.

Listing 12-9. GenericEventHandler Class Review 2

```
1 if (handler != null) {
2     handler.HandleGenericEvent(new GenericEventMessage(ScreenSplash.
    EVENT_DISPLAY_COMPLETE, null, GetGameState()));
3 }
```

As you can see, to fire an event, we call the HandleGenericEvent method of the assigned event handler, and we send it a GenericEventMessage object to process. The next line of code shows us how the ScreenLoading class fires off its event.

Listing 12-10. GenericEventHandler Class Review 3

```
1 if (handler != null) {
2     handler.HandleGenericEvent(new GenericEventMessage(ScreenLoading.
      EVENT_LOAD_COMPLETE, null, GetGameState()));
3 }
```

In a similar fashion to the way it's handled by the ScreenSplash class, the ScreenLoading class calls the HandleGenericEvent method and passes it a GenericEventMessage with an EVENT_LOAD_COMPLETE event ID to process.

Event Handlers: LoadResourceUpdateMessage

The LoadResourceUpdateMessage class is used to send resource loading events to a target LoadResourceMessage handler. Events of this type are used to convey information about the progress of the resource load.

Class Fields

The LoadResourceUpdateMessage class has two class fields for us to review listed in the following.

Listing 12-11. LoadResourceUpdateMessage Class Fields 1

```
public int pos;
public int len;
```

The first field listed is the pos field. This field indicates the current position of the resource load in terms of how many files have been loaded out of the total number of files to load. The len field represents the total number of resource files to load.

Support Method Details

The LoadResourceUpdateMessage has two sets of get and set methods for us to review.

Listing 12-12. LoadResourceUpdateMessage Support Method Details 1

```
public int GetPos() { ... }
public void SetPos(int Pos) { ... }
public int GetLen() { ... }
public void SetLen(int Len) { ... }
```

These are basic get and set methods that allow access to the class' fields. There's not much more to it than that. Let's take a look at the class constructor next.

Main Method Details

There is only one main method for us to review, the class constructor.

Listing 12-13. LoadResourceUpdateMessage Main Method Details 1

```
public LoadResourceUpdateMessage(int Pos, int Len) { ... }
```

The constructor is very basic and assigns argument values to each class field.

Demonstration: LoadResourceUpdateMessage Class

For the demonstration section of the LoadResourceUpdateMessage class, we'll take a look at the event handler that receives this type of event. The example code for this section is from the ScreenLoading class' HandleUpdate method from the MmgCore API. Let's take a look at some code.

Listing 12-14. LoadResourceUpdateMessage Class Demonstration 1

```
01 public void HandleUpdate(LoadResourceUpdateMessage obj) {
02     if (obj != null) {
03         float prct = (float) obj.GetPos() / (float) obj.GetLen();
04
05         if (GetLoadingBar() != null) {
06             GetLoadingBar().SetFillAmt(prct);
07         }
08
```

```
09          if (GetLoadComplete() == true) {
10              if (handler != null) {
11                  handler.HandleGenericEvent(new GenericEventMessage(Screen
                    Loading.EVENT_LOAD_COMPLETE, null, GetGameState()));
12              }
13          }
14      }
15 }
```

This method receives events from the RunResourceLoad class as it loads sounds and images into the engine's resource cache. If the event, obj, is not null, then we calculate the resource load's progress on line 3. If the loading bar is defined, we update the percentage complete. On lines 9–11, if the resource load is complete, a generic event is fired indicating it's time to change game states. We'll take a look at the source of these events when we review the LoadResourceUpdateHandler class next.

Event Handlers: LoadResourceUpdateHandler

The LoadResourceUpdateHandler is implemented as an interface, and we can list the entire interface right here. Let's take a look at some code!

Listing 12-15. LoadResourceUpdateHandler Class Review

```
1 public interface LoadResourceUpdateHandler {
2     public void HandleUpdate(LoadResourceUpdateMessage obj);
3 }
```

This interface is very similar to the GenericEventHandler interface. It's very simple in nature. Any class that implements the interface must define a HandleUpdate method and can receive LoadResourceUpdateMessage events if the class is registered to do so.

Demonstration: LoadResourceUpdateHandler Class

The snippet of example code listed in the following is from the RunResourceLoad class' run method from the MmgCore API. The code is part of the resource loading process run on a separate thread by the game's loading screen.

Listing 12-16. LoadResourceUpdateHandler Class Demonstration 1

```
01 MmgHelper.GetBasicCachedBmp(adFiles.get(i).getPath(), adFiles.get(i).
   getName());
02 readPos = i * loadMultiplier;
03
04 if (update != null) {
05     update.HandleUpdate(new LoadResourceUpdateMessage(readPos,
       readLen));
06 }
07
08 try {
09     Thread.sleep(slowDown);
10 } catch (Exception e) {
11     MmgHelper.wrErr(e);
12 }
13
14 if(exitLoad) {
15     break;
16 }
```

Because this snippet of code is part of the resource loading process, the first line of code loads the target resource file into the engine's resource cache. The current loading progress is calculated on line 2. Note that the read position is artificially increased by the loadMultiplier field.

This is done to make sure the calculations work with very few resources. A new LoadResourceUpdateMessage event is created and sent to the registered event handler if one exists on line 5. If the exitLoad field is set to true, we exit the loading process.

Event Handlers: HandleMainMenuEvent

The HandleMainMenuEvent class is used to represent a main menu event action. Instances of this class are generated when the user selects a main menu option.

Static Class Members

The class' static fields are used to define some default main menu events. You don't have to use these event IDs; you can create your own set to accommodate your needs. Let's take a look at the static fields listed in the following.

Listing 12-17. HandleMainMenuEvent Static Class Members 1

```
public static int MAIN_MENU_EVENT_TYPE = 0;
public static int MAIN_MENU_EVENT_START_GAME = 0;
public static int MAIN_MENU_EVENT_SETTINGS = 1;
public static int MAIN_MENU_EVENT_ABOUT = 2;
public static int MAIN_MENU_EVENT_HELP = 3;
public static int MAIN_MENU_EVENT_EXIT_GAME = 4;
public static int MAIN_MENU_EVENT_START_GAME_1P = 5;
public static int MAIN_MENU_EVENT_START_GAME_2P = 6;
```

The first static field listed in the preceding is a type value for main menu events. The next seven entries are default event IDs for a default set of menu items. These defaults should serve you well for most of your games as the options presented are very standard. Let's take a look at the class fields next.

Class Fields

The HandleMainMenuEvent class has only two fields for us to talk about.

Listing 12-18. HandleMainMenuEvent Class FIelds 1

```
private MmgGameScreen cApp;
private GamePanel owner;
```

This event class is intimately tied to the MmgGameScreen class of the MmgBase API. Recall that the MmgGameScreen class has a built-in menu system support. The HandleMainMenuEvent class is designed to work with the default menu system. As such, the first class field listed in the preceding references the MmgGameScreen that this event originates from. The second class field references the GamePanel that manages the game screen listed in the cApp field. This class has no support methods to speak of, so we'll move on to the main method review.

Main Method Details

The HandleMainMenuEvent class has two main methods for us to discuss.

Listing 12-19. HandleMainMenuEvent Main Method Details

```
public HandleMainMenuEvent(MmgGameScreen CApp, GamePanel Owner) { ... }

public void MmgHandleEvent(MmgEvent e) { ... }
```

The first method listed is the class constructor. It updates class fields based on the constructor arguments. The next method listed is the MmgEventHandler method, and it's used to process and respond to menu events.

Demonstration: HandleMainMenuEvent Class

The demonstration code listed in the following is from the MmgCore API's ScreenMainMenu class. I should mention that the HandleMainMenuEvent class is a little bit different than previous classes we've reviewed in that the event handler is a class, not an interface. This is due to the predictable nature of the menu event system and the tight integration the menu system has with the MmgGameScreen class.

Listing 12-20. HandleMainMenuEvent Class Demonstration 1

```
1 handleMenuEvent = new HandleMainMenuEvent(this, owner);
```

The menu event handler is initialized, as shown in the preceding, in the ScreenMainMenu class' LoadResources method. Let's take a look at how the menu items are initialized in this game screen. The next snippet of code is from the class' DrawScreen method.

Listing 12-21. HandleMainMenuEvent Class Demonstration 2

```
1 if (menuStartGame != null) {
2     mItm = MmgHelper.GetBasicMenuItem(handleMenuEvent, "Main Menu
      Start Game", HandleMainMenuEvent.MAIN_MENU_EVENT_START_GAME,
      HandleMainMenuEvent.MAIN_MENU_EVENT_TYPE, menuStartGame);
3     mItm.SetSound(menuSound);
4     menu.Add(mItm);
5 }
```

If the menu item image is defined, we create a new menu item using the `MmgHelper` class' `GetBasicMenuItem` method. Notice that the first argument is the class' menu handler. When this menu item is selected, an event is sent to the registered menu event handler.

Chapter Conclusion

In this chapter, we took a deep dive into the MmgCore API events and event handlers. We learned how the `ScreenSplash` class used generic events to communicate to the `GamePanel` class that it was time to change screens. We saw a similar implementation in the `ScreenLoading` class with its own resource load complete generic event.

We also got to see how the load resource message events were used to send information to the `ScreenLoading` class about the progress of the game's resource load and how the game screen fired off an event of its own to tell the `GamePanel` the load process was complete and to change states to the main menu.

The details of these events and event handlers are important. You should know how the default game screens are wired up to the `GamePanel,` and you should understand the different types of event systems at your disposal. Let's take a look at a summary of the MmgCore API classes covered in this chapter:

- GenericEventMessage: An MmgCore API class used to represent a generic event with the event associated to a game state. This class provides generic event support to the API.

- GenericEventHandler: An MmgCore API interface that is implemented to support receiving generic events from registered sources. This interface provides generic event handling support to the API.

- LoadResourceUpdateMessage: An MmgCore API message that is used to send information about a resource loading process to a registered event handler. This class provides resource loading event message support to the API.

- LoadResourceUpdateHandler: An MmgCore API interface that is implemented to support receiving load resource update events. This interface provides load resource update event handling support to the API.

- HandleMainMenuEvent: An MmgCore API class used to support menu system events. These events are fired by the menu system when a menu item is selected. The events are processed by a class and not an interface. This class provides basic menu support to the API.

There are some very subtle but important points in the classes we reviewed during this chapter. One take-away is the way you can use events to facilitate inter–game screen and game screen-to-game panel communication. Using the event systems and the different techniques outlined in this chapter, you will be able to create your own events to manage game states – a key aspect of any game.

The other main take-away, I would say, is just getting used to working with events and event handlers. You will encounter events time and time again, from game engine to game engine, so it's good to get experience working with them in your own games. Furthermore, you'll gain invaluable experience learning when to use events. There shouldn't be many events in your game. Events are reserved for cross-class communication where a user action requires that a game screen ask the game panel to do something for it. Follow this general rule of thumb but realize there are always exceptions.

CHAPTER 13

Resource Loading

Resource loading and access is one of the most important aspects of any game engine. It's difficult to make a 2D game without any images. In this chapter, we'll cover, in detail, the game engine's runtime code for loading resources. You'll see how sounds and images are accessed explicitly, globally, or through game-specific resource folders.

In the upcoming sections, we'll review the resource loading process and the exact code to load resources for use in your game screens. In this chapter, we'll review the following classes and topics:

- RunResourceLoad

- Topic: Accessing Explicit Resources

- Topic: Accessing Auto Load Resources

- Topic: Accessing Game-Specific Resources

Resource Loading: RunResourceLoad

The RunResourceLoad class is designed to run in its own thread and is used to load game resources, like sounds and images, into the game engine's resource cache. The resource cache is governed by the MmgBase API's MmgMediaTracker class. Before we get into the class review, let's take a look at the Java and C# class definitions for the RunResourceLoad class.

Listing 13-1. RunResourceLoad Class Intro 1

```
//Java implementation
public class RunResourceLoad implements Runnable { ... }

//C# implementation
public class RunResourceLoad { ... }
```

© Victor G Brusca 2021

V. G. Brusca, *Introduction to Video Game Engine Development*, https://doi.org/10.1007/978-1-4842-7039-4_13

Notice that the Java version of the class implements the Runnable interface. This is a framework-level interface that is used to execute the class' functionality in a separate thread. Don't worry. The same threading functionality exists in the C# implementation. It's just gone about slightly differently as there is no equivalent Runnable interface used. I just wanted to point out this slight difference before we began the class review.

Class Fields

The RunResourceLoad class has a few class fields regarding the resource loading process. Let's have a look!

Listing 13-2. RunResourceLoad Class Fields 1

```
public boolean readResult;
public boolean readComplete;
public int readPos;
public int readLen;
public int loadMultiplier = 1000;
public LoadResourceUpdateHandler update;
public long slowDown;
public boolean exitLoad;
```

The first two fields listed in the preceding are used to report the result of resource load operations. The readResult field holds a true value if any sound or image was loaded during the resource processing operation. The readComplete field is set to true if the entire load process has finished. The readPos and readLen fields track the current position in the resource loading process and the total number of files to load, respectively.

The loadMultiplier field is used to artificially increase the sizes of the numbers we're working with. All this does is help with the progress percentage in the case that there are very few resources to load. The slowDown field is used to artificially slow down the loading process by adding a small time sink into the operations. This helps greatly when you only have a few resources to load and you want to verify your loading bar is working correctly. Adding in a slowdown value makes it so you can see the progress bar a lot easier.

Support Method Details

The RunResourceLoad class' support methods are listed in the following group in the same order as their corresponding fields.

Listing 13-3. RunResourceLoad Support Method Details 1

```
public boolean GetReadResult() { ... }
public boolean GetReadComplete() { ... }
public int GetPos() { ... }
public int GetLen() { ... }
public void SetUpdateHandler(LoadResourceUpdateHandler Update) { ... }

public long GetSlowDown() { ... }
public void SetSlowDown(long l) { ... }
public void StopLoad() { ... }
```

The first four support methods are just get methods for their associated class fields. The method following that group is the SetUpdateHandler method. It's used to set the class' update field. The slowDown field has a pair of get and set methods followed by the StopLoad method. The StopLoad method will force the resource loading process to exit on the next loop iteration.

Main Method Details

The RunResourceLoad class has two main methods I want to review.

Listing 13-4. RunResourceLoad Main Method Details 1

```
public RunResourceLoad() { ... }
public void run() { ... }
```

The first entry is the class constructor. It takes no arguments and prepares the class for immediate use. The second method listed in the preceding is the heart of the resource loading process. This method is defined by the Runnable interface and is called as part of the thread start process. You can, however, call the method directly yourself if need be.

Demonstration: RunResourceLoad Class

For the RunResourceLoad class' demonstration section, we'll take a look at the sound and image resource loading process – specifically, the part of the process where the target resource files to load are identified. The steps are identical for sounds and images, so I'll only detail the image loading steps in the following.

Listing 13-5. RunResourceLoad Class Demonstration 1

```
01 adld = new File(GameSettings.AUTO_IMAGE_LOAD_DIR);
02 if(adld.exists()) {
03     srcFiles = adld.listFiles();
04     clnFiles = new ArrayList();
05
06     for(j = 0; j < srcFiles.length; j++) {
07         if(srcFiles[j].getName().charAt(0) != '.' && (srcFiles[j].
           getName().toLowerCase().indexOf(".png") != -1 || srcFiles[j].
           getName().toLowerCase().indexOf(".jpg") != -1 || srcFiles[j].
           getName().toLowerCase().indexOf(".bmp") != -1)) {
08             clnFiles.add(srcFiles[j]);
09         }
10     }
11
12     adFiles.addAll(clnFiles);
13     if(adFiles != null && adFiles.size() > 0) {
14         readLen = (adFiles.size() - 1) * loadMultiplier;
15     }
16 }
```

The process we're about to outline is run on the GameSettings class' AUTO_IMAGE_LOAD_DIR field as well as the PROGRAM_IMAGE_LOAD_DIR field. This means that for sound and image resources, we process an auto load directory as well as a game-specific directory. If the target resource folder exists, line 2, then we initialize an array of files found in the folder on line 3. On line 4, the clnFiles local variable is reset to an empty ArrayList. This data structure will hold valid resource files for future processing.

The loop on lines 6–10 iterates over all the files in the srcFiles array checking the file name and extension to make sure the file is a valid resource. If so, the file is stored in the clnFiles data structure on line 8. The set of clean files we've found are added to the main list of image files to load on line 12. If valid resource files have been found, the readLen field is updated to reflect the new total file count. Again, keep in mind that this process is performed for sound and image files.

The next snippet of code up for review shows the image resource processing step. This step loads the image resource files into the game's resource cache.

Listing 13-6. RunResourceLoad Class Demonstration 2

```
01    tlen = adFiles.size();
02
03    for(i = 0; i < tlen; i++) {
04        MmgHelper.wr("RunResourceLoad: Found auto_load file: " + adFiles.
          get(i).getName() + " Path: " + adFiles.get(i).getPath());
05        MmgHelper.GetBasicCachedBmp(adFiles.get(i).getPath(), adFiles.
          get(i).getName());
06        readPos = i * loadMultiplier;
07
08        if (update != null) {
09            update.HandleUpdate(new LoadResourceUpdateMessage(readPos,
              readLen));
10        }
11
12        try {
13            Thread.sleep(slowDown);
14        } catch (Exception e) {
15            MmgHelper.wrErr(e);
16        }
17
18        if(exitLoad) {
19            break;
20        }
21    }
22 }
```

We've seen this snippet of code before during the Chapter 12 review of resource loading events and event handlers. I won't spend a lot of time on this example code. The main take-away from this snippet is that for each vetted file to load, the MmgHelper class' GetBasicCachedBmp method is called, line 5. This method is responsible for loading the image into the cache if it doesn't already exist.

Topic: Accessing Explicit Resources

In this topic section, we're going to review the details involved with manually accessing resources. You might be wondering why we need to access resources directly when they are loaded into the game's resource cache for us.

Think about the game screens that display before the loading screen. They also need to access resources but can't rely on the engine's cache. In that case, we have to manually load resources into a game screen. The following snippet demonstrates directly accessing resources.

Listing 13-7. Topic: Accessing Explicit Resources 1

```
MmgHelper.GetBasicBmp("../cfg/drawable/popup_window_base.png");

MmgHelper.GetBasicSound("../cfg/playable/jump1.wav");
```

In the preceding short example, we're doing a direct resource load. The only requirement here is that the resource must exist. The next section is a slight permutation of this resource access approach.

Topic: Accessing Auto Load Resources

We're going to take a look at the code used to load resources that were placed in the auto load directory. Recall that there are three levels of resources for both sounds and images: explicit resources, auto load resources, and game-specific resources. Think of the auto load resources as belonging to the game engine, for instance, default images and default sounds that are included with the game engine's project.

Listing 13-8. Topic: Accessing Auto Load Resources 1

```
MmgHelper.GetBasicBmp(GameSettings.IMAGE_LOAD_DIR + "file_name.png");

MmgHelper.GetBasicSound(GameSettings.SOUND_LOAD_DIR + "file_name.png");
```

While this example is very similar to the first topic section, there are some subtle but important points I want to discuss. The first thing I'd like to point out is the path value stored in the game settings class. There is a hidden agreement here that the path variable, IMAGE_LOAD_DIR, ends with a path separation character. Thus, when used, you need only append the file name. Make sure you are aware of and consistent with how you use your resource paths.

The previous two examples demonstrate direct resource loading. The precedent with regard to direct resources is to place them at the root of the corresponding resource folder. For instance, a direct image resource should be placed in the root of the drawable folder. Similarly, the sound resource is placed in the root of the playable folder. The next examples demonstrate accessing cached resources. These resources reside in **auto_load** directories in the **drawable** and **playable** folders.

Listing 13-9. Topic: Accessing Auto Load Resources 2

```
MmgHelper.GetBasicCachedBmp(GameSettings.IMAGE_LOAD_DIR + "file_name.png",
"file_name.png");
MmgHelper.GetBasicCachedBmp("file_name.png");

MmgHelper.GetBasicCachedSound(GameSettings.SOUND_LOAD_DIR + "file_name.
png", "file_name.wav");
MmgHelper.GetBasicCachedSound("file_name.wav");
```

In the code example listed in the preceding, the first entry loads a resource and stores it in the game engine's resource cache if it doesn't already exist. It also returns the new image resource for use. The next method entry will only pull a cached image resource for use if it exists. The same functionality exists for sound resources and is also listed in the preceding.

Topic: Accessing Game-Specific Resources

Let's take a look at the game-specific resource access calls. The game-specific folder exists in the root of the **drawable** and **playable** folders next to the **auto_load** directory and direct load resources. There is a nuance as to how this aspect of the resource system works. Let's take a look at a few lines of code from the MmgApiGame class' main method from the MmgCore API.

Listing 13-10. Topic: Accessing Game-Specific Resources 1

```
GameSettings.PROGRAM_IMAGE_LOAD_DIR += GameSettings.NAME;
GameSettings.PROGRAM_SOUND_LOAD_DIR += GameSettings.NAME;
```

The code listed in the preceding is default functionality built into the template static main class. The thing you need to be aware of is that the game's name, GameSettings. NAME, must be a valid folder name and the game-specific resource folder must match. Once that is taken care of, the game resources in the program-specific resource folder will be loaded as part of the game's startup process.

Listing 13-11. Topic: Accessing Game-Specific Resources 2

```
MmgHelper.GetBasicCachedBmp("game_file_name.png");
MmgHelper.GetBasicCachedSound("game_file_name.wav");
```

The two lines of code listed in the preceding demonstrate how to access resources loaded from the game-specific resource folder. The process is the same as with the auto load resources. That concludes our review of the different ways you can access game resources.

Chapter Conclusion

In this chapter, we took a moment to talk about an important aspect of the game engine, resource loading and resource access. You will encounter this topic when working with any game engine. There are all kinds of approaches to handling game resources.

Some engines will load resources into an intermediate format and preprocess the resources during the editing phase of the game. Our engine is designed to work directly off of the file system, hopefully making the use of game sounds and images quick and easy. Let me summarize the classes and topics we've reviewed in this chapter:

- RunResourceLoad: An MmgCore API class that is responsible for scanning the auto load and game-specific directories listed in the GameSettings file. A set of target files to load is created as a result of the scan. The individual files are processed and loaded into the game engine's image and sound resource caches.

- Topic: Accessing Explicit Resources: A demonstration of how to access sound and image resources directly with just a file path.

- Topic: Accessing Auto Load Resources: A demonstration of how to access sound and image resources that have been processed as an auto load resource.

- Topic: Accessing Game-Specific Resources: A demonstration of how to access sound and image resources that have been processed as a game-specific resource.

This chapter was a short but important chapter. We covered all the different ways you can access resources and use them in your game screens. Notice the flexibility in accessing resources; there are a few different ways for you to do things, which is always beneficial when designing a new game. I hope you have a good understanding of how the engine handles loading resources of different types and have the ability to access them from different screens in your games.

CHAPTER 14

Game Screens

The focus of this chapter is to review and understand how the MmgCore API's game screen and frame rate classes work with the GamePanel class to drive the game engine's drawing routine. We'll also want to review some subtle details about the set of game screens that have been implemented in the MmgCore API.

These game screens are more concrete in their implementation than those we encountered in the MmgBase API and are designed to plug into the engine's game panel class. A summary of the classes covered in this chapter is as follows:

- RunFrameRate

- ScreenSplash

- ScreenLoading

- ScreenMainMenu

- Screen

Game Screens: RunFrameRate

The RunFrameRate class is only used by the Java version of the game engine. The RunFrameRate class is designed to, as one might expect, drive the engine's frame rate. Because the C# version of the engine sits on top of the MonoGame API, the frame rate control is built into that framework's Game class.

In that case, you can adjust the frame rate by simply setting a class field, TargetElapsedTime. It's important for us to understand frame rates and how threading is used to drive the Java version of the game engine's drawing routine and subsequently the game's frame rate. Let's jump into some code!

© Victor G Brusca 2021
V. G. Brusca, *Introduction to Video Game Engine Development*, https://doi.org/10.1007/978-1-4842-7039-4_14

Static Class Members

There are two static class fields for us to review. These entries are used to control the frame rate thread and its main execution loop.

Listing 14-1. RunFrameRate Static Class Members 1

```
public static boolean PAUSE = false;
public static boolean RUNNING = true;
```

The first field listed in the preceding is the PAUSE field. This field is used to prevent the class' main execution loop from redrawing the current game screen. The RUNNING field controls the class' main loop. If this field is set to false, the frame rate thread will exit immediately. Let's move on to the class' static methods next.

Listing 14-2. RunFrameRate Static Class Members 2

```
public static boolean IsPaused() { ... }
public static void Pause() { ... }
public static void UnPause() { ... }
public static void StartRunning() { ... }
public static void StopRunning() { ... }
```

The static methods are listed in the preceding in the same order as their associated class fields. The methods are self-explanatory for the most part. The IsPaused method provides static get access to the PAUSE field. The next two entries provide static control methods for pausing or unpausing the main loop. Similarly, the StartRunning and StopRunning entries provide static control methods for starting and stopping the main execution loop and subsequently the engine's drawing routine.

Class Fields

There are a number of class fields for us to look at. They deal mainly with measuring frame timing. I've broken them up into two groups and listed the first group in the following.

Listing 14-3. RunFrameRate Class Fields 1

```
public final MainFrame mf;
public final long tFps;
public final long tFrameTime;
public long aFps;
public long rFps;
```

The first class field listed is a reference to the game's MainFrame object, mf. The following entry, tFps, represents the target frames per second the game is set to run at. The tFrameTime field is the target frame time in milliseconds. This value is calculated from the target frames per second. If you set your game to run at 30 frames per second, FPS, then a new frame will be drawn to the screen every 33.3 milliseconds.

This means that you have that much time to prepare the game's next frame. This small amount of time may seem like hardly enough time to do anything, but believe me it's a lot of time. Not only can you draw the next game frame in this amount of time but you can also run all necessary update calls.

The next two fields provide measurements about how the game is running. The first such field, aFps, indicates the frame rate the game would run at if it wasn't being throttled to the target FPS. This essentially shows you how fast your game would run if it was running at full speed. The following field, rFps, represents the real frame rate; and its value shows you how close to the target FPS your game is running.

Listing 14-4. RunFrameRate Class Fields 2

```
public long frameStart;
public long frameStop;
public long frameTime;
public long frameTimeDiff;
```

The next group of class fields are also used in frame timing calculations. As you can see, this class is mainly concerned with running the game at a consistent frame rate. The frameStart and frameStop fields mark the beginning and end times of the current frame.

The frameTime field holds the calculated total time it took to process the frame. The last entry, frameTimeDiff, measures the difference in milliseconds between how much time the frame took to process and the amount of time allotted for a given game frame. If there's any time left over, we sleep the thread for that amount of time before starting on the next frame.

279

Support Method Details

The RunFrameRate class has only two support methods for us to look at.

Listing 14-5. RunFrameRate Support Method Details 1

```
public long GetActualFrameRate() { ... }
public long GetTargetFrameRate() { ... }
```

The two methods listed in the preceding are simply access methods for the tFps and aFps fields, respectively.

Main Method Details

There are two main methods for us to cover listed in the following.

Listing 14-6. RunFrameRate Main Method Details 1

```
public RunFrameRate(MainFrame Mf, long Fps) { ... }
public void run() { ... }
```

The mf and tFps fields are set from the class' constructor arguments. The tFrameTime is calculated and set based on the target FPS provided. The run method is where all the work is done. This method is called as part of the Java framework's Runnable interface. The run method gets called automatically as part of starting a new thread. That's it, short and sweet. The class is ready to use.

Demonstration: RunFrameRate Class

For the RunFrameRate demonstration section, we'll take a look at three snippets of code. The first snippet is from the MmgCore API's MmgApiGame class at the bottom of the main method.

Listing 14-7. RunFrameRate Class Demonstration 1

```
1 fr = new RunFrameRate(mf, FPS);
```

In the line of code listed in the preceding, we are shown the initialization of the RunFrameRate class. It takes a MainFrame object and a frame rate as arguments. The FPS variable shown in the preceding is a class field that can be adjusted by command-line arguments and game engine config files.

Listing 14-8. RunFrameRate Class Demonstration 2

```
1 t = new Thread(fr);
2 t.start();
```

In the next snippet of code, also from the MmgApiGame class' main method, the frame rate thread is started. This starts the game engine's drawing routine and calls the RunFrameRate class' run method.

Listing 14-9. RunFrameRate Class Demonstration 3

```
01 while (RunFrameRate.RUNNING == true) {
02     frameStart = System.currentTimeMillis();
03
04     if (RunFrameRate.PAUSE == false) {
05         mf.Redraw();
06     }
07
08     frameStop = System.currentTimeMillis();
09     frameTime = (frameStop - frameStart) + 1;
10     aFps = (1000 / frameTime);
11
12     frameTimeDiff = tFrameTime - frameTime;
13     if (frameTimeDiff > 0) {
14         try {
15             Thread.sleep((int) frameTimeDiff);
16         } catch (Exception e) {
17             MmgHelper.wrErr(e);
18         }
19     }
20
```

```
21      frameStop = System.currentTimeMillis();
22      frameTime = (frameStop - frameStart) + 1;
23      rFps = (1000 / frameTime);
24      mf.SetFrameRate(aFps, rFps);
25 }
```

Notice on the preceding first line that the class' main execution loop only executes if the RUNNING field is set to true. The RunFrameRate class is started through the use of the Java framework's Thread class, shown in the previous snippet. This causes the RunFrameRate class' run method to execute in a new thread. On line 2, the frameStart field is updated with the current time. This value will be used to determine how much time this frame takes to process.

The if statement on lines 4–6 checks to see if the RunFrameRate class is paused or not. If the class is paused, then no work is done on this frame, and the main loop carries on as normal. The value of frameStop is updated on line 8, and the total time to process the frame is calculated on line 9. Why do you think we update the calculated time and add one millisecond? Think about the phrase "calculated frame time." One issue that stands out is we might end up with a frame time of zero milliseconds.

This would cause a divide by zero exception on line 10, and we simply can't have that. By adding one millisecond to the frameTime, we essentially set the floor for the timing to one instead of zero. Subsequently on line 10, the value of the actual frame rate field, aFps, is calculated. As you can see, the value reflects only the time it took to draw the current frame.

The block of code on lines 12–19 sleeps the current thread for the excess time on this game frame. For instance, if we want the game to run at 30 FPS, then we have 33 milliseconds to draw the current frame, including running update calls. If it only takes us 20 milliseconds to do all of that work, then we have to sleep the thread for 13 milliseconds. That's what this code does. The code on lines 21–23 updates the frameStop field and calculates a new runtime FPS. This time the measurement is taken after the frame is created, and the thread is slept for a few milliseconds.

What this means is that this calculation is the real frame rate, or the frame rate experienced by the player. Lastly, on line 24, a call to SetFrameRate updates the debug header with fresh frame rate statistics.

Game Screens: ScreenSplash

The ScreenSplash class is the concrete implementation of the MmgSplashScreen class. What I mean by concrete implementation is that the general class, MmgSplashScreen, has its generic functionality extended to plug into the runtime code –specifically, the GamePanel class. Let's see how it's done!

Static Class Members

There is only one static class member to look at listed in the following line of code.

Listing 14-10. ScreenSplash Static Class Members 1

```
public static int EVENT_DISPLAY_COMPLETE = 0;
```

This static field is used as an event ID that marks an event object as indicating that the splash screen's display time is up.

Class Fields

The ScreenSplash class has four fields for us to review.

Listing 14-11. ScreenSplash Class Fields 1

```
public GameStates state;
public GenericEventHandler handler;
public GamePanel owner;
public Hashtable<String, MmgCfgFileEntry> classConfig;
```

The first field, state, is used to represent what game state this game screen is associated with. The handler field receives any generic events generated by this class. Subsequently, the owner field represents the GamePanel object that this game screen belongs to. Lastly, the classConfig data structure is used to hold config file data that drives runtime screen customization.

Support Method Details

The class support methods, listed in the following, provide access to pertinent class fields.

Listing 14-12. ScreenSplash Support Method Details 1

```
public GameStates GetGameState() { ... }
public GenericEventHandler GetGenericEventHandler() { ... }

public void SetGenericEventHandler(GenericEventHandler Handler) { ... }
```

I've listed the support methods in the same order as their corresponding class fields. The methods are straightforward, so I won't cover them in any detail here. The first entry provides access to the gameState field, while the next two are get and set methods for the handler field. Let's move on to review the class' main methods.

Main Method Details

The class' main methods handle MmgSplashScreen events, drawing the screen, and loading or unloading screen resources.

Listing 14-13. ScreenSplash Main Method Details 1

```
public ScreenSplash(GameStates State, GamePanel Owner) { ... }

public void MmgDraw(MmgPen p) { ... }
public void MmgHandleUpdate(Object obj) { ... }
public void LoadResources() { ... }
public void UnloadResources() { ... }
```

The first entry, as we expect, is a class constructor. The constructor takes a game state and a game panel as arguments. The MmgDraw method is one we've seen before during the MmgBase API review in Part 1 of this text. This method hasn't come up too much during our review of the MmgCore API. The reason for this is that only MmgCore game screens plug into the GamePanel class for display. As such, these are the only API classes where we'll encounter the MmgUpdate and MmgDraw methods.

The following method, MmgHandleUpdate, is used to respond to the MmgSplashScreen's internal timer that controls how long the screen displays for. The last two methods are used to load and unload all of the resources used by this game screen.

Demonstration: ScreenSplash Class

The ScreenSplash class' demonstration section starts with a code snippet from the GamePanel's constructor. Navigate to that file and open it in your IDE. Let's review some code!

Listing 14-14. ScreenSplash Class Demonstration 1

```
1 screenSplash = new ScreenSplash(GameStates.SPLASH, this);

2 screenSplash.SetGenericEventHandler(this);
```

The use of the class constructor shows us how the ScreenSplash class is initialized. Notice that it takes a game state and a game panel for arguments. The second line of code registers the GamePanel class as the splash screen's generic event handler. This means that the game panel can receive certain events from the splash screen class. The next snippet of code is from the GamePanel class' SwitchGameState method.

Listing 14-15. ScreenSplash Class Demonstration 2

```
1 } else if (prevGameState == GameStates.SPLASH) {
2     MmgHelper.wr("Hiding SPLASH screen.");
3     screenSplash.Pause();
4     screenSplash.SetIsVisible(false);
5     screenSplash.UnloadResources();
6 }
```

In this snippet, the GamePanel's prevGameState field is used to clean up the previous game state before changing to the new state. Note that the game screen is paused and hidden and its resources released all as part of deactivating the screen.

Listing 14-16. ScreenSplash Class Demonstration 3

```
1 } else if (gameState == GameStates.SPLASH) {
2     MmgHelper.wr("Showing SPLASH screen.");
3     screenSplash.LoadResources();
4     screenSplash.UnPause();
5     screenSplash.SetIsVisible(true);
6     screenSplash.StartDisplay();
7     currentScreen = screenSplash;
8 }
```

The final snippet of demonstration code is also from the SwitchGameState method. This code shows how the splash screen is activated for display. Notice the order in which the screen's methods are called. First, the screen's resources are loaded. Then the screen is unpaused and made visible. A screen-specific method, StartDisplay, is called to start the splash screen's internal timer. The final line of code is very important. This line sets the game screen as the active game screen for the GamePanel class, line 7.

Game Screens: ScreenLoading

The ScreenLoading class is similar to the ScreenSplash class in that they are both concrete implementations of an MmgBase class. In this case, the ScreenLoading class extends the MmgLoadingScreen class. The ScreenLoading class extends its super class adding support for game screens and game panels.

Static Class Members

The ScreenLoading class has one static class member just like its splash screen counterpart.

Listing 14-17. ScreenLoading Static Class Members 1

```
public static int EVENT_LOAD_COMPLETE = 0;
```

In the same fashion as the ScreenSplash class, the ScreenLoading class' static field is used as an event ID that marks an event object as indicating the screen is done loading resources.

Class Fields

Some of the class fields listed in the following snippet should be familiar from our review of the MmgLoadingScreen and RunResourceLoad classes.

Listing 14-18. ScreenLoading Class Fields 1

```
public RunResourceLoad datLoad;
public GameStates state;
public GenericEventHandler handler;
public GamePanel owner;
public long slowDown;
public Hashtable<String, MmgCfgFileEntry> classConfig;
```

The datLoad field is responsible for running the resource load in a new thread. The state field is the game state this game screen is associated with. Next, the handler field receives any generic events generated by the ScreenLoading class. Lastly, the owner field is the GamePanel object this screen belongs to.

The slowDown field that follows should look familiar. This value is used to artificially sleep the resource loading thread so that the loading screen's progress bar is easier to see during small resource loads. The last entry is the classConfig field. This field is used to hold class config file data if any exists.

Support Method Details

The ScreenLoading class has a number of support methods that give you access to pertinent class fields, start and stop the resource load, and set up the generic event handler. Let's take a look!

Listing 14-19. ScreenLoading Support Method Details 1

```
public RunResourceLoad GetLoader() { ... }
public void SetLoader(RunResourceLoad DatLoad) { ... }

public boolean GetLoadComplete() { ... }
public boolean GetLoadResult() { ... }
public GameStates GetGameState() { ... }
public GenericEventHandler GetGenericEventHandler() { ... }
```

```
public void SetGenericEventHandler(GenericEventHandler Handler) { ... }

public long GetSlowDown() { ... }
public void SetSlowDown(long l) { ... }
public boolean GetResourceFileData() { ... }
public void StartDatLoad() { ... }
public void StopDatLoad() { ... }
```

I've listed the support methods in the preceding in roughly the same order as the class fields previously reviewed. The first two entries are get and set methods for the datLoad field. The GetLoadComplete and GetLoadResults methods provide access to resource load status information. We've seen the GetGameState method before. It provides access to the screen's game state value. The next four methods are two get and set pairs for the handler and slowDown fields, respectively.

The GetResourceFileData method's only purpose is to determine if there are any resources to load. It doesn't perform any advanced scans; it's just looking for at least one resource to load. The last two methods are responsible for starting and stopping the resource load process, the StartDatLoad and StopDatLoad methods. Keep an eye out for those two methods in the class' demonstration section.

Main Method Details

The ScreenLoading class has a standard set of main methods for us to look at, listed in the following group.

Listing 14-20. ScreenLoading Main Method Details 1

```
public ScreenLoading(MmgLoadingBar LoadingBar, float lBarOff, GameStates
State, GamePanel Owner) { ... }

public ScreenLoading(GameStates State, GamePanel Owner) { ... }

public void HandleUpdate(LoadResourceUpdateMessage obj) { ... }

public void LoadResources() { ... }
public void UnloadResources() { ... }
public void MmgDraw(MmgPen p) { ... }
```

The first constructor listed lets you set the loading bar's positioning offset. Remember these fields from our review of the MmgLoadingScreen class. It also takes arguments for the game state and the game panel this game screen belongs to. The second constructor listed is an abridged version that doesn't take any loading bar arguments. You'll be expected to set them on your own before you use the class.

The HandleUpdate main method is used to process resource load update events. These are used to set the values of the loading bar. The next two entries we've seen a few times before. The LoadResources method sets up all the class' resources so it's ready to be displayed. The UnloadResources method releases all class resources. The last entry is the MmgDraw method, which is called by the GamePanel class as part of the engine's drawing routine. The MmgDraw method renders the game screen to the display.

Demonstration: ScreenLoading Class

The ScreenLoading class' demonstration starts with a code snippet from the GamePanel class' constructor.

Listing 14-21. ScreenLoading Class Demonstration 1

```
1 screenLoading = new ScreenLoading(GameStates.LOADING, this);
2 screenLoading.SetGenericEventHandler(this);
3 screenLoading.SetSlowDown(500);
```

The use of the class constructor demonstrates how the ScreenLoading class is initialized. Notice that it takes a game state and a game panel for arguments. The second line of code registers the GamePanel as the class' generic event handler. This means that the game panel can receive certain events from the loading screen. On line 3, the loading class' slowDown field is set. This will add a time sink into the loading process making it take longer. The next snippet of code is from the GamePanel class' SwitchGameState method.

Listing 14-22. ScreenLoading Class Demonstration 2

```
1 } else if (prevGameState == GameStates.LOADING) {
2     MmgHelper.wr("Hiding LOADING screen.");
3     screenLoading.Pause();
4     screenLoading.SetIsVisible(false);
5     screenLoading.UnloadResources();
6 }
```

In the snippet of code listed in the preceding, the GamePanel's prevGameState field is used to clean up the game screen associated with the previous game state before switching to the new game state. Note than when the game screen is deactivated, the screen is paused and hidden and its resources released.

Listing 14-23. ScreenLoading Class Demonstration 3

```
1 } else if (gameState == GameStates.LOADING) {
2     MmgHelper.wr("Showing LOADING screen.");
3     screenLoading.LoadResources();
4     screenLoading.UnPause();
5     screenLoading.SetIsVisible(true);
6     screenLoading.StartDatLoad();
7     currentScreen = screenLoading;
8 }
```

The final snippet of demonstration code is also from the SwitchGameState method. This code shows you how the loading screen is activated for display. Note that the order in which the loading screen's methods are called is important. First, the screen's resources are loaded. The screen is unpaused and made visible. A screen-specific method, StartDatLoad, is called to start the resource load. The final line of code is important. This line sets the game screen as the active screen.

Game Screens: ScreenMainMenu

The ScreenMainMenu class extends the MmgBase API's MmgGameScreen class. This class provides a main menu screen that is aware of the game state and game panel aspects of the MmgCore API. You'll notice some similarities between this screen and the previous two game screens we've reviewed.

Class Fields

This class' fields are a mix of some standard fields we've seen before and a set of fields that power the screen's menu system. I've separated the fields into the two groups listed in the following code snippet.

Listing 14-24. ScreenMainMenu Class Fields 1

```
//Standard fields
public GameStates state;
public GamePanel owner;
public Hashtable<String, MmgCfgFileEntry> classConfig;

//Menu system fields
public MmgBmp menuTitle;
public MmgBmp menuSubTitle;
public MmgBmp menuStartGame;
public MmgBmp menuExitGame;
public MmgBmp menuFooterUrl;
public MmgBmp menuCursor;
public MmgMenuContainer menu;
public MmgSound menuSound;
public MmgFont version;
public HandleMainMenuEvent handleMenuEvent = null;
```

The first group of class fields are some standard fields we've seen before in this chapter. The state and owner fields are there to associate the screen with a game panel and game state value. The third entry, classConfig, is there to hold class config data, if any, loaded up at runtime.

The second set of fields are there to power the screen's menu system. The first five fields are MmgBmp, image objects, used to represent five visual elements of the main menu. Those elements are the title, subtitle, start game option, exit game option, and footer. The menuCursor field is also an MmgBmp image used to draw the menu system's cursor.

The MmgMenuContainer field menu is used to hold the menu items that are based on the first five fields of the menu group. The menuSound field holds a sound effect that will be played if a menu item is selected. The version field is another visual element that displays a version string on the lower left-hand side of the menu screen. The final entry listed, handleMenuEvent, is a class field that provides event handling to the menu system.

Support Method Details

The ScreenMainMenu class has a small set of support methods for us to review. Let's take a look!

Listing 14-25. ScreenMainMenu Support Method Details 1

```
public GameStates GetGameState() { ... }
public boolean GetIsDirty() { ... }
public void SetIsDirty(boolean b) { ... }
public void DrawScreen() { ... }
```

The GetGameState method returns the game state value assigned to the game screen. The next two methods are get and set methods of the class' isDirty field. The field is used to enable the class' MmgUpdate method to run on the next game frame. The last method for us to review is the DrawScreen method. This method is called as part of the class' update call; it redraws the screen usually in response to user input.

Main Method Details

The class' main methods include constructors, input methods, resource management methods, and drawing methods that are part of the game engine's drawing routine.

Listing 14-26. ScreenMainMenu Main Method Details 1

```
public ScreenMainMenu(GameStates State, GamePanel Owner) { ... }

public boolean ProcessAClick(int src) { ... }
public boolean ProcessDpadRelease(int dir) { ... }
public void LoadResources() { ... }
public void UnloadResources() { ... }
public boolean MmgUpdate(int updateTick, long currentTimeMs, long
msSinceLastFrame) { ... }

public void MmgDraw(MmgPen p) { ... }
```

The first entry, as to be expected, is a class constructor. The constructor takes the same arguments we've seen before in the ScreenSplash and ScreenLoading class reviews. The constructor expects a game state and a game panel as arguments. The next two main methods listed are input handlers ProcessAClick and ProcessDpadRelease.

These methods are defined and wired into the screen's menu system. The ProcessAClick input handler is mainly for detecting when a menu option is selected. The ProcessDpadRelease input handler is mainly for processing direction pad input and using it to move the cursor around the menu.

The next two methods are the screen resource management methods LoadResources and UnloadResources. The LoadResources method prepares all of the screen's resources so the class is ready for display. The UnloadResources method reverses this process and releases all the class' resources.

Last but not least, we have the MmgUpdate and MmgDraw methods we know and love. The MmgUpdate method responds to the game engine drawing routine's update call and is responsible for preparing the screen's menu system. The MmgDraw method renders the screen to the display.

Demonstration: ScreenMainMenu Class

The demonstration code for this class is from the MmgCore API's GamePanel class, specifically the class constructor.

Listing 14-27. ScreenMainMenu Class Demonstration 1

```
screenMainMenu = new ScreenMainMenu(GameStates.MAIN_MENU, this);
```

This snippet of code shows us how to instantiate the class and what the constructor arguments look like. Let's take a look at this game screen's deactivation and activation code from the GamePanel class' SwitchGameState method.

Listing 14-28. ScreenMainMenu Class Demonstration 2

```
1 } else if (prevGameState == GameStates.MAIN_MENU) {
2     MmgHelper.wr("Hiding MAIN GAME screen.");
3     screenMainMenu.Pause();
4     screenMainMenu.SetIsVisible(false);
5     screenMainMenu.UnloadResources();
6 }
```

Just like the previous game screens we've reviewed, the screenMainMenu class is paused and hidden, and its resources are released. Notice that the game state used to represent the main menu screen is the MAIN_MENU state. I want to cover the activation part of this process because you'll use very similar code for every screen in your game. The next snippet demonstrates the screen's activation code.

Listing 14-29. ScreenMainMenu Class Demonstration 3

```
1 } else if (gameState == GameStates.MAIN_MENU) {
2     MmgHelper.wr("Showing MAIN_MENU screen.");
3     screenMainMenu.LoadResources();
4     screenMainMenu.UnPause();
5     screenMainMenu.SetIsVisible(true);
6     currentScreen = screenMainMenu;
7 }
```

This snippet of demonstration code is also from the SwitchGameState method, and it's a block of code that you should be familiar with. This code shows you the proper process for activating the main menu screen. I want to mention that there really aren't a lot of example lines of code in the GamePanel class with regard to the ScreenMainMenu.

This is because a lot of the functionality we're using is hidden by the ScreenMainMenu class' super class, the MmgGameScreen class. This lets us just plug our menu screen right into the existing system setup in the GamePanel class.

Game Screens: Screen

The Screen class is very similar to the other game screens we've reviewed in this chapter. The previous classes, ScreenSplash, ScreenLoading, and ScreenMainMenu, were all specific game screens that are designed to function a certain way. The Screen class is a general game screen. There is no specific built-in functionality like a splash screen or loading bar to speak of.

Class Fields

The Screen class' fields are very similar to those that we've seen before in this chapter. This is the last MmgCore game screen for us to review, so let's jump into some code.

Listing 14-30. Screen Class Fields 1

```
public GameStates state;
public GamePanel owner;
public Hashtable<String, MmgCfgFileEntry> classConfig;
```

The first two class fields are used to identify the GameStates value assigned to this game screen as well as the GamePanel, owner, that this game screen belongs to. The last field, classConfig, is used to hold class config data, if any exists. Class config files are processed at runtime. It's up to you to implement the class config code as you see fit.

Support Method Details

The Screen class' support methods are a familiar group we've come across before.

Listing 14-31. Screen Support Method Details 1

```
public GameStates GetGameState() { ... }
public boolean GetIsDirty() { ... }
public void SetIsDirty(boolean b) { ... }
public void DrawScreen() { ... }
```

The first method listed returns the Screen's associated game state value. The next two methods are a pair of get and set methods that allow you to access the screen's isDirty flag. The isDirty flag controls if the screen's MmgUpdate method executes on the next game frame. The last entry in the preceding list is the DrawScreen method. This method is responsible for updating the game screen and is called from the MmgUpdate method if the screen is marked as dirty.

Main Method Details

The Screen class' main methods are a familiar group we've come across before. Let's take a look at the class' main methods.

Listing 14-32. Screen Main Method Details 1

```
public Screen(GameStates State, GamePanel Owner) { ... }

public void LoadResources() { ... }
public void UnloadResources() { ... }
public void HandleGenericEvent(GenericEventMessage obj) { ... }

public boolean MmgUpdate(int updateTick, long currentTimeMs, long
msSinceLastFrame) { ... }

public void MmgDraw(MmgPen p) { ... }
```

The class constructor follows the same pattern we've seen with the ScreenSplash, ScreenLoading, and ScreenMainMenu classes. The State argument is the game state value associated with the game screen. The LoadResources and UnloadResources methods are responsible for preparing and releasing the screen's resources. The HandleGenericEvent method is part of the class' implementation of the GenericEventHandler interface, which requires that the method be defined.

The Screen class is able to register for and process generic events. The last two methods shown in the preceding are the MmgUpdate and MmgDraw methods that are called as part of the game engine's drawing routine. The MmgUpdate method is called first and is responsible for running the game screen's update logic, if any. The MmgDraw method is responsible for rendering the game screen to the display.

Demonstration: Screen Class

The demonstration section for the Screen class is from the PongClone game project included with the game engine. Open the ScreenGame class of the Chapter15_ CompleteGame package, or namespace if you're following along in C#, and direct your attention to the class definition.

Listing 14-33. Screen Class Demonstration 1

```
public class ScreenGame extends Screen { ... }
```

You'll notice from the class definition that the ScreenGame class extends the Screen class. The main thing to notice about the Screen class is that it doesn't have any built-in functionality in the same way that the ScreenSplash and ScreenMainMenu classes did. The next snippet of code is from the MmgCore API's Screen class, specifically the MmgUpdate method.

Listing 14-34. Screen Class Demonstration 2

```
01 if (pause == false && isVisible == true) {
02     if (super.MmgUpdate(updateTick, currentTimeMs, msSinceLastFrame) ==
       true) {
03         lret = true;
04     }
05
06     if (isDirty == true) {
07         lret = true;
08         DrawScreen();
09     }
10 }
```

The MmgUpdate method only executes if the screen isn't paused and currently is visible, line 1. The focus of the code snippet listed in the preceding is on line 8 where the DrawScreen call is made. If the isDirty flag is set to true, the screen will update on each game frame. This is the main difference between this game screen and the previous ones we reviewed in this chapter.

The Screen class is configured to run updates on every game frame, so it's perfect for a game screen that requires update calls for animation. That's what the main purpose of the Screen class is, a starting point for animation-heavy game screens.

Chapter Conclusion

In this chapter, we took a look at the MmgCore API's screen classes. Although these classes are based on classes from the MmgBase API, they have been extended to support functionality that the MmgBase API isn't aware of. For instance, each game screen we've covered has a few things in common. One of those things is the gameState and owner class fields. These fields are necessary for the screen to plug into the MmgCore API's GamePanel class.

We also took a moment to review the `RunFrameRate` class, which is responsible for driving the game engine's drawing routine and subsequently the frame rate in the Java version of the game engine.

- RunFrameRate: An MmgCore API class that is responsible for running the game engine's drawing routine. This class is responsible for enforcing the frame rate for the Java version of the game engine.

- ScreenSplash: An MmgCore API implementation of the MmgSplashScreen class that is aware of both GameStates and GamePanel classes and can plug into the GamePanel class' screen management system.

- ScreenLoading: An MmgCore API implementation of the MmgLoadingScreen class that is aware of both GameStates and GamePanel classes and can plug into the GamePanel class' screen management system.

- ScreenMainMenu: An MmgCore API implementation of the MmgGameScreen class that is aware of both GameStates and GamePanel classes and can plug into the GamePanel class' screen management.

- Screen: The MmgCore API's Screen class is similar to other game screen classes but is slightly different in that it's designed to be used as a main game screen.

Don't be discouraged if you don't quite feel like you have a handle on the MmgCore's game screen classes. First, there are literally a ton of examples throughout the game engine project. I would take some time to look at a few of them. Keep in mind that functionality presented by the super class, or base class if you're following along in C#, may not be readily apparent.

Make sure you take a moment to trace through the classes you are using to power your game screens. Be aware of how the super class, base class in C#, functions and how it will interact with your extended classes. Keep this in mind when you're working with overridden methods or methods that rely on super class functionality.

PART 3

CHAPTER 15

Game Build Introduction

Welcome to Part 3 of this text. If you've made it this far, then you're an expert at the intricate details of the game engine, and it's time to put that knowledge to use. In this part of the text, we're going to build two games from the ground up. This will be an exciting journey. We'll start literally from scratch with an outline of the game. Then we'll add functionality in phases until we have a finished product.

The first game that we'll create is called PongClone, and as the name would suggest, it's a clone of the classic video game Pong. The PongClone game build will get your feet wet with game development. You'll learn first-hand how quickly and easily you can get a game project up and running. With the power of the MmgBase and MmgCore APIs at your fingertips, you can create a feature-filled game with just a few classes.

With this project, you'll gain invaluable experience setting up game projects, handling user input, animating graphics, working with one- and two-player games, and much more. For the second game build, we'll create a slightly more intricate game, DungeonTrap. In DungeonTrap, you control a character stuck in an enchanted dungeon vault fighting off waves of bad guys.

I hope these projects sound interesting to you. The main goal here is to gain experience building games using only the IDE and the game engine reviewed in Parts 1 and 2 of this text. I won't focus on game engine–specific topics during these game builds, and I'll try to stay away from the more rigid class review format I've used in the previous parts of the book.

We'll focus explicitly on the game. If you find a piece of code to be unfamiliar, take a moment to read over the material on that class and the example code provided with the project. We'll outline the details of our two game projects in the following sections. We'll start with the PongClone game.

© Victor G Brusca 2021
V. G. Brusca, *Introduction to Video Game Engine Development*, https://doi.org/10.1007/978-1-4842-7039-4_15

PongClone Game Outline

If we're going to sit down in front of the computer and write a game, we'd better have some idea of what we're trying to do. The best way to do that is to outline the features of the game in a list. This gives you a starting point in your game development. Simple games may only require a few bullet points before you can start writing your code.

More complex games will require a lot of planning before you can comfortably begin development. I wish there was a rule of thumb that I can impart upon you so you can better decide how much planning is adequate for a given game. The simple fact is that you'll have to develop this instinct on your own, over time, after you have a few games under your belt. With that, let's take a look at the first game's outline.

PongClone General Game Specifications

- General Description: The PongClone game consists of two players, each with a paddle positioned at the left or right edge of the screen. The players compete to get the game ball past their opponent's paddle scoring a point. The first player to score seven points wins.

- Number of Players: The game should support one or two players.

- Win Condition: First player to score seven points.

- Lose Condition: Opponent scores seven points before you can.

- Game Screens:

  - Splash screen

  - Loading screen

  - Main menu screen

  - Game screen

- Game Screen Details:

  - Splash Screen: A splash screen with a logo that displays for a few seconds.

  - Loading Screen: A loading screen with a logo and a loading bar.

- Main Menu Screen: A menu screen with title, subtitle, one player, two players, exit game menu options, and a version number feature.

- Game Screen: A game screen with an instructions sub-screen that has a countdown feature. The game should also support a game exit sub-screen, a game over screen, player scores, and an AI opponent when in one-player mode.

- Game Input Details:

  - Player One Input: Up and down keyboard arrow keys

  - Player Two Input: Keyboard keys, mouse input

That concludes our outline for the PongClone game. Look over the details of the specification list and think about what game engine features can be used to address the different game requirements.

DungeonTrap Game Outline

The second game we'll build in this part of the text is DungeonTrap. This game is a bit more complex than the PongClone game you'll start with. Even so, the game specification should not be overly detailed. The chapters for this game build are independent and available as a download from the book's GitHub repository.

For instance, I'll mention the game's requirement for random item drops, but I won't specifically list what they are even though I have a good idea of what I want to implement. My reasoning here is that the item drops will function almost identically, so I don't really need to specify a concrete list of items at this point in time. This is a fine line you'll learn how to walk as you get more experience building games.

DungeonTrap General Game Specifications

- General Description: The DungeonTrap game consists of one or two players trapped in a dungeon vault where waves of enemies enter the room in stages. Players collect points as they fight off the enemy hordes using weapons, items, and objects. As the enemies are defeated, random items are dropped for the players to pick up. Defeat all the enemy waves to escape the DungeonTrap!

- Number of Players: The game should support one or two players.

- Win Condition: Survive ten waves of enemies.

- Lose Condition: Take lethal damage from enemies.

- Game Screens:

  - Splash screen

  - Loading screen

  - Main menu screen

  - Game screen

- Game Screen Details:

  - Splash Screen: A splash screen with a logo that displays for a few seconds.

  - Loading Screen: A loading screen with a logo and a loading bar.

  - Main Menu Screen: A menu screen with title, subtitle, one player, two players, exit game menu options, and a version number feature.

  - Game Screen: A game screen with an instructions sub-screen that has a countdown feature. The game should also support a game exit sub-screen, a game over screen, player stats HUD, and AI opponents.

- Game Input Details:

  - Player One Input: Up, down, left, and right keyboard arrow keys and A and B keys for input

  - Player Two Input: Four keyboard keys mimicking arrow keys and A/B input.

Notice that the outline isn't too much longer than that of the previous game even though the game is most certainly more complex. I think this is an indication of a good game outline. We don't try to solve any implementation problems or specify any in-depth details – just high-level ideas. One last thought: Don't be afraid to stray from your initial plans. Building games is challenging, and with any sufficiently challenging experience, you will ultimately have to adapt to overcome the challenge.

Game Resources

When it comes to game resources, I have you covered. I'll provide a base set of resources including sounds, images, and class config files. The main focus of this text is to build games in code, using only an IDE and a game engine. As such, I won't require you to edit or create resources for the games we create here. That being said, images and sounds are integral aspects of most games.

Start thinking about different ways you can access resources for your game. You can search online for sites that have game resources, create your own, or work with friends. Don't be discouraged if you're not an artist. There're a lot of options out there for you. Trust me.

I'd also like to mention that there are example game projects for each chapter in this part of the book. You can open up and view the complete implementation of the game for your specific chapter. The chapter projects are included with the game engine's main project. This can help you resolve bugs in your code, so be sure to keep it in mind. And with that, we've reached the conclusion of this intro. Happy coding!

CHAPTER 16

PongClone Project Setup

Before I begin the chapter I want to list some general project notes to help make sure you have things setup correctly and can address the most common issues quickly. The notes are as follows:

Java:

1. The game project should be configured with a working directory set to './dist' in the project's 'Run' settings.

Java and C#:

1. The ENGINE_CONFIG_FILE field of the static main class should point to the game project's config file in the 'cfg' directory with a relative path from the project's working directory.

2. The game engine config file should have a NAME entry with a value that is the same as its associated project and that project's resource folder.

3. To turn off the gamepad 1 input add this line to your game engine config file:

```
<entry key="GAMEPAD_1_ON" val="false" type="bool"
from="GameSettings" />
```

© Victor G Brusca 2021

V. G. Brusca, *Introduction to Video Game Engine Development*, https://doi.org/10.1007/978-1-4842-7039-4_16

In this chapter, I will walk you through setting up a new game development project in Java or C#. You can use this chapter as a reference for both versions of the game engine. We'll also prepare the game's resources including images, sounds, and class config files used by the game screens for data-driven customization.

We're going to approach the project in steps. This chapter represents our first step. Because we want something functional at the end of a development step, I've designed the development process so that you'll have a program that will compile and run at the end of each chapter. I should mention that this might not be the case in the real world.

There will be times where you're working hard to implement a feature and you'll have a project that might not compile or work properly. This is perfectly normal. Don't think video game development is always as cut and dried as the game builds we're working on here. I want to take a moment to mention two caveats with regard to following along on OSX-based computers. The first thing is that you may encounter a security exception in the NetBeans IDE when trying to load and run the game project.

The error message I get says something about the file "libjnidispatch-440.jnilib" causing a "cannot be opened because the developer cannot be verified" error. Open your Mac's system preferences and go to the security section. You'll notice an application security exception entry pops up when the error is encountered in the IDE. Accept the security exception both for the IDE and when you run the game for testing. The messages will stop appearing after that adjustment.

The second issue you might run into has to do with the OSX keyboard key context menu. This menu pops up when you hold a key down for a few seconds. It allows you to choose different versions of a key with different language accent marks. Look up online how to turn this feature on and off for your version of OSX. Make sure to turn it **off** before testing your game, or you may lock one of the keyboard keys inadvertently when the context menu is triggered, but doesn't actually display, during game play.

Setting Up a New Project: Java/NetBeans IDE

In this section, we'll review the steps necessary to create a brand-new game development project, in Java, that uses the game engine API you just finished reviewing. First up, we'll outline the process for the Java version of the game engine; then we'll take a look at the process for C#. Fire up the NetBeans IDE, and let's get to work! Make sure you have the MmgGameApiJava project opened in the IDE.

Once that is done, select "File ➤ New Project …" from the application menu and create a new project in the directory where you keep your NetBeans projects. Select the "Java with Ant" category from the "New Project" popup. From the "Projects" list, select the "Java Application" option and click the "Next >" button.

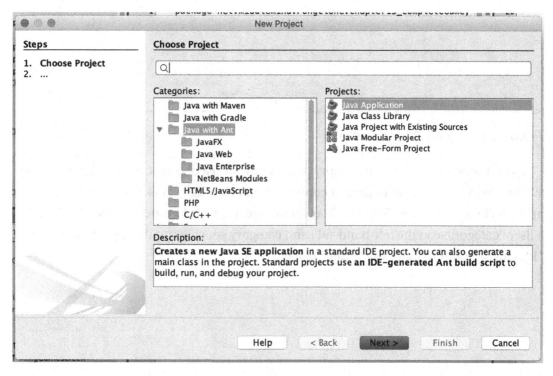

Figure 16-1. *Java Project Setup 1*

Set the "Project Name" field to "PongClone." Make sure that the "Project Location" and "Project Folder" fields have the correct values. Keep the "Use Dedicated Folder for Storing Libraries" and "Create Main Class" options unchecked, as shown in the following image, and then click the "Finish" button.

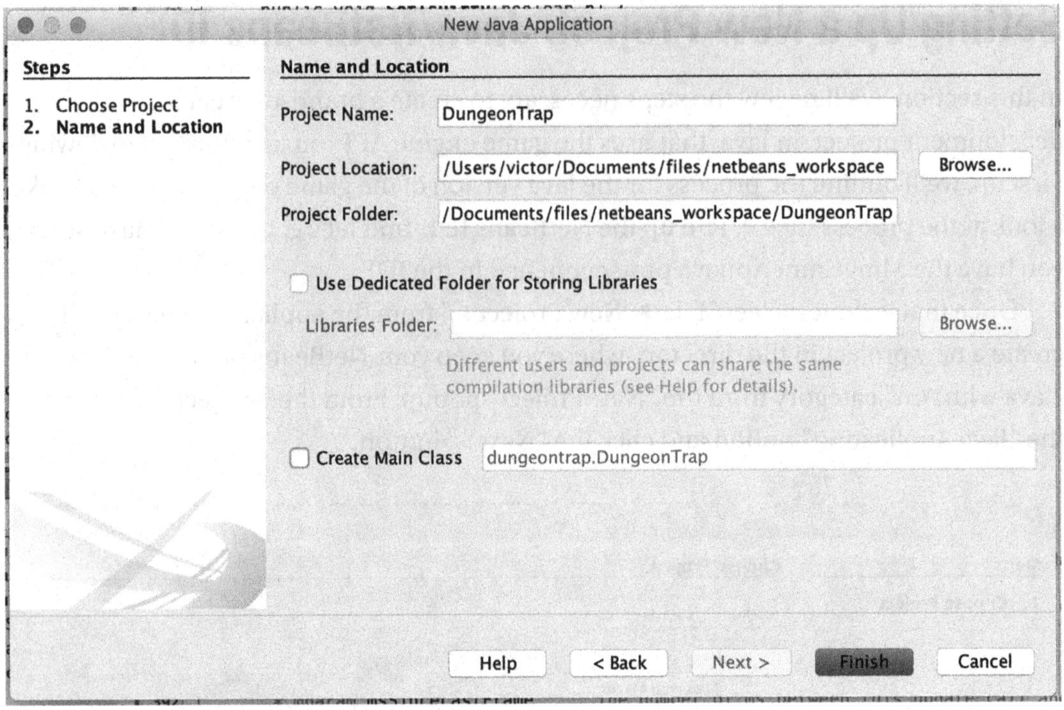

Figure 16-2. *Java Project Setup 2*

You should now have a new empty project in your list of projects named PongClone. We'll have to do a little bit of project configuration next. Right-click your new project and select the "Properties" option. You should see a "Project Properties" popup with a list of categories on the left-hand side and category specifics on the right. Select the "Packaging" option under the "Build" category.

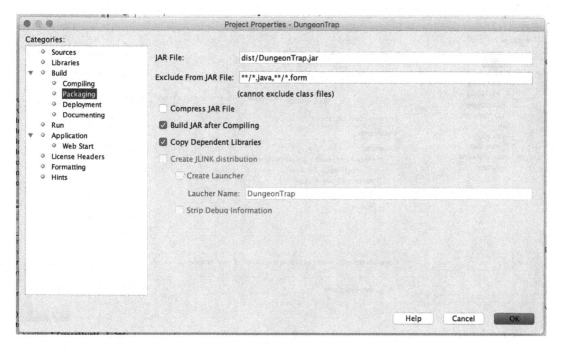

Figure 16-3. *Java Project Setup 3*

Make sure that your project's "JAR File" is set to "dist/PongClone.jar." Make sure your project has the working directory set to "./dist/" under the project's "Run" settings. Also, make sure the "Build JAR after Compiling" and "Copy Dependent Libraries" options are checked as shown in the preceding. Now we need to set up our project resources. You'll need to have the MmgGameApiJava project loaded if it hasn't been already. Click the "Files" tab next the project listing. If you don't see it there, you can also access the Files view by clicking the "Window" menu option and selecting the "Files" entry.

Open the MmgGameApiJava folder and locate a folder inside named "cfg." Open the "cfg" directory and locate the "asset_src" folder. In this folder, there should be a folder called "pong_clone_resources." Open it and find the folder inside named "cfg." Copy this folder and paste it into the root of the PongClone game's project folder. Your new game project now has a full set of resources ready to use.

We're just about ready to start writing some code, but there're still a few things we must attend to first. We'll need to get our project's libraries sorted out. First, let's add a reference to the game engine API. Open up the PongClone project's properties popup again. This time, select the "Libraries" category from the left-hand side's list of categories. Under the "Compile" tab, locate the "Classpath" section as shown in the following.

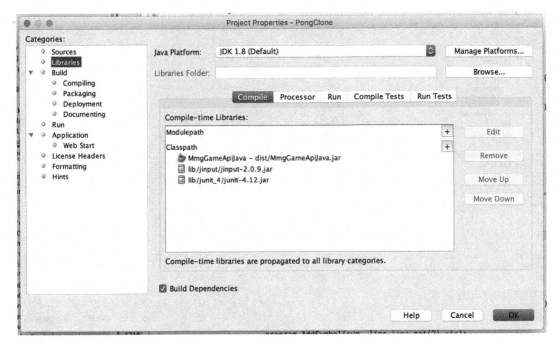

Figure 16-4. *Java Project Setup 4*

Click the "+" button and select the "Add project" option. Choose the "MmgGameApiJava" project from the list, and you should now see the game engine project listed under the "Classpath" section. Close the Project Properties popup. Reopen the "Files" view. Find the game engine project folder again and open it. You should see a folder named "lib" in the project's root directory.

Copy the folder and go back one directory to the project listing. Find the "PongClone" folder and paste the "lib" folder into the project's root directory. We have just two more libraries to register, and the project configuration is done. Open the PongClone project's properties popup again. Select the "Libraries" category and find the "Classpath" section.

Click the "+" button and select the "Add JAR/Folder" option. Navigate to the PongClone project folder and open the "libs" directory you just pasted there. Find and open the "jinput" folder and select the file "jinput-2.0.9.jar"; click the "Choose" button and then click the "Ok" button. Repeat the process except this time find and open the "junit_4" folder and select the "junit-4.12.jar" file. Click the "Choose" button and then click the "Ok" button. That's it. The PongClone project is set up and configured. We're ready to code!

Setting Up a New Project: C#/Visual Studio IDE

In this section, we'll review the steps necessary to create a brand-new game development project, in C#, that uses the game engine API you just finished reviewing. We'll outline the process for the C# version of the game engine.

You'll need to open up a terminal program for this next part. Please refer to the Internet for details on finding the terminal program for your particular operating system. At the terminal, run the following command to ensure that you have the MonoGame project templates installed. Again, refer to Chapter 1 for more information on how to set up the C#/MonoGame environment:

```
dotnet new -i MonoGame.Templates.CSharp::3.8.0.1641
```

Once that is done, navigate to the directory where you keep your Visual Studio projects. You should have the MmgGameApiCS project in this folder. Run the following command to create a new MonoGame development project for the "PongClone" game:

```
dotnet new mgdesktopgl -o PongClone
```

When the command is done running, you should have a new project folder in your Visual Studio project directory named "PongClone." In the next few steps, we'll be working on getting the game project properly configured. First off, let's get a copy of the game's resource folder and add it to the project.

Using your preferred folder navigator, locate and open the "MmgGameApiCs" folder in your Visual Studio project directory. Find the "cfg" folder inside and open it. You should see a folder named "asset_src"; open it and locate the folder named "pong_clone_resources." Open that directory and copy the "cfg" folder inside.

Now, navigate to the "PongClone" project folder you just created. Paste the "cfg" directory into the project's root folder. Next up, we have to configure the "PongClone" project and add some libraries to it that give us access to the game engine API. For this next part, we must make sure that the game engine project has been built so we can reference the resulting .Net library.

To do this, open the "MmgGameApiCs" project; and once it's done loading, select "Build" from the IDE's menu and then choose "Rebuild." Allow the project to compile and make sure that you see successful build results in the IDE's "Build Output" view. Now that we have a library to reference, close the "MmgGameApiCs" project and open the "PongClone" project you just created.

When it's done loading, right-click the "Dependencies" folder in the "Solution" view and select "Add Reference ..." from the context menu. From the "References" popup, click the ".Net Assembly" tab and click the "Browse ..." button. Navigate to the "MmgGameApiCs" folder in your Visual Studio project directory. Find the following file and add it to your project's references. Click the "Ok" button to close the "References" popup:

```
./MmgGameApiCs/bin/Debug/netcoreapp3.1/MmgGameApiCs.dll
```

Your project "References" popup should look like the following screenshot.

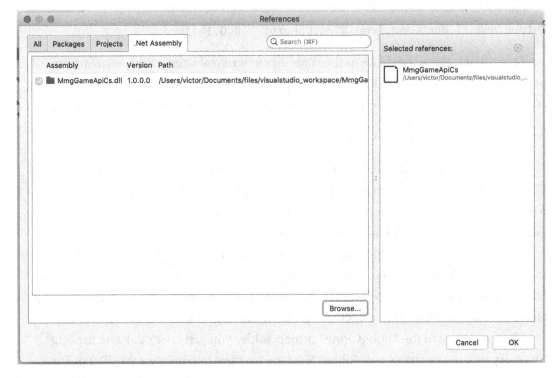

Figure 16-5. *C# Project Setup 1*

We have a few NuGet packages to add to our project before we can start coding. Select "Project" from the IDE menu and click the "Manage NuGet Packages ..." option. When the "Manage NuGet Packages" popup is done loading, search for the package "MonoGame.Framework.Content.Pipeline" by using the search bar in the top right-hand corner of the popup.

Look for the package in the list on the left and check the box next to the package entry. Next, search for the package named "MSTest.TestFramework." Check the box next to that package listing as well and click the "Add Package" button in the bottom right-hand corner of the popup. Accept any popup dialogs with licensing prompts, and the packages will be installed and ready to go.

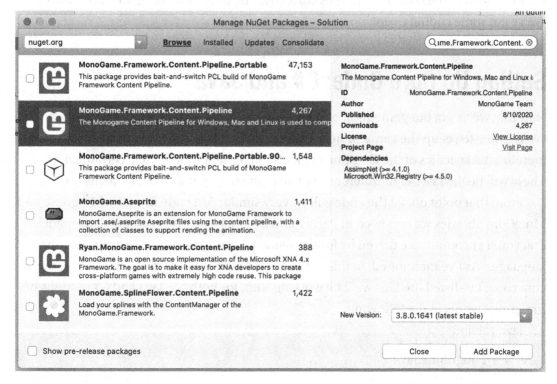

Figure 16-6. *C# Project Setup 2*

There's one last thing for us to do before we can start coding: add the MonoGame content resource file. The content file contains font data for font sizes 1–50 that the C# version of the game engine uses. Recall that the C# version uses this font data to emulate the more fluid font functionality of the Java version.

Using the file system navigator of your choice, locate and open the "MmgGameApiCs" project folder. Copy the "Content" folder and paste it into the root of the "PongClone" project folder. Overwrite the current "Content" folder, if necessary, and open the project in Visual Studio when the folder is done copying.

Once the project is done loading, expand the "Content" folder listed in the "Solution" view. Right-click the file named "Content.mgcb" and select the "Open With ..." option. Click the entry named "mgcb-editor." This will open the content database in a special editing application.

Find the "Rebuild" button, third from the right in the program's button bar. Click it and verify that the content compiles correctly. The project is configured and ready. We've got some coding to do!

Setting Up Core Code: C# and Java

Now that we've got our game project set up and configured, it's time to start coding. We're going to set up the game project's core code in this section. I'll make sure to mention the specifics of the C# game engine's implementation up to a certain point. These will be the last major difference between the two projects that I'll focus on.

From that point on, all the code will be very similar API code from the MmgBase and MmgCore libraries we reviewed in Parts 1 and 2 of this text. The only real discrepancies that you'll encounter are driven by fundamental differences in the two programming languages. As I've mentioned, in this section, we'll be setting up the PongClone game's core code. I've listed the files we'll be working with, for both the Java and C# versions of the game engine, in the following:

Java version

- PongClone.java

- MainFrame.java

- GamePanel.java

C# version

- PongClone.cs

- GamePanel.cs

We'll want to create a new package for the project code. Right-click the project and select "Add ..."; then choose "New Package." Name the new package "game.jam. PongClone." Notice the slight difference in the files listed in the preceding. Do you know why this is? Recall from our review of the MmgCore API that the C# implementation doesn't need a MainFrame class due to the underlying framework's implementation.

The first class we'll add to the project is the static main class. It just so happens we have a static main class all set up and ready to use. Copy the MmgApiGame class from the game engine project's MmgCore library. Paste the file into the PongClone project and rename the file and class so they are both named PongClone. There is one reference to the MmgGameApi class in the file. Search for it and replace it with the PongClone class' name.

Make sure to update the ENGINE_CONFIG_FILE field so that it has this value, "../cfg/engine_config_mmg_pong_clone.xml", which is our game specific engine config file. You also have to open the engine config file and change the value of the NAME entry from MmgPongClone to PongClone. Now your new game is plugged into the proper engine config file and resource directories, all of which are named "PongClone." Make sure to rebuild the project once it compiles for either C# or Java. This will ensure a project output directory is created.

You can perform this refactoring operation automatically in the NetBeans IDE if you have both projects open. If so, you can choose to use the "Refactor Paste" option, which will take care of renaming the class for you. Add the following import to the top of the PongClone.java class below the other import listings:

```
import net.middlemind.MmgGameApiJava.MmgCore.*;
```

This will import all the MmgCore API classes we need. In the C# version of the PongClone project, you'll need to delete the Game1.cs and Program.cs files from the project before pasting a copy of the MmgApiGame.cs file into the project. Add the following folders to the project: "src/game/jam/PongClone." This is where we'll keep our class files, and it loosely mimics the Java version's packages. You'll have to refactor the file name. Right-click the new file and select the "Rename ..." option. Rename the file and the class to "PongClone."

You can refactor the class name by opening the file and selecting the class' name; right-click it and select the "Rename ..." option from the context menu. Type in the name "PongClone" and press Enter. You'll have to add the following library reference to the top of the file at the bottom of the current list:

```
using net.middlemind.MmgGameApiCs.MmgCore;
```

The class' header for the PongClone.cs class should look similar to the following snippet.

Listing 16-1. PongClone Class Definition 1

```
1 namespace game.jam.PongClone {
2 {
3      public static class PongClone
4      { ... }
5 }
```

Next up, we'll make adjustments to the Java and C# projects. If you're following along in Java, open up the NetBeans IDE and the PongClone project. Right-click the project and open the properties popup. Select the "Run" option from the categories list. Find the "Main Class" text field and click the "Browse ..." button.

Select the PongClone class as the default main class. The adjustment that is necessary for the C# version of the PongClone project is to open the PongClone class and change the name of the AltMain method to Main.

Now that we have a foundation built, we can add a few more classes to move the project along. These classes are actually defined in the MmgCore API, but we want to extend those classes and define them locally so that we can have full control over the game's code. The next class we'll work on is the MainFrame class. Again, this only applies to the Java version of the game project.

The C# version does not have an equivalent MainFrame class. The underlying framework's implementation is such that only the GamePanel class is necessary. With regard to the Java version, however, we want to extend the MmgCore API's MainFrame class and preserve its functionality. Create a new empty class in the PongClone project. It should reside in the same package and folder as the static main class. The class is concise, so I'll list it here.

Listing 16-2. MainFrame Java Setting Up Core Code 1

```
01 public class MainFrame extends net.middlemind.MmgGameApiJava.MmgCore.
   MainFrame {
02
03     public MainFrame(int WinWidth, int WinHeight, int PanWidth, int
       PanHeight, int GameWidth, int GameHeight) {
04         super(WinWidth, WinHeight, PanWidth, PanHeight, GameWidth,
           GameHeight);
05     }
06
```

```
07      public MainFrame(int WinWidth, int WinHeight) {
08          super(WinWidth, WinHeight);
09      }
10  }
```

Notice that I don't import the MmgCore library in this class. If I did that, there would be two classes named MainFrame in the current scope, and that could get confusing. By not importing the library, it forces my references to be explicit. You can clearly see where I'm using the MmgCore API's MainFrame class and where I'm not. Note that we define the same class constructors that exist in the API's MainFrame class, and we use the super keyword to call the super class' constructor.

What we've done here is bring the functionality of the MmgCore API's MainFrame class into the current project's package through class extension as shown in the preceding. That takes care of the second main step we needed to complete. The next class for us to work on is the GamePanel class.

We're going to be using a similar technique of extending super class functionality, or base class functionality if you're following along in C#. By extending and customizing the MmgCore API's GamePanel class, we can leverage all the existing code and add new, project-specific functionality at the same time.

Taking a look at the game's general specifications, I can see that I need to support four game screens. I know that the default GamePanel class has support for a splash screen, a loading screen, and a main menu screen. I also know that the splash and loading screens use generic events, from the MmgCore API, to indicate when the game state needs to change.

Now if all that information seemed to be pulled out of thin air, it wasn't. A lot of it was covered in Part 2 of this text. Remember I have the added benefit of hindsight so I can rattle off class features only because I've already done all the difficult work of figuring everything out ahead of time.

I wanted to mention this because software development, and especially video game development, rarely goes as smoothly as the game builds we encounter in this text. So don't be discouraged if you run into some rough patches during your game's development. They are a perfectly natural occurrence.

Back to the task at hand. At this point in the project, after reviewing the game's general specifications, we know that we'll need to customize the game panel class' constructor along with the SwitchGameState and HandleGenericEvent methods. Let's start a class outline. I've listed the code in the following snippet.

Listing 16-3. GamePanel Java Setting Up Core Code 2

```
public class GamePanel extends net.middlemind.MmgGameApiJava.MmgCore.
GamePanel {

public GamePanel(MainFrame Mf, int WinWidth, int WinHeight, int X, int Y,
int GameWidth, int GameHeight) { ... }

@Override
        public void SwitchGameState(GameStates g) { ... }

@Override
        public void HandleGenericEvent(GenericEventMessage obj) { ... }
}
```

We'll use the same process for the C# version of the game with some slight, language-based differences.

Listing 16-4. GamePanel C# Setting Up Core Code 3

```
public class GamePanel : net.middlemind.MmgGameApiJava.MmgCore.GamePanel {

public GamePanel(int WinWidth, int WinHeight, int X, int Y, int GameWidth,
int GameHeight) { ... }

public override void SwitchGameState(GameStates g) { ... }

public override void HandleGenericEvent(GenericEventMessage obj) { ... }
}
```

Notice how similar the two class outlines are. The only differences we've seen so far are based on differences between the two programming languages, Java and C#. Indeed, the code used to complete the outlined constructor and class methods will also be very similar. Let's fill in the class constructor first. As usual, I'll work with the Java version here.

Listing 16-5. GamePanel Java Setting Up Core Code 4

```
1 public GamePanel(MainFrame Mf, int WinWidth, int WinHeight, int X, int Y,
int GameWidth, int GameHeight) {
2     super(Mf, WinWidth, WinHeight, X, Y, GameWidth, GameHeight);
3     screenSplash.SetGenericEventHandler(this);
```

```
4      screenLoading.SetGenericEventHandler(this);
5      screenLoading.SetSlowDown(500);
6 }
```

Because we're using the GamePanel class' built-in functionality, we have access to the splash screen and loading screen class fields. I want to make sure the classes' event handlers are wired up correctly. To do so, I explicitly set them on the preceding lines 3 and 4. I also want to add a slight loading slowdown so that I can verify that the loading bar is working properly. On line 5, the loading screen's slowdown value is set. Let's take a look at the C# version of this method.

Listing 16-6. GamePanel C# Setting Up Core Code 5

```
1 public GamePanel(int WinWidth, int WinHeight, int X, int Y, int
GameWidth, int GameHeight) :
2      base(WinWidth, WinHeight, X, Y, GameWidth, GameHeight) {
3      screenSplash.SetGenericEventHandler(this);
4      screenLoading.SetGenericEventHandler(this);
5      screenLoading.SetSlowDown(500);
6 }
```

As you can see, the constructor implementations are nearly identical. Keep in mind that this is where we'll initialize our game screens. We didn't need to create any new class fields because screenSplash and screenLoading are available by default. This will change as we add new game screens that are outside of the default functionality.

Next up, we'll tackle the SwitchGameState method. I'm going to follow the default implementation almost line for line as you'll see in the following code block. The code will be almost identical for the Java and C# versions of the game, so I'll try to cover both right now.

Listing 16-7. GamePanel Setting Up Core Code 6

```
//Java method signature
@Override
public void SwitchGameState(GameStates g) { ... }

//C# method signature
public override void SwitchGameState(GameStates g) { ... }
```

```
01      if (gameState != prevGameState) {
02          prevGameState = gameState;
03      }
04
05      if (g != gameState) {
06          gameState = g;
07      } else {
08          return;
09      }
10
11      if (prevGameState == GameStates.BLANK) {
12          MmgHelper.wr("Hiding BLANK screen.");
13
14      } else if (prevGameState == GameStates.SPLASH){
15          MmgHelper.wr("Hiding SPLASH screen.");
16          screenSplash.Pause();
17          screenSplash.SetIsVisible(false);
18          screenSplash.UnloadResources();
19
20      } else if (prevGameState == GameStates.LOADING){
21          MmgHelper.wr("Hiding LOADING screen.");
22          screenLoading.Pause();
23          screenLoading.SetIsVisible(false);
24          screenLoading.UnloadResources();
25
26      } else if (prevGameState == GameStates.MAIN_MENU) {
27          MmgHelper.wr("Hiding MAIN_MENU screen.");
28          screenMainMenu.Pause();
29          screenMainMenu.SetIsVisible(false);
30          screenMainMenu.UnloadResources();
31
32      }
33
34      if (gameState == GameStates.BLANK) {
35          MmgHelper.wr("Showing BLANK screen.");
36
```

```
37      } else if (gameState == GameStates.SPLASH) {
38          MmgHelper.wr("Showing SPLASH screen.");
39          screenSplash.LoadResources();
40          screenSplash.UnPause();
41          screenSplash.SetIsVisible(true);
42          screenSplash.StartDisplay();
43          currentScreen = screenSplash;
44
45      } else if (gameState == GameStates.LOADING) {
46          MmgHelper.wr("Showing LOADING screen.");
47          screenLoading.LoadResources();
48          screenLoading.UnPause();
49          screenLoading.SetIsVisible(true);
50          screenLoading.StartDatLoad();
51          currentScreen = screenLoading;
52
53      } else if (gameState == GameStates.MAIN_MENU) {
54          MmgHelper.wr("Showing MAIN_MENU screen.");
55          screenMainMenu.LoadResources();
56          screenMainMenu.UnPause();
57          screenMainMenu.SetIsVisible(true);
58          currentScreen = screenMainMenu;
59
60      }
61  }
```

This class method should look familiar from our review of the MmgCore API. Notice that the three game screens in use, screenSplash, screenLoading, and screenMainMenu, are all built into the MmgCore API's GamePanel class. We have one more method to work on; then we'll compile and test our project. Let's take a look at the HandleGenericEvent method. This code will be the same in the Java and C# versions of the game.

The HandleGenericEvent method is designed to process game screen events from the splash and loading screens. We're going to start with the same code that exists in the MmgCore API's GamePanel class method. As we progress with the development of the game, we'll add any new code needed to the methods and constructor we've just outlined. Let's jump into some code!

Listing 16-8. GamePanel Setting Up Core Code 7

```
//Java method signature
@Override
public void HandleGenericEvent(GenericEventMessage obj) { ... }

//C# method signature
public override void HandleGenericEvent(GenericEventMessage obj) { ... }
```

Again, the only difference here is driven by the underlying programming language. I won't list the nuanced differences, like method signatures, moving forward. We'll reserve our time for deeper, more complex differences if we encounter any. Let's take a look at the method's contents in the following code snippet.

Listing 16-9. GamePanel Setting Up Core Code 8

```
01 if (obj != null) {
02     MmgHelper.wr("TestSpace.HandleGenericEvent " + obj.GetGameState());
03     if (obj.GetGameState() == GameStates.LOADING) {
04         if (obj.GetId() == ScreenLoading.EVENT_LOAD_COMPLETE) {
05             //Final loading steps
06             DatExternalStrings.LOAD_EXT_STRINGS();
07         }
08
09     } else if (obj.GetGameState() == GameStates.SPLASH) {
10         if (obj.GetId() == ScreenSplash.EVENT_DISPLAY_COMPLETE) {
11             SwitchGameState(GameStates.LOADING);
12         }
13     }
14 }
```

Again, this code should be very familiar from our review of the MmgCore API. Add the code shown in the preceding to your GamePanel class and then save and build your project. Make sure you address any typos or bugs. We're going to run the project and see what we've got. To run the Java version of the project, simply right-click the game project's static main class and select "Run." You should see a window popup with your game running in it in just a few seconds.

If you're following along in C#, you're going to want to run the game from a terminal window. Open up your favorite terminal and navigate to your game's root directory. Make sure you build your game in Visual Studio by clicking "Build" and selecting "Rebuild All" from the IDE menu. You should then see the following folder in the project directory:

```
/bin/Debug/netcoreapp3.1/PongClone.dll
```

Run the following command to launch your game:

```
cd /bin/Debug/netcoreapp3.1/
dotnet PongClone.dll
```

You should see images similar to those shown in the following depending on your OS and programming language choices.

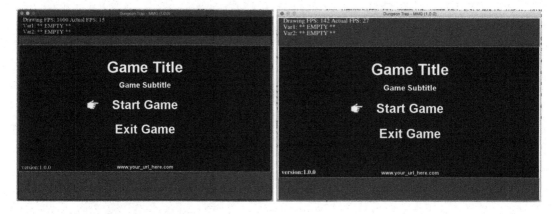

Figure 16-7. *PongClone Game 1*

Wow, we're off to a great start. Three small classes, two if you're following along in C#, and our project now supports a splash screen, a loading screen, and a default main menu screen. Not too bad! Keep in mind this is a project in development; so if you try hard enough, or at all, you'll probably find a way to get it to crash. No worries, we're only at the start of our game project.

CHAPTER 17

PongClone Main Menu Screen

In this chapter, we'll move the project even further along by adding a custom main menu screen to the game. We'll wire up the main menu and make sure it's functional. Let's start things off by taking a look at the main menu screen and what we need to do to get it set up.

The following process should work fine with both the Java and C# versions of the project. Create a new class and name it "ScreenMainMenu." We want this class to extend the MmgCore API's ScreenMainMenu class. Keep in mind that we'll have access to that functionality as we define how our local ScreenMainMenu class works. Because the screen's default implementation includes the following features – title, subtitle, single player, game start, game exit, footer, and version number – we won't have to worry too much about them.

PongClone: ScreenMainMenu Code Review

Let's take a look at our game's general specification list and see if we're missing anything. One thing that stands out to me is that the game is defined as supporting both one- and two-player modes. However, the default main menu screen only has an option for starting a single-player game. We'll have to adjust things a bit. I'll start by listing the class headers in the following code snippet. You may need to add an import/using statement for the GamePanel class' GameStates enumeration. The IDE should detect this error and provide a solution automatically. You can also just explicitly reference the GameStates enumeration.

Listing 17-1. ScreenMainMenu Class Code 1

```
//Java lib references and class header
import net.middlemind.MmgGameApiJava.MmgBase.*;
import net.middlemind.MmgGameApiJava.MmgCore.*;
```

© Victor G Brusca 2021
V. G. Brusca, *Introduction to Video Game Engine Development*, https://doi.org/10.1007/978-1-4842-7039-4_17

```
public class ScreenMainMenu extends net.middlemind.MmgGameApiJava.MmgCore.
ScreenMainMenu {
```

```
//C# lib references and class header
using net.middlemind.MmgGameApiCs.MmgBase;
using net.middlemind.MmgGameApiCs.MmgCore;
```

```
public class ScreenMainMenu : net.middlemind.MmgGameApiCs.MmgCore.
ScreenMainMenu {
```

```
//Class outline
private MmgBmp menuStartGame1P;
private MmgBmp menuStartGame2P;
private boolean lret;
```

```
public ScreenMainMenu(GameStates State, GamePanel Owner) { ... }
```

```
@Override
public void LoadResources() { ... }
```

```
@Override
public boolean ProcessAClick(int src) { ... }
```

```
@Override
public boolean ProcessDpadRelease(int dir) { ... }
```

```
@Override
public void DrawScreen() { ... }
```

```
@Override
public void UnloadResources() { ... }
```

```
@Override
public GameStates GetGameState() { ... }
```

```
@Override
public boolean GetIsDirty() { ... }
```

```
@Override
public void SetIsDirty(boolean b) { ... }
```

```
public void MakeDirty() { ... }
```

```
@Override
public void MmgDraw(MmgPen p) { ... }
```

```
@Override
public boolean MmgUpdate(int updateTick, long currentTimeMs, long
msSinceLastFrame) { ... }
```

The methods outlined in the preceding should be familiar to you from our review of the MmgCore API's game screen classes. We're going to be methodically building up this class over the next few pages. Let's start with the class' constructor, shall we? Again, I won't be addressing the slight differences between the Java and C# versions.

We'll stick to working with the Java code in the text. If you run into trouble following along in either Java or C#, then please check the example project in the MmgTestSpace library or the completed chapter projects included with the game engine project.

Listing 17-2. ScreenMainMenu Class Code 2

```
1 public ScreenMainMenu(GameStates State, GamePanel Owner) {
2       super(State, Owner);
3       isDirty = false;
4       pause = false;
5       ready = false;
6       state = State;
7       owner = Owner;
8 }
```

The constructor, much like in other screen classes we've reviewed, calls the super class constructor and prepares all the class fields as shown in the preceding. I think we should get the class' support methods out of the way first. I'll list the methods in the following code block; please add them to your ScreenMainMenu class along with the constructor outlined in the preceding.

Listing 17-3. ScreenMainMenu Class Code 3

```
@Override
1 public GameStates GetGameState() {
2       return state;
3 }
```

```
@Override
1 public boolean GetIsDirty() {
2      return isDirty;
3 }
```

```
@Override
1 public void SetIsDirty(boolean b) {
2      isDirty = b;
3 }
```

```
1 public void MakeDirty() {
2      isDirty = true;
3 }
```

Some of these methods are already defined by the super class, or base class in C#. We didn't need to override them and redefine them in this class, but I wanted to make sure that the code was local in case I needed to make customizations. In the end, it's only a few lines of code, so let's not worry too much about it. Next up, let's take a look at the class' input methods. Notice that in this case we're overriding the super class and not using super class functionality. We're letting the local class take full control.

Listing 17-4. ScreenMainMenu Class Code 4

```
@Override
01 public boolean ProcessAClick(int src) {
02      int idx = GetMenuIdx();
03      MmgMenuItem mmi;
04      mmi = (MmgMenuItem) menu.GetContainer().get(idx);
05
06      if (mmi != null) {
07          ProcessMenuItemSel(mmi);
08          return true;
09      }
10
11      return false;
12 }
```

```
@Override
01 public boolean ProcessDpadRelease(int dir) {
02     if (dir == GameSettings.UP_KEYBOARD || dir ==
       GameSettings.UP_GAMEPAD_1) {
03         MoveMenuSelUp();
04     } else if (dir == GameSettings.DOWN_KEYBOARD || dir ==
       GameSettings.DOWN_GAMEPAD_1) {
05         MoveMenuSelDown();
06     }
07
08     return true;
09 }
```

Review the input methods listed in the preceding and add them to your
ScreenMainMenu class. This adds input handling to the menu screen. The next set of class
methods for us to implement are the LoadResources and UnloadResources methods.
If you recall from the ScreenMainMenu class' review, the LoadResources method is
responsible for loading and configuring the screen's resources. Let's take a look at a
snippet of code from this method.

Listing 17-5. ScreenMainMenu Class Code 5

```
@Override
01 public void LoadResources() {
02     pause = true;
03     SetHeight(MmgScreenData.GetGameHeight());
04     SetWidth(MmgScreenData.GetGameWidth());
05     SetPosition(MmgScreenData.GetPosition());
06
07     classConfig = MmgHelper.ReadClassConfigFile(GameSettings.CLASS_
       CONFIG_DIR + GameSettings.NAME + "/screen_main_menu.txt");
08
09     MmgBmp tB = null;
10     MmgPen p;
11     String key = "";
12     String imgId = "";
13     String sndId = "";
```

```
14      MmgBmp lval = null;
15      MmgSound sval = null;
16      String file = "";
17
18      p = new MmgPen();
19      p.SetCacheOn(false);
20      handleMenuEvent = new HandleMainMenuEvent(this, owner);
21
22      key = "soundMenuSelect";
23      if(classConfig.containsKey(key)) {
24          file = classConfig.get(key).str;
25      } else {
26          file = "jump1.wav";
27      }
28
29      sndId = file;
30      sval = MmgHelper.GetBasicCachedSound(sndId);
31      menuSound = sval;
32
33      tB = MmgHelper.CreateFilledBmp(w, h, MmgColor.GetBlack());
34      if (tB != null) {
35          SetCenteredBackground(tB);
36      }
37
38      key = "bmpGameTitle";
39      if(classConfig.containsKey(key)) {
40          file = classConfig.get(key).str;
41      } else {
42          file = "game_title.png";
43      }
44
45      imgId = file;
46      lval = MmgHelper.GetBasicCachedBmp(imgId);
47      menuTitle = lval;
48      if (menuTitle != null) {
```

```
49        MmgHelper.CenterHor(menuTitle);
50        menuTitle.GetPosition().SetY(GetPosition().GetY() + MmgHelper.
          ScaleValue(40));
51        menuTitle = MmgHelper.ContainsKeyMmgBmpScaleAndPosition(
          "menuTitle", menuTitle, classConfig, menuTitle.GetPosition());
52        AddObj(menuTitle);
53    }
```

This is quite a long method, so take your time with it. I recommend copying the full version of this method from the Chapter 17 project included with the game engine project. The main take-away from the preceding listing is on lines 45–53. The code block shows how resources are loaded and processed. The same steps are applied to each image resource on this screen. It's redundant and we've seen similar code during the MmgCore API review, so I won't go over it again here.

Listing 17-6. ScreenMainMenu Class Code 6

```
@Override
01 public void UnloadResources() {
02     isDirty = false;
03     pause = true;
04
05     SetIsVisible(false);
06     SetBackground(null);
07     SetMenu(null);
08     ClearObjs();
09
10     menuStartGame = null;
11     menuStartGame1P = null;
12     menuStartGame2P = null;
13     menuExitGame = null;
14     menuTitle = null;
15     menuFooterUrl = null;
16     menuCursor = null;
17     menuSound = null;
18
```

```
19      handleMenuEvent = null;
20      classConfig = null;
21
22      super.UnloadResources();
23
24      menu = null;
25      ready = false;
26 }
```

The UnloadResources method is used to reverse what the LoadResources method does and clear any class resources. Notice that there is one line in the method that stands out a bit. Remember the class you're working on extends a super class, so we must be sure to call the super class' UnloadResources method to ensure all resources have been released. There is a specific call to the super class method on line 22.

We're just about finished with this class, but we still have a bit of work to do. The next method we'll work on is the DrawScreen method. We've reviewed this method before as well, but in case you're a little fuzzy on its details, think of this method as a runtime configuration method. It will redraw the screen in response to an MmgUpdate call if the class is marked as dirty. Let's take a look at some code!

Listing 17-7. ScreenMainMenu Class Code 7

```
@Override
01 public void DrawScreen() {
02      pause = true;
03      menu = new MmgMenuContainer();
04      menu.SetMmgColor(null);
05      isDirty = false;
06
07      MmgMenuItem mItm = null;
08
09      if (menuStartGame1P != null) {
10          mItm = MmgHelper.GetBasicMenuItem(handleMenuEvent, "Main Menu
            Start Game 1P", HandleMainMenuEvent.MAIN_MENU_EVENT_START_GAME_1P,
            HandleMainMenuEvent.MAIN_MENU_EVENT_TYPE, menuStartGame1P);
```

```
11          mItm.SetSound(menuSound);
12          menu.Add(mItm);
13      }
14
15      if (menuStartGame2P != null) {
16          mItm = MmgHelper.GetBasicMenuItem(handleMenuEvent, "Main Menu
            Start Game 2P", HandleMainMenuEvent.MAIN_MENU_EVENT_START_GAME_2P,
            HandleMainMenuEvent.MAIN_MENU_EVENT_TYPE, menuStartGame2P);
17          mItm.SetSound(menuSound);
18          menu.Add(mItm);
19      }
20
21      if (menuExitGame != null) {
22          mItm = MmgHelper.GetBasicMenuItem(handleMenuEvent, "Main Menu
            Exit Game", HandleMainMenuEvent.MAIN_MENU_EVENT_EXIT_GAME,
            HandleMainMenuEvent.MAIN_MENU_EVENT_TYPE, menuExitGame);
23          mItm.SetSound(menuSound);
24          menu.Add(mItm);
25      }
26
27      SetMenuStart(0);
28      SetMenuStop(menu.GetCount() - 1);
29
30      SetMenu(menu);
31      SetMenuOn(true);
32      pause = false;
33 }
```

Notice that the DrawScreen method is responsible for setting up the menu items after the first call to the MmgUpdate method when the class is marked as dirty. Add this method to the ScreenMainMenu class, and we'll move on to tackle the drawing routine methods MmgDraw and MmgUpdate. Let's take a look at the MmgDraw method next.

Listing 17-8. ScreenMainMenu Class Code 8

```
1 public void MmgDraw(MmgPen p) {
2       if (pause == false && GetIsVisible() == true) {
3             super.MmgDraw(p);
4       }
5 }
```

Add the MmgDraw method listed in the preceding to your ScreenMainMenu class and save your work. Please remember to save early and save often. The last method we have to work on is the MmgUpdate method listed next.

Listing 17-9. ScreenMainMenu Class Code 9

```
01 public boolean MmgUpdate(int updateTick, long currentTimeMs, long
msSinceLastFrame) {
02      lret = false;
03
04      if (pause == false && isVisible == true) {
05           if (super.MmgUpdate(updateTick, currentTimeMs, msSinceLastFrame)
             == true) {
06                lret = true;
07           }
08
09           if (isDirty == true) {
10                lret = true;
11                DrawScreen();
12           }
13
14      }
15
16      return lret;
17 }
```

We're almost ready to compile and test our project, but we have a few more steps to complete before the new ScreenMainMenu game screen is plugged into the game. Open up the GamePanel class and add the following line of code to the bottom of the list of class fields:

```
public ScreenMainMenu screenMainMenu;
```

You'll also need to add the following code to the GamePanel class' constructor. This will initialize the main menu screen along with the other game screens.

Listing 17-10. GamePanel Class Code 1

```
1 screenMainMenu = new ScreenMainMenu(GameStates.MAIN_MENU, this);
```

To connect the game screen into the GamePanel's known states, we need to add the following code to the cleanup section of the SwitchGameState method. Add in the following code if it doesn't already exist.

Listing 17-11. GamePanel Class Code 2

```
1 } else if (prevGameState == GameStates.MAIN_MENU) {
2     MmgHelper.wr("Hiding MAIN_MENU screen.");
3     screenMainMenu.Pause();
4     screenMainMenu.SetIsVisible(false);
5     screenMainMenu.UnloadResources();
6
7 }
```

We're almost there. We still need to add the game state preparation code that's responsible for getting the main menu screen ready to display. Again, add in the following code if it doesn't already exist.

Listing 17-12. GamePanel Class Code 3

```
1 } else if (gameState == GameStates.MAIN_MENU) {
2     MmgHelper.wr("Showing MAIN_MENU screen.");
3     screenMainMenu.LoadResources();
4     screenMainMenu.UnPause();
5     screenMainMenu.SetIsVisible(true);
6     currentScreen = screenMainMenu;
7
8 }
```

Now the new main menu screen is fully wired into the GamePanel class and subsequently the game. Once you're done adding in the SwitchGameState method updates, make sure your project compiles correctly. Address any errors if you encounter them, and if you run into real trouble, take a look at the example project for this chapter and double-check your code. Run your project using the same steps outlined in the previous chapter.

If you're following along in C#, then use the terminal to run your newly compiled project. If you're working with the Java version of the game, you can run the project directly in the IDE. Notice that the main menu is visible just like in the previous chapter, but in this case, it's now customized for our game.

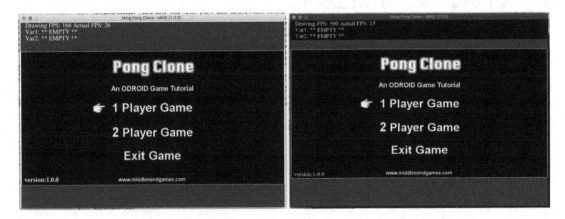

Figure 17-1. *PongClone Game 1*

That brings us to the conclusion of this chapter. We've addressed a number of points from the PongClone game's specification list. In the next chapter, we'll implement the game screen and address all the game-specific details on the specification list.

CHAPTER 18

PongClone Game Screen

The game is coming along nicely. We've actually covered a lot of ground. Most of the game screens have been implemented, and the last few bullet points are all associated with the main game screen. This is where the actual game play occurs. We'll also have to link the new game screen into the project's GamePanel class. There is a lot going on in the game screen, so we'll proceed carefully and methodically.

PongClone: ScreenGame Class Header and Fields

We'll start with the class headers listed in the following snippet for both the Java and C# versions of the project.

Listing 18-1. ScreenGame Class Header 1

```
import net.middlemind.MmgGameApiJava.MmgCore.*;
import net.middlemind.MmgGameApiJava.MmgBase.*;
import java.util.Random;

public class ScreenGame extends Screen { ... }
```

If you're following along in C#, the class header will look like the following code snippet.

Listing 18-2. ScreenGame Class Header 2

```
using System;
using net.middlemind.MmgGameApiCs.MmgBase;
using net.middlemind.MmgGameApiCs.MmgCore;
using static net.middlemind.MmgGameApiCs.MmgCore.GamePanel;

public class ScreenGame : Screen { ... }
```

© Victor G Brusca 2021

V. G. Brusca, *Introduction to Video Game Engine Development*, https://doi.org/10.1007/978-1-4842-7039-4_18

I won't always list every library reference used by a class. This is in regard to the import and using statements in Java and C# class files, respectively. Both Visual Studio and NetBeans have the ability to suggest a library reference if it's the cause of an error in the class you're working on.

Just something to keep in the back of your mind as you build the PongClone game. You can always open up the chapter project found in the associated game engine project and check the class header. Next, we'll take a look at the ScreenGame class' fields. Take a moment to add a new class to your project and enter in the class header listed in the preceding. Be sure to name the class and the corresponding file "ScreenGame," as shown in the examples.

Listing 18-3. ScreenGame Class Fields 1

```
private enum NumberState {
    NONE,
    NUMBER_1,
    NUMBER_2,
    NUMBER_3
};

private NumberState numberState = NumberState.NONE;
private long timeNumberMs = 0L;
private long timeNumberDisplayMs = 1000;
private long timeTmpMs = 0L;
private MmgBmp number1;
private MmgBmp number2;
private MmgBmp number3;
```

The enumeration and class fields listed in the preceding are used to drive the game's countdown numbers that are displayed before game play begins and in-between rounds of play. The game start sub-screen displays information about the game, while both the game start and game re-start countdown sub-screens provide a few seconds for the players to get ready.

Add these lines of code to your new class. Try and take a moment to understand what the fields represent, but don't worry too much if they don't seem clear. You'll see them in action in just a bit when you add the in-game functionality.

Listing 18-4. ScreenGame Class Fields 2

```
private enum State {
    NONE,
    SHOW_GAME,
    SHOW_COUNT_DOWN,
    SHOW_COUNT_DOWN_IN_GAME,
    SHOW_GAME_OVER,
    SHOW_GAME_EXIT
};

private GameType gameType = GameType.GAME_ONE_PLAYER;
private State statePrev = State.NONE;
private State state = State.NONE;
```

The next set of class fields listed in the preceding are game state–related class fields. A few of them have been encountered before, during the review of game screen classes in Part 2 of this text. These fields are used to define the current state of the game screen. You may need to add a reference, import/using statement, for the GamePanel class' GameType enumeration. This applies to both the C# and Java projects. The IDE should provide a suggestion to resolve any reference errors with regard to this enumeration. The next block of class fields are used in the popup window formatting and display. There is also a class field used to describe the position of the game screen.

Listing 18-5. ScreenGame Class Fields 3

```
private MmgBmp bgroundPopupSrc;
private Mmg9Slice bgroundPopup;
private MmgFont txtOk;
private MmgFont txtCancel;
private int popupTotalWidth = MmgHelper.ScaleValue(300);

private int popupTotalHeight = MmgHelper.ScaleValue(120);

private int lastX;
private int lastY;
private boolean mousePos = true;
private MmgVector2 screenPos;
```

One of the in-game features mentioned in the game's general specifications is an exit prompt. This feature can also be used to pause the game play. The fields listed in the preceding are used to define this feature. The first few field entries are used to position and draw the exit prompt. The last few entries are used to track mouse input and the game's screen position.

Listing 18-6. ScreenGame Class Fields 4

```
private MmgBmp paddleLeft;
private MmgBmp paddleRight;
private MmgVector2 paddle1Pos;
private MmgVector2 paddle2Pos;
private int paddle1MovePerFrame = GetSpeedPerFrame(400);

private boolean paddle1MoveUp = false;
private boolean paddle1MoveDown = false;
private int paddle2MovePerFrame = GetSpeedPerFrame(400);

private boolean paddle2MoveUp = false;
private boolean paddle2MoveDown = false;
```

There are a few game features that aren't explicitly listed in the game's general specifications. Some features are implicitly defined as part of the game's description or in the description of other game features. The preceding fields are used to define the players' paddles. Notice that there are class fields for the paddle images and positions. These are used to render the paddles at specific positions on the screen as the players move them. The next three class fields describe the movement of paddle 1. Similarly, the remaining fields are used to describe the movement of paddle 2.

I'd like to take a moment to talk about the paddle 1 and 2 move-per-frame class fields. Notice that the value of the fields is the result of a static method call, GetSpeedPerFrame, that calculates how much the paddle moves on any given frame. This technique is important because it ensures that the paddle movement is locked to the frame rate. This means the game will run at just about the same speed even if the game's frame rate changes. This is a very important detail you should keep in mind when working with movement in your games.

Listing 18-7. ScreenGame Class Fields 5

```
private MmgSound bounceNorm;
private MmgSound bounceSuper;
private MmgBmp bground;
private MmgBmp ball;
private MmgVector2 ballPos;
private int ballMovePerFrameMin = GetSpeedPerFrame(150);

private int ballMovePerFrameMax = GetSpeedPerFrame(425);

private int ballDirX = 1;
private int ballDirY = 1;
private int ballMovePerFrameX = 0;
private int ballMovePerFrameY = 0;
private Random rand;
private int ballNewX;
private int ballNewY;
private boolean bounced = false;
private boolean infiniteBounce = false;
```

The block of class fields listed in the preceding are fields that manage how the ball moves on the game board and in response to bouncing off of a player's paddle or the game screen walls. The first two fields listed are used to play a sound when the ball bounces. A different sound is played depending on the ball's speed. The next two fields, bground and ball, are the images drawn during game play for those game features.

The ballPos field is an MmgVector2 object that represents the position of the ball. The following two entries, ballMovePerFrameMin and ballMovePerFrameMax, are set up similarly to the paddle's movement fields. Note that they're also locked to the game's frame rate. The ballDirX and ballDirY fields are used to track the ball's direction of movement. We need to have class fields that keep track of what the ball's current speed is; ballMovePerFrameX and ballMovePerFrameY take care of that for us.

The rand field is used to generate any random values we need in the game. For instance, the rand field is used to generate the ball's initial direction of movement. The last four entries are used to calculate the ball's next position and if it bounced or not. Lastly, the infiniteBounce field is used to allow the ball to bounce around the screen indefinitely. This is a great tool for debugging the game's physics.

Listing 18-8. ScreenGame Class Fields 6

```
private int scoreGameWin = 7;
private MmgFont scoreLeft;
private int scorePlayerLeft = 0;
private MmgFont scoreRight;
private int scorePlayerRight = 0;
private int aiMaxSpeed = 425;
```

We're almost done working through the class' fields. We have only two sets of fields left to add to our class and a few more game specifications that have to be addressed. We'll need a way to keep track of the player's score for one thing. The fields listed in the preceding will track the player's scores as integer values, scorePlayerLeft and scorePlayerRight, and the string representation of the scores is handled by the scoreLeft and scoreRight fields. The preceding last entry, aiMaxSpeed, is used to regulate the maximum speed of the AI player's paddle.

Listing 18-9. ScreenGame Class Fields 7

```
private MmgFont exit;
private MmgBmp exitBground;
private MmgFont txtGoal;
private MmgFont txtDirecP1;
private MmgFont txtDirecP2;
private MmgFont txtGameOver1;
private MmgFont txtGameOver2;
private int padding = MmgHelper.ScaleValue(4);
```

The last set of class fields for us to look at are listed in the preceding. The exit and exitBground fields are used to display the exit prompt. The next few fields, txtGoal, txtDirectP1, txtDirectP2, txtGameOver1, and txtGameOver2, are used to present information in the game start and game end sub-screens. The game's rules are displayed on the game start sub-screen, while the game's results are reported on the game over sub-screen.

That completes all the class fields we'll need for this game screen. Make sure to carefully add them to your ScreenGame class. Address any errors that pop up. Once everything's settled and error-free, make sure all your work is saved. Note that there may be errors that you can't address until you implement more of the game class' code. Don't worry about these. Take care of any syntax errors and other errors you can address.

PongClone: ScreenGame Support Methods

We're going to outline the class methods next. It's good practice to try and plan out your class' functionality before you actually sit down to code. This is something most people don't do; and to be honest, the experienced coders out there actually do this almost subconsciously, but they still do it. I use pen and paper sometimes with more complex classes or vague ideas I'm trying to bring to code.

Listing 18-10. ScreenGame Class Outline 1

```
//Main methods
public ScreenGame(GameStates State, GamePanel Owner) { ... }

public void LoadResources() { ... }
public void UnloadResources() { ... }
private void ResetGame() { ... }
public void DrawScreen() { ... }
public void MmgDraw(MmgPen p) { ... }

//Support methods
public GameType GetGameType() { ... }
public void SetGameType(GameType gt) { ... }
private void SetState(State inS) { ... }
private void SetScoreLeftText(int score) { ... }
private void SetScoreRightText(int score) { ... }
private static int GetSpeedPerFrame(int speed) { ... }

//Input methods
public boolean ProcessAClick(int src) { ... }
public boolean ProcessBClick(int src) { ... }
public void ProcessDebugClick() { ... }
public boolean ProcessKeyPress(char c, int code) { ... }

public boolean ProcessKeyRelease(char c, int code) { ... }

public boolean ProcessDpadPress(int dir) { ... }
public boolean ProcessDpadRelease(int dir) { ... }
public boolean ProcessMouseMove(int x, int y) { ... }
```

Take a look at the class outline listed in the preceding. There are 20 methods listed in three groups. A lot of these methods will look familiar to you from our previous class reviews. Review the list and spend a few minutes thinking about what each method will do. Recall the class fields we've outlined for this class and think about how they might be used in the methods listed. We'll work on the methods in the support group first. Add each method to your ScreenGame class as we outline them here.

Listing 18-11. ScreenGame Support Methods 1

```
001 public void SetGameType(GameType gt) {
002      gameType = gt;
003 }

001 public GameType GetGameType() {
002      return gameType;
003 }

001 private void SetState(State inS) {
002      //clean up prev state
003      switch(statePrev) {
004          case NONE:
005              break;
006
007          case SHOW_GAME:
008              break;
009
010          case SHOW_COUNT_DOWN:
011              break;
012
013          case SHOW_COUNT_DOWN_IN_GAME:
014              break;
015
016          case SHOW_GAME_OVER:
017              break;
018
```

```
019        case SHOW_GAME_EXIT:
020            break;
021    }
022
023    statePrev = state;
024    state = inS;
025
026    switch(state) {
027        case NONE:
028            ResetGame();
029
030            ball.SetIsVisible(false);
031            paddleLeft.SetIsVisible(false);
032            paddleRight.SetIsVisible(false);
033            bground.SetIsVisible(false);
034            number1.SetIsVisible(false);
035            number2.SetIsVisible(false);
036            number3.SetIsVisible(false);
037            txtGoal.SetIsVisible(false);
038            txtDirecP1.SetIsVisible(false);
039            txtDirecP2.SetIsVisible(false);
040            scoreLeft.SetIsVisible(false);
041            scoreRight.SetIsVisible(false);
042            exit.SetIsVisible(false);
043            bgroundPopup.SetIsVisible(false);
044            txtOk.SetIsVisible(false);
045            txtCancel.SetIsVisible(false);
046
047            scorePlayerRight = 0;
048            scorePlayerLeft = 0;
049            SetScoreRightText(scorePlayerRight);
050            SetScoreLeftText(scorePlayerLeft);
051
```

```
052              pause = false;
053              isDirty = false;
054              break;
055
056          case SHOW_GAME_OVER:
057              ball.SetIsVisible(true);
058              paddleLeft.SetIsVisible(true);
059              paddleRight.SetIsVisible(true);
060              bground.SetIsVisible(false);
061              number1.SetIsVisible(false);
062              number2.SetIsVisible(false);
063              number3.SetIsVisible(false);
064              txtGoal.SetIsVisible(false);
065              txtDirecP1.SetIsVisible(false);
066              txtDirecP2.SetIsVisible(false);
067              scoreLeft.SetIsVisible(true);
068              scoreRight.SetIsVisible(true);
069              exit.SetIsVisible(true);
070              bgroundPopup.SetIsVisible(false);
071              txtOk.SetIsVisible(false);
072              txtCancel.SetIsVisible(false);
073
074              if(scorePlayerRight == scoreGameWin) {
075                  txtGameOver1.SetIsVisible(true);
076                  txtGameOver2.SetIsVisible(false);
077
078              } else if(scorePlayerLeft == scoreGameWin) {
079                  txtGameOver1.SetIsVisible(false);
080                  txtGameOver2.SetIsVisible(true);
081
082              }
083              numberState = NumberState.NONE;
084
085              pause = false;
086              isDirty = true;
087              break;
```

```
088
089        case SHOW_GAME:
090            if(statePrev != State.SHOW_GAME_EXIT) {
091                timeNumberMs = System.currentTimeMillis();
092                ResetGame();
093            }
094
095            ball.SetIsVisible(true);
096            paddleLeft.SetIsVisible(true);
097            paddleRight.SetIsVisible(true);
098            bground.SetIsVisible(true);
099            number1.SetIsVisible(false);
100            number2.SetIsVisible(false);
101            number3.SetIsVisible(false);
102            txtGoal.SetIsVisible(false);
103            txtDirecP1.SetIsVisible(false);
104            txtDirecP2.SetIsVisible(false);
105            scoreLeft.SetIsVisible(true);
106            scoreRight.SetIsVisible(true);
107            exit.SetIsVisible(true);
108            bgroundPopup.SetIsVisible(false);
109            txtOk.SetIsVisible(false);
110            txtCancel.SetIsVisible(false);
111            txtGameOver1.SetIsVisible(false);
112            txtGameOver2.SetIsVisible(false);
113
114            if(statePrev != State.SHOW_GAME_EXIT) {
115                if(rand.nextInt(11) % 2 == 0) {
116                    ballDirX = 1;
117                } else {
118                    ballDirX = -1;
119                }
120                ballMovePerFrameX = ballMovePerFrameMin;
121
```

```
122                    if(rand.nextInt(11) % 2 == 0) {
123                        ballDirY = 1;
124                    } else {
125                        ballDirY = -1;
126                    }
127                    ballMovePerFrameY = ballMovePerFrameMin;
128                }
129
130            pause = false;
131            isDirty = true;
132            break;
133
134        case SHOW_COUNT_DOWN_IN_GAME:
135            ball.SetIsVisible(true);
136            paddleLeft.SetIsVisible(true);
137            paddleRight.SetIsVisible(true);
138            bground.SetIsVisible(true);
139
140            if(statePrev != State.SHOW_GAME_EXIT) {
141                number1.SetIsVisible(false);
142                number2.SetIsVisible(false);
143                number3.SetIsVisible(false);
144            }
145
146            txtGoal.SetIsVisible(false);
147            txtDirecP1.SetIsVisible(false);
148            txtDirecP2.SetIsVisible(false);
149            scoreLeft.SetIsVisible(true);
150            scoreRight.SetIsVisible(true);
151            exit.SetIsVisible(true);
152            bgroundPopup.SetIsVisible(false);
153            txtOk.SetIsVisible(false);
154            txtCancel.SetIsVisible(false);
155            txtGameOver1.SetIsVisible(false);
156            txtGameOver2.SetIsVisible(false);
157
```

```
158              if(statePrev != State.SHOW_GAME_EXIT) {
159                  numberState = NumberState.NONE;
160              } else {
161                  //reset this number count down
162                  timeNumberMs = System.currentTimeMillis();
163              }
164
165              pause = false;
166              isDirty = true;
167              break;
168
169          case SHOW_COUNT_DOWN:
170              ball.SetIsVisible(false);
171              paddleLeft.SetIsVisible(false);
172              paddleRight.SetIsVisible(false);
173              bground.SetIsVisible(false);
174
175              if(statePrev != State.SHOW_GAME_EXIT) {
176                  number1.SetIsVisible(false);
177                  number2.SetIsVisible(false);
178                  number3.SetIsVisible(false);
179                  txtGoal.SetIsVisible(false);
180                  txtDirecP1.SetIsVisible(false);
181                  txtDirecP2.SetIsVisible(false);
182              }
183
184              scoreLeft.SetIsVisible(true);
185              scoreRight.SetIsVisible(true);
186              exit.SetIsVisible(true);
187              bgroundPopup.SetIsVisible(false);
188              txtOk.SetIsVisible(false);
189              txtCancel.SetIsVisible(false);
190              txtGameOver1.SetIsVisible(false);
191              txtGameOver2.SetIsVisible(false);
192
```

```
193                 if(statePrev != State.SHOW_GAME_EXIT) {
194                     numberState = NumberState.NONE;
195                 } else {
196                     //reset this number count down
197                     timeNumberMs = System.currentTimeMillis();
198                 }
199
200                 pause = false;
201                 isDirty = true;
202                 break;
203
204             case SHOW_GAME_EXIT:
205                 bgroundPopup.SetIsVisible(true);
206                 txtOk.SetIsVisible(true);
207                 txtCancel.SetIsVisible(true);
208                 isDirty = true;
209                 break;
210         }
211 }
```

```
001 private void SetScoreLeftText(int score) {
002     String tmp = score + "";
003     if(tmp.length() != 2) {
004         tmp = "0" + tmp;
005     }
006     scoreLeft.SetText(tmp);
007 }
```

```
001 private void SetScoreRightText(int score) {
002     String tmp = score + "";
003     if(tmp.length() != 2) {
004         tmp = "0" + tmp;
005     }
006     scoreRight.SetText(tmp);
007 }
```

```
001 private static int GetSpeedPerFrame(int speed) {
002     return (int)(speed/(MmgPongClone.FPS - 4));
003 }
```

The first two methods listed are get and set methods for the gameType class field. Add these methods to your ScreenGame class. The SetState method is used a lot like the SwitchGameState method from the GamePanel class. This method is long, and although it's listed here so you can type it up by hand, feel free to just copy and paste the code from the chapter's completed project found in the associated game engine's project folder.

Whatever path you choose, make sure you read over and understand what the code is doing. Basically, the code is based on the screen's internal state. Different MmgObj-based fields are set to visible or not visible depending on that state. Pay special attention to what screen features are being turned on or off and for what game state. The SetScoreLeftText and SetScoreRightText methods are used to update the left and right scores presented to the player by the MmgFont object fields scoreLeft and scoreRight.

The last method entry is very important. The GetSpeedPerFrame static method is used to calculate a speed per frame value based on the provided movement speed. Make sure that you add the methods listed in the preceding to your ScreenGame class and take care of any errors that may come up. Please refer to the completed chapter project, if necessary, to resolve any issues.

PongClone: ScreenGame Input Methods

The next set of methods that we'll tackle are the input methods. These methods are going to be a little bit more complicated than the first group of methods we've worked through. You should take the time to interpret and understand how the input methods work and how they can be used to drive aspects of the game. Let's take a look at some input code!

Listing 18-12. ScreenGame Input Methods 1

```
@Override
01 public boolean ProcessAClick(int src) {
02      if(state == State.SHOW_GAME_EXIT) {
03           owner.SwitchGameState(GameStates.MAIN_MENU);
04           return true;
05
06      } else if(state == State.SHOW_GAME_OVER) {
07           owner.SwitchGameState(GameStates.MAIN_MENU);
08           return true;
09
10      }
11
12      return false;
13 }

@Override
01 public boolean ProcessBClick(int src) {
02      if(state == State.SHOW_GAME_OVER) {
03           owner.SwitchGameState(GameStates.MAIN_MENU);
04           return true;
05
06      } else {
07           if(state != State.SHOW_GAME_EXIT) {
08                SetState(State.SHOW_GAME_EXIT);
09                return true;
10
11           } else {
12                SetState(statePrev);
13                return true;
14           }
15      }
16 }
```

```
@Override
01 public void ProcessDebugClick() {
02     if(scoreGameWin > 1) {
03         MmgHelper.wr("Setting game win score to 1.");
04         scoreGameWin = 1;
05     } else if(scoreGameWin == 1 && infiniteBounce == false) {
06         MmgHelper.wr("Setting infinite bounce to true.");
07         infiniteBounce = true;
08     } else if(scoreGameWin == 1 && infiniteBounce == true) {
09         MmgHelper.wr("Setting game win score to 7 and infinite bounce to
           false.");
10         scoreGameWin = 7;
11         infiniteBounce = false;
12     }
13 }

@Override
01 public boolean ProcessKeyPress(char c, int code) {
02     if(state == State.SHOW_GAME && pause == false) {
03         if(gameType == GameType.GAME_TWO_PLAYER) {
04             if(c == 'x' || c == 'X') {
05                 paddle1MoveUp = false;
06                 paddle1MoveDown = true;
07                 return true;
08
09             } else if(c == 's' || c == 'S') {
10                 paddle1MoveUp = true;
11                 paddle1MoveDown = false;
12                 return true;
13
14             }
15         }
16     }
17
18     return false;
19 }
```

```
@Override
01 public boolean ProcessKeyRelease(char c, int code) {
02      if(state == State.SHOW_GAME && pause == false) {
03          if(gameType == GameType.GAME_TWO_PLAYER) {
04              if(c == 'x' || c == 'X') {
05                  paddle1MoveDown = false;
06                  return true;
07
08              } else if(c == 's' || c == 'S') {
09                  paddle1MoveUp = false;
10                  return true;
11
12              }
13          }
14      }
15
16      return false;
17 }
```

```
@Override
01 public boolean ProcessDpadPress(int dir) {
02      if(state == State.SHOW_GAME && pause == false) {
03          if(dir == GameSettings.DOWN_KEYBOARD) {
04              paddle2MoveUp = false;
05              paddle2MoveDown = true;
06              return true;
07
08          } else if(dir == GameSettings.UP_KEYBOARD) {
09              paddle2MoveUp = true;
10              paddle2MoveDown = false;
11              return true;
12
```

```
13          } else if(this.gameType == GameType.GAME_TWO_PLAYER) {
14              if(dir == GameSettings.DOWN_GAMEPAD_1 || dir ==
                GameSettings.DOWN_GPIO) {
15                  if(dir == GameSettings.DOWN_GPIO) {
16                      MmgHelper.wr(("GPIO Gamepad Down Button Event"));
17                  }
18
19                  paddle1MoveUp = false;
20                  paddle1MoveDown = true;
21                  return true;
22
23              } else if(dir == GameSettings.UP_GAMEPAD_1 || dir ==
                GameSettings.UP_GPIO) {
24                  if(dir == GameSettings.UP_GPIO) {
25                      MmgHelper.wr(("GPIO Gamepad Up Button Event"));
26                  }
27
28                  paddle1MoveUp = true;
29                  paddle1MoveDown = false;
30                  return true;
31
32              }
33          }
34      }
35
36      return false;
37 }

@Override
01 public boolean ProcessDpadRelease(int dir) {
02      if(state == State.SHOW_GAME && pause == false) {
03          if(dir == GameSettings.DOWN_KEYBOARD) {
04              paddle2MoveDown = false;
05              return true;
06
```

```
07              } else if(dir == GameSettings.UP_KEYBOARD) {
08                  paddle2MoveUp = false;
09                  return true;
10
11          } else if(this.gameType == GameType.GAME_TWO_PLAYER) {
12              if(dir == GameSettings.DOWN_GAMEPAD_1 || dir ==
                GameSettings.DOWN_GPIO) {
13                  paddle1MoveDown = false;
14                  return true;
15
16              } else if(dir == GameSettings.UP_GAMEPAD_1 || dir ==
                GameSettings.UP_GPIO) {
17                  paddle1MoveUp = false;
18                  return true;
19
20              }
21          }
22      }
23
24      return false;
25 }

@Override
01 public boolean ProcessMouseMove(int x, int y) {
02      if(state == State.SHOW_GAME && pause == false) {
03          if(gameType == GameType.GAME_TWO_PLAYER) {
04              if(y >= screenPos.GetY() && y <= (screenPos.GetY() +
                GetHeight() - paddleLeft.GetHeight())) {
05                  lastX = x;
06                  lastY = y;
07                  mousePos = true;
08                  return true;
09              }
10          }
11      }
12
```

```
13     mousePos = false;
14     return false;
15 }
```

Take the time to add the input methods listed in the preceding to the ScreenGame class. The first two methods handle A and B button input. This input is used to interact with the exit game and game over sub-screens. Notice that in the ProcessAClick method, the game panel is used to change the current game state. This is used to exit the game. Notice on line 8 of the ProcessBClick method that it's the game screen's state that is changed causing the exit popup to display.

I should mention that the ProcessDebugClick method can be used to toggle some useful debugging settings. Take a moment to review the method and understand how it works. Basically, pressing the debug key, D key, once turns on a one-point win condition in the game. This is used to speed up testing game ending states. Pressing it a second time will turn on infinite bounce as well. Now the game can't be won because the ball will bounce around infinitely. Lastly, if you press the key a third time, the original settings will be restored.

There are four keyboard-driven input methods for you to add to the class. The ProcessKeyPress and ProcessKeyRelease methods are designed to support input from the X and S keys. The keys are used to move the paddle up and down, respectively. Similarly, the ProcessDpadPress and ProcessDpadRelease methods are used to process directional pad input from the keyboard, a GPIO gamepad, and a USB gamepad.

The game supports a decent number of control options. Speaking of which, the mouse is also supported as a source of input. Take a look at the ProcessMouseMove method. If the game type is two players, then the mouse can be used to move the second player's paddle. Look over how the input methods are structured. Do you notice anything? For the most part, we don't handle any update code in our input handlers.

Notice how each input method analyzes the input data and then sets class fields to track what's happening with the user input. We then process this info in the class' update method, DrawScreen. Recall that the DrawScreen method is automatically called by the super class, or base class in C#, the MmgCore API's Screen class.

This class is designed to work with frequent animations, so the DrawScreen method is already plugged into the game engine's drawing routine, the MmgDraw and MmgUpdate methods, for us. Take your time to add these methods to your ScreenGame class. Be sure to save your work, but don't worry if you have errors. We're still working on things. We'll focus on the main method group next.

PongClone: ScreenGame Main Methods

We'll dive into the class' main methods next. Because we have limited space and because we've seen screen class constructors and LoadResources and UnloadResources methods many times before, we're going to take a little shortcut. Take a moment to read over the methods and understand how they function.

Let's copy and paste this code from the finished version of this game, included in the main game engine project's "Chatper15_CompleteGame" package – specifically, the ScreenGame class' ScreenGame constructor and LoadResources, UnloadResources methods. For the most part, these methods are very direct, but there is one line of code from the LoadResources method that I want you to be aware of.

Listing 18-13. ScreenGame LoadResources Method 1

```
1 SetState(State.SHOW_COUNT_DOWN);
2 ready = true;
3 pause = false;
```

Notice that the three lines at the end of the method, listed in the preceding, kick things off by setting up the game screen to show the number countdown sub-screen and unpausing the game screen. Now that we have that out of the way, let's take a look at the code for the main methods in the following code block.

Listing 18-14. ScreenGame Main Methods 1

```
@Override
01 public void MmgDraw(MmgPen p) {
02      if (pause == false && isVisible == true) {
03          super.GetObjects().MmgDraw(p);
04      }
05 }

01 private void ResetGame() {
02      ball.SetIsVisible(true);
03      MmgHelper.CenterHorAndVert(ball);
04      ballPos = ball.GetPosition();
05      ballMovePerFrameX = ballMovePerFrameMin;
06      ballMovePerFrameY = ballMovePerFrameMin;
```

```
07
08      paddleLeft.SetIsVisible(true);
09      MmgHelper.CenterVert(paddleLeft);
10      paddle1Pos = paddleLeft.GetPosition();
11      paddle1MoveDown = false;
12      paddle1MoveUp = false;
13
14      paddleRight.SetIsVisible(true);
15      MmgHelper.CenterVert(paddleRight);
16      paddle2Pos = paddleRight.GetPosition();
17      paddle2MoveDown = false;
18      paddle2MoveUp = false;
19
20      lastX = 0;
21      lastY = 0;
22      mousePos = false;
23 }
```

The two main methods listed in the preceding are the MmgDraw method and the ResetGame method. Notice how deceptively simple the MmgDraw method looks. Don't be deceived. We're leveraging a lot of code from the classes we're extending. Add these two methods to your ScreenGame class, and let's get ready to look at the brain of the entire game, the DrawScreen method.

Recall from our review of the Screen class that it's designed more for game screens with lots of animations; thus, the DrawScreen method is automatically called by the super class, or base class in C#. That means all our game logic will either reside in or be called from the DrawScreen method. Because of the importance of this method, we're going to cover the material by building it up from a skeleton of the method. I'll list the skeleton in the following code block.

Listing 18-15. ScreenGame DrawScreen Skeleton 1

```
@Override
001 public void DrawScreen() {
002     //ran each game frame
003     pause = true;
004
```

```
005      switch(state) {
006          case NONE:
007              break;
008
009          case SHOW_GAME_EXIT:
010              break;
011
012          case SHOW_COUNT_DOWN_IN_GAME:
013          case SHOW_COUNT_DOWN:
014              switch(numberState) {
015                  case NONE:
016                      break;
017
018                  case NUMBER_1:
019                      ...
020
021                  case NUMBER_2:
022                      ...
023
024                  case NUMBER_3:
025                      ...
026
027              }
028              break;
029
030          case SHOW_GAME:
031              //<editor-fold>
032              //player two movement
033              if(gameType == GameType.GAME_TWO_PLAYER) {
034                  ...
035              } else {
036                  //AI
037                  ...
038              }
039
```

```
040          //player one movement
041          if(paddle2MoveUp) {
042              ...
043          } else if(paddle2MoveDown) {
044              ...
045          }
046
047          //calculate where the ball will be
048          ballNewX = ballPos.GetX() + (ballMovePerFrameX * ballDirX);
049          ballNewY = ballPos.GetY() + (ballMovePerFrameY * ballDirY);
050
051          //board collision
052          if(ballNewY < screenPos.GetY()) {
053              //top
054              ...
055          } else if(ballNewY + ball.GetHeight() > screenPos.GetY() +
             GetHeight()) {
056              //bottom
057              ...
058          }else if(ballNewX < screenPos.GetX()) {
059              //left
060              ...
061          } else if(ballNewX + ball.GetWidth() > screenPos.GetX() +
             GetWidth()) {
062              //right
063              ...
064          }
065
066          bounced = false;
067          //paddle1 collision
068          if(ballNewX <= paddle1Pos.GetX() + paddleLeft.GetWidth() &&
             ballDirX == -1) {
069              ...
070          }
071
```

```
072                     //paddle2 collision
073                     if(ballNewX + ball.GetWidth() >= paddle2Pos.GetX() &&
                        ballDirX == 1) {
074                         ...
075                     }
076
077                     //set limits on the ball's speed
078                     if(ballMovePerFrameX > ballMovePerFrameMax) {
079                         ballMovePerFrameX = ballMovePerFrameMax;
080                     }
081
082                     if(ballMovePerFrameY > ballMovePerFrameMax) {
083                         ballMovePerFrameY = ballMovePerFrameMax;
084                     }
085
086                     //handle bounce sound
087                     if(bounced) {
088                         if(ballMovePerFrameY == ballMovePerFrameMax ||
                            ballMovePerFrameX == ballMovePerFrameMax) {
089                             bounceSuper.Play();
090                         } else {
091                             bounceNorm.Play();
092                         }
093                     }
094
095                     //update ball's position
096                     ballPos.SetX(ballNewX);
097                     ballPos.SetY(ballNewY);
098                     break;
099                     // </editor-fold>
100             }
101
102         pause = false;
103 }
```

Let's review the skeleton before we start adding in the missing blocks of code. The first line of code, line 3, pauses the game screen from drawing or updating while this method executes. We want to do this to prevent drawing the screen while it's in the middle of being updated. This method should only take a few milliseconds to run; make sure your update methods are as efficient as possible. The next few lines of code define a switch statement, line 5, which controls the behavior of the DrawScreen method.

As you can see, there is an entry for each game state. The NONE and SHOW_GAME_EXIT states require no work, so we break out of the main switch statement immediately. The general idea of how things are set up is that the SetState method is used to prepare the visible elements of the state that's being switched to. This is very similar to the way the GamePanel class handles game screens just on a smaller scale. The DrawScreen method is responsible for processing the current screen state each game frame if the current state requires it.

The next two screen states, SHOW_COUNT_DOWN and SHOW_COUNT_DOWN_IMAGE, are used to show a countdown timer from 3 to 1 over a few seconds. This will give our players a chance to reset before the next round of play. It also gives the players a few moments to read the game's instructions. Take a look at line 14. Note how a second switch statement is used to control the number countdown state. The code you place here will control changing the countdown number after the proper time interval has passed.

Following these two game screen states, we have the most important screen state, the SHOW_GAME state, line 30. You guessed it. This state is responsible for making sure the game updates. This includes moving the paddles for each player, moving the ball, calculating collisions and bounces, and keeping track of scores among other things.

A little sidenote: If you're using the NetBeans IDE, direct your attention to line 31. You can use this comment and its associated closing tag to create a custom code fold in the class file. This can come in handy with large complex methods like the DrawScreen method. Let's move on to the block of code on lines 32–38 in the preceding method skeleton. These if statements are the placeholders for processing player one, player two, and AI input.

Similarly, on lines 40–45, we have the placeholders for processing player one's input. On lines 43 and 44, the ball's new position is calculated from its speed and direction. This information is not used to reposition the game ball until we check for collisions. On lines 51–64, we have the skeleton in place for handling the ball's collision with the game board's edges. Take a moment to review and ponder the simple calculations used to determine the game ball's boundaries.

We're almost done with this method's skeleton outline. There are just a few more points I'd like to draw your attention to. The next such point is on lines 66–75. This block of code scaffolding is used to determine if the ball will collide with any of the players' paddles. Again, take a moment to review and understand the calculations used to determine if a paddle collision has occurred. On lines 77–84 is the section of the skeleton that controls the ball's maximum speed in the X and Y directions.

This is followed by a snippet of code on lines 86–93 responsible for playing sound effects. If the ball is traveling at a lower speed when it hits a player's paddle, it will make a different sound than if it's travelling at maximum speed. Finally, on lines 96 and 97, the ball's position coordinates are updated with the newly calculated, you don't have that code in place just yet, ball's direction and speed. Let's summarize the method's responsibilities in the order they are handled.

Listing 18-16. ScreenGame DrawScreen Skeleton 2

- GameStart timer countdown

- RoundStart timer countdown

- Player 2/AI paddle movement

- Player 1 paddle movement

- Calculating the ball's new position

- Board edge collision detection

- Paddle 1 collision detection

- Paddle 2 collision detection

- Limiting ball's max speed

- Playing paddle bounce sounds

- Updating ball's position

Looking at the game's general specifications, this class update method wraps up the last set of requirements and adds a new feature or two. Instead of me printing out each block of code and reviewing it before we add it to our ScreenGame class, I want you to add in the missing code either by typing it in by hand, while looking at the completed version of the game, or by copying and pasting it in.

Be extra careful and complete each code block without error. Review the code and make sure you understand it. When you are finished, you should be able to compile the project without error. Don't go trying to play the game just yet. We still have one more task to complete before we can compile and run the project.

Please take your time when working through the ScreenGame code. Reference the completed project, net.middlemind.PongClone.Chapter18_CompleteGame, in the main game engine project. A similar directory exists in the C# version of the project. If you run into trouble start over and copy/paste in each class method, one at a time, making sure you understand each method as you do so. At the end of this process you'll have a complete version of the ScreenGame class.

PongClone: Register ScreenGame

Now that the game's main game screen class is complete, we need to link it into the GamePanel class so that the player can start a one- or two-player game and the main game screen will display and run properly. Open up your game project's GamePanel class and add the following field to the class:

```
public ScreenGame screenGame;
```

You'll also need to add the following line of code to the class' constructor:

```
screenGame = new ScreenGame(GameStates.MAIN_GAME, this);
```

To connect the game screen into the GamePanel's known states, we need to add the following code to the cleanup section of the SwitchGameState method.

Listing 18-17. GamePanel Screen Registration 1

```
01 else if (prevGameState == GameStates.MAIN_GAME_1P || prevGameState ==
GameStates.MAIN_GAME)
02 {
03     MmgHelper.wr("Hiding MAIN GAME 1P screen.");
04     screenGame.Pause();
05     screenGame.SetIsVisible(false);
06     screenGame.UnloadResources();
07
08 }
```

```
09 else if (prevGameState == GameStates.MAIN_GAME_2P)
10 {
11     MmgHelper.wr("Hiding MAIN GAME 2P screen.");
12     screenGame.Pause();
13     screenGame.SetIsVisible(false);
14     screenGame.UnloadResources();
15
16 }
```

We're almost there. We still need to add the game state preparation code that's responsible for getting the main game screen ready to display. Notice that the code is designed to work with one-player or two-player game states.

Listing 18-18. GamePanel Screen Registration 2

```
01 else if (gameState == GameStates.MAIN_GAME_1P || gameState ==
   GameStates.MAIN_GAME)
02 {
03     MmgHelper.wr("Showing MAIN GAME 1P screen.");
04     screenGame.SetGameType(GameType.GAME_ONE_PLAYER);
05     screenGame.LoadResources();
06     screenGame.UnPause();
07     screenGame.SetIsVisible(true);
08     currentScreen = screenGame;
09
10 }
11 else if (gameState == GameStates.MAIN_GAME_2P)
12 {
13     MmgHelper.wr("Showing MAIN GAME 2P screen.");
14     screenGame.SetGameType(GameType.GAME_TWO_PLAYER);
15     screenGame.LoadResources();
16     screenGame.UnPause();
17     screenGame.SetIsVisible(true);
18     currentScreen = screenGame;
19
20 }
```

Add the two code snippets listed in the preceding to the SwitchGameState method of the GamePanel class as instructed. Now the new game screen class is fully wired into the GamePanel and subsequently the game. Save your files, address any errors, and compile your PongClone game project. If you run into any issues, take a look at the code in the "Chapter15_CompleteVersion" package included in the game engine's main project. Now let's run the game!

If you've been following along in C#, then compile the project and open up a terminal program. Navigate to your project's directory and find the local copy of "PongClone.dll." This file should reside in the following folder in the root directory of the PongClone project:

```
./bin/Debug/netcoreapp3.1/PongClone.dll
```

Navigate to the root directory of your project and run the following command to launch your game:

```
dotnet ./bin/Debug/netcoreapp3.1/PongClone.dll
```

If you've been following along in Java, then you only need to run the project from the IDE. If you've implemented everything correctly, then you should be able to run your project by right-clicking the PongClone.java class and selecting "Run File" from the context menu. You can also select the IDE's "Run" menu option and choose the "Run Project" context menu option. Make sure that the project listed in the context menu command is your PongClone project.

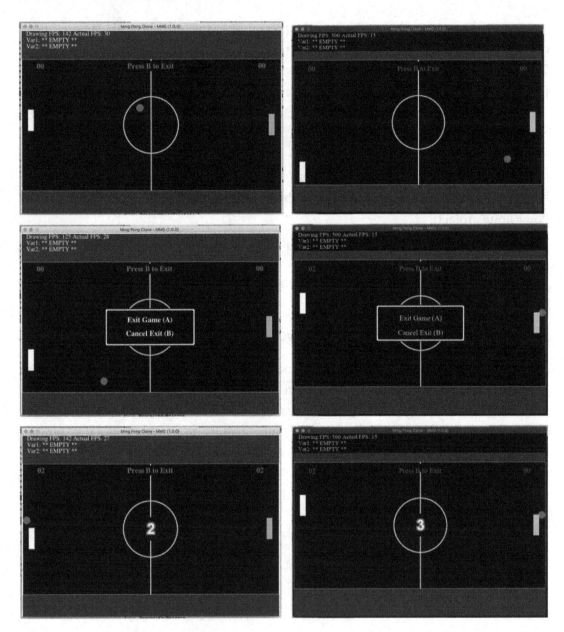

Figure 18-1. *PongClone Game 1*

Take a moment to let it soak in. Congratulations! You've just written your first game with the Mmg game engine! Take a moment to think about the complexity of your code when compared to the complexity of the resulting game. I must say not bad for a couple of classes and a few lines of code. Don't go away just yet. We have another game build to work on next, DungeonTrap.

CHAPTER 19

Conclusion

Congratulations! If you've made it this far and have completed Parts 1, 2, and 3 of this text, then you've accomplished no small feat. I'd like to take a few moments to step back and look at what we've managed to accomplish together over the course of this text.

Accomplishments

The first major accomplishment we've achieved is the introduction to, and detailed explanation of a fairly robust, 2D game engine API. We worked literally from the ground up reviewing each game engine class in turn as we completed our review of the MmgBase API. During this review, we got to witness the power of a well-designed super class, or base class if you're following along in C#, in the MmgObj class.

We also saw first-hand how to design and build not only a 2D game engine API but any advanced API really. The examples of consistent naming conventions, globally supported features like cloning and comparison, and well-documented code are foundational to any good API and any good software development project.

The second major accomplishment we've achieved together through this text is the detailed review of the MmgCore API. We saw how to separate the MmgBase API features from the MmgCore API's application-level features like user input, screen management, and the main drawing loop. We also learned how to launch our games and demo the MmgBase API functionality through the use of the MmgTestScreens API's example application.

Last but not least, we applied literally everything we learned to build two games, PongClone and DungeonTrap, from the ground up. With PongClone, we started from an empty project. We pulled in our API code to create a game that we could launch and play with just a few class files. The DungeonTrap game build is available as an additional download from the book's GitHub repository. I highly recommend that you download and complete the DungeonTrap game.

© Victor G Brusca 2021
V. G. Brusca, *Introduction to Video Game Engine Development*, https://doi.org/10.1007/978-1-4842-7039-4_19

For the DungeonTrap game, we got to build out a complex class hierarchy that properly encapsulated and exposed functionality from super classes to child classes. We managed to review over 40 classes and complete the game in just a few chapters. Take a moment for yourself and enjoy what you've accomplished. I'd like to acknowledge the artists and websites I used for resources in some of the book's projects.

Acknowledgments

First off, I'd like to thank Pipoya for creating some great, low-cost, 2D video game art. You can access Pipoya's free RPG character sprites at the following URL. Be sure to support and check out all of the great work this artist has to offer:

Pipoya's Free RPG Character Sprites 32x32 (`https://pipoya.itch.io/pipoya-free-rpg-character-sprites-32x32`)

The next content creator I'd like to thank is O_lobster. I used one of O_lobster's free dungeon tile sets to build the DungeonTrap board. You can access O_lobster's work at the following URL:

Simple Dungeon Crawler 16x16 Pixel Art Asset Pack (`https://o-lobster.itch.io/simple-dungeon-crawler-16x16-pixel-pack?download`)

I'd like to thank Robinhood76 and Leszek_Szary for the sound effects they shared on `https://freesound.org`. The two small sound effects are the only sounds used in the game jams within and can be found at the following URLs:

FreeSound Sound Effect 1 (`https://freesound.org/people/Robinhood76/sounds/95557/`)

FreeSound Sound Effect 2 (`https://freesound.org/people/Leszek_Szary/sounds/146726/`)

Lastly, I would also like to thank Chasersgaming and Zintoki, both from `https://itch.io`, for their artwork, which was used in the MmgTestSpace API's game engine demo application. All of the source artwork along with their original download URLs can be found in the "cfg/asset_src" folder in the game engine's project directory.

Where You Go From Here

So now that you've completed this book and you have some game engine and 2D game building experience, you might be wondering, *Where can I go from here?* Obviously, this question depends a lot on you, but I can certainly make some suggestions.

Add to the PongClone Game

Take the time to customize the PongClone game. You can add new game features like multi-ball, super-speed, larger paddles, you name it. You could also modify the game to support different modes. Think about different win conditions or a penalty shot mode. It's really up to you.

Add to the DungeonTrap Game

You could spend a little bit of time working on customizing your DungeonTrap game. For instance, there are items like the bomb and the treasure chest that exist but aren't implemented in the game. Similarly, there are unused weapons, the axe and the sword, and the ability for enemy characters to use weapons. All of these could be used to customize and refine the game. At the very least, you should be sure to adjust the level, enemy wave, parameters to make the game a little more playable.

Add to the Game Engine API

You could add new functionality to the game engine project, either at the MmgBase API level where you could define more widgets and tools to use or at the MmgCore API level where you could create game screens that are specialized for side scrolling games or 2D top-down shooters. The sky is the limit really.

Learn Cross-Platform Coding

You can utilize this text's included projects to learn a new programming language, Java or C#, or to gain experience with cross-platform API design and implementation. Because you have so much experience working with the game engine's API-level code, you'll be able to see the cross-platform design decisions and programming language–driven differences more readily. I highly recommend setting aside some time to review the cross-platform aspects of the included game engine projects.

Build More Games and Have Fun

Last but not least, you could simply build more games and just have fun. After all, what's the point in learning about 2D game engine design and implementation if you can't just have fun and build a few games.

Saying Goodbye

I sincerely hope that you enjoyed this book and that you derived some modicum of joy, knowledge, wisdom, and/or experience from it. Happy coding!

Index

© Victor G Brusca 2021
V. G. Brusca, *Introduction to Video Game Engine Development*, https://doi.org/10.1007/978-1-4842-7039-4

Printed in the United States
by Baker & Taylor Publisher Services